D1449252

How to Draw

David Brody, M.F.A.

THE
GREAT
COURSES®

PUBLISHED BY:

THE GREAT COURSES
Corporate Headquarters
4840 Westfields Boulevard, Suite 500
Chantilly, Virginia 20151-2299
Phone: 1-800-832-2412
Fax: 703-378-3819
www.thegreatcourses.com

David Brody, M.F.A.
Professor of Painting and Drawing
University of Washington

Professor David Brody has been a Professor of Painting and Drawing at the University of Washington in Seattle since 1996. He did undergraduate work at Columbia University and Bennington College and received his graduate degree in painting from Yale University in 1983. Professor Brody has received numerous awards. He has been a Fulbright Scholar and a Guggenheim Fellow and has received the Basil H. Alkazzi Award for Excellence in Painting, a grant from the Elizabeth Foundation for the Arts, and two fellowships from the Massachusetts Cultural Council. At the University of Washington, he received two Royalty Research Fund grants and three Milliman Endowment for Faculty Excellence awards.

Professor Brody's paintings and drawings have been shown in close to 100 exhibitions in the United States and Europe. These include solo shows at Gallery NAGA in Boston, the Esther Claypool Gallery in Seattle, Gescheidle in Chicago, and Galeria Gilde in Portugal. His group exhibitions include shows at the Chicago Center for the Print; the Frye Art Museum and Prographica Gallery in Seattle; The Museum of Fine Arts at Florida State University; and The Painting Center, The Alternative Museum, and Bridgewater Fine Arts in New York City. His work has also been shown at ARCO Art Fair in Madrid, the RipArte Art Fair in Rome, the Trevi Flash Art Museum, the FAC Art Fair in Lisbon, and Art Chicago in the United States.

Professor Brody's work has been published and written about in two monographs and in many articles and reviews. An exhibit at the Esther Claypool Gallery in Seattle was described by *Seattle Weekly* as "daring, humorous, and superbly executed." According to *Artforum*, "Brody's … paintings … provide a stunning visual punch … [and] are rendered with a bravura that is both compelling and hypnotic." And *Art in America* concluded, "A highly intelligent artist … Brody is absolutely serious about technique. An emphasis on fine drawing, delicate surfaces and careful considerations of color and light informs all his pictures." In addition, Brody has been written about in many other publications, including *The Boston Globe*, the *New Art Examiner*, the Spanish journal *Lapiz*, and the Lisbon daily *O Público*.

Professor Brody has lectured or been a visiting critic at Carnegie Mellon University, the Massachusetts Institute of Technology, The University of Chicago, Harvard University, Capital Normal University in Beijing, and the China Art Academy in Hangzhou.

Professor Brody has had a parallel career in music. He has published five books on traditional music, including the best-selling *The Fiddler's Fakebook: The Ultimate Sourcebook for the Traditional Fiddler*. He has performed at festivals in the United States, Europe, and Canada; at Avery Fisher Hall and Symphony Space in New York City; and on Garrison Keillor's radio show *A Prairie Home Companion*. He has recorded with the Klezmer Conservatory Band and other artists on the Rounder, Vanguard, and Flying Fish labels. ∎

Table of Contents

Table of Contents

SUPPLEMENTAL MATERIAL

How to Draw

Scope:

Т he 36 lectures in this course are distilled from four decades of study, studio work, and teaching and communicate the most important and useful things to know about drawing—information that will greatly benefit novice artists.

The course presents drawing as a language and, as in many language courses, introduces ideas one at a time to allow you to fully examine each piece of the puzzle. The lectures progress cumulatively in a step-by-step fashion, with each new idea building on the previous ones. We'll start from simple units and move up to ever-greater complexity.

Each lecture or set of lectures deals with a key idea, concept, material, or technique that has been historically important to artists over the long history of drawing. As we'll see, although there have certainly been changes with time and place, there has also been a great degree of continuity in the language of drawing across continents and over the millennia that human beings have been making drawings.

The approach in this course is simple. Each lecture begins by describing and explaining a new concept or technique, which is then situated it in its historical context and illustrated with visual examples. The examples include both masterworks from a range of periods and traditions in art history and student drawings meant to demonstrate that learning to draw is eminently attainable. The lectures themselves run about 18 hours, but working through all the exercises and projects could well keep you occupied for many months.

The course is divided into six sections. The first section, Lectures 1 through 3, introduces the long history of drawing, starting with some lines scratched into a piece of ochre found in a cave in South Africa dating back some 80,000 years or more and bringing us up to the present day. The introductory section presents the course in broad strokes and quickly gets you experimenting with the materials you'll be using throughout.

The second section, Lectures 4 through 14, focuses on the underlying grammar of drawing, referred to as *formal language*. Here, you'll learn to draw with different types of line, including contour, cross-contour, construction line, and gestural line. You'll learn how line creates shapes, both positive and negative, and how you can use simple shapes to draw many complex objects. You'll also see how you can use cross-contour line to transform flat shape into three-dimensional volume.

As we begin to draw more complex groupings of objects, we'll delve into composition. We'll learn how famous artists—spanning the Song dynasty in China, the Italian Renaissance, the French Impressionist period, and beyond—structured their drawings in this regard.

In Lectures 12 through 14, we'll learn how such artists as Leonardo, Dürer, Eakins, and Van Gogh used practical systems to arrive at accurate proportions and a convincing illusion of volume and three-dimensional space. You'll apply these same methods and techniques to your own drawing projects.

In the third section, Lectures 15 through 19, we'll learn about linear perspective. This powerful drawing system, developed during the Renaissance, radically changed the way future generations around the world would draw. It's not only at the heart of what Raphael and his Renaissance contemporaries were able to accomplish but has become ubiquitous in everything from the contemporary works of such artists as Anselm Kiefer, to video games and manga, to animated cartoons, such as *The Simpsons*.

In the fourth section, Lectures 20 through 30, we'll return to complete our examination of formal language, learning to incorporate value, texture, and color into drawings. You'll learn how artists think about palettes of value and how palettes suggest light and mood. You'll also learn to use value as a compositional tool and how you can create the illusion of volume, space, and light through modulations of light and dark. You'll see how you can further affect the feel of a drawing thorough mark-making and the use of texture. And you'll learn about textural approaches to creating value, including hatching, cross-hatching, and other mark-making systems.

We'll conclude the fourth section with an exploration of color. We'll learn about color properties and study the basics of color theory. As with value, we'll see how artists use these ideas and conceive of color in terms of palettes—groupings or limitations of color that help create specific qualities of light and mood. As we did with value, we'll learn how we can use color compositionally to create a visual hierarchy with focal areas and focal points. And you'll apply all these ideas in your own drawings to create different qualities of mood, light, and form.

In the fifth section, we'll focus on the human figure. The approach in this section is geared to help you draw figures from both observation and your imagination. We'll start with an examination of canons of proportion. Here, you'll learn how to build a figure using a set of measures. We'll complement this with a study of artistic anatomy, including both the skeletal and muscular systems. You'll also learn techniques for approaching the foreshortened figure. We'll combine what we learn about the figure with what we learned in our study of linear perspective, giving you the tools you need to draw figures from your imagination in imagined environments. This is just what Leonardo and Dürer did during the Renaissance, and it is the same method many contemporary animators and game designers use to develop their characters and environments.

In the final section, devoted to advanced projects, we'll look at some of the changes that occurred between the late 19th century and the present. We'll see how Renaissance spatial constructs evolved to include a broader understanding of pictorial space and how this related to many movements in art, including Impressionism, Cubism, and abstraction. We'll close with a discussion and a set or projects designed to help you identify the kind of art you want to make and some thoughts on how you can work toward that goal. ∎

An Introduction to Drawing
Lecture 1

The ability to draw naturalistically did not come easily to human beings. It took us tens of thousands of years to get a figure proportionate and believably seated in a chair, the chair on the carpet, and the carpet on the floor. The knowledge and methods we use to do these things today were developed and codified during the Renaissance. And you could argue that they represent the greatest set of technical advances the field has known. Many people, when they think about "learning to draw," want to develop just these skills—getting the proportions right, getting the things to sit on the table, and perhaps even drawing a group of figures from the imagination. Although these skills are often mystified, they can, to an overwhelming degree, be learned, and with practice, you can make the ideas and methods your own. Those are our goals for this course.

The Renaissance
Although just about every people and culture has produced beautiful and expressive artworks, discoveries in 15th-century Europe changed drawing forever. Before the Renaissance, no one had figured out how to create anything as remotely naturalistic as this watercolor (*John Biglin in a Single Scull*) by Thomas Eakins:

Bits and pieces had been learned and practiced for a period, but local advances were often swallowed up by time and forgotten. For example, from about the late 1st century B.C.E. to perhaps the 3rd century C.E., some Egyptians had their portraits painted on wooden panels, which were then attached to their mummies when the subjects died. These paintings, known as Fayum Portraits, are amazingly naturalistic for their time. But after about the 3rd century, this kind of naturalism would not appear again for hundreds of years.

In Europe, between the 1300s and the late 1400s, a group of artists figured out how to create a believable and proportionate illusion of three dimensions on a two-dimensional surface. Interestingly, the drawing concepts and techniques developed during the Renaissance and used by Leonardo da Vinci, Raphael, and others are commonly used today by cartoonists, video game designers, and animators.

But we mustn't think that people were visually challenged for tens of thousands of years and then, suddenly, from the Renaissance to the present, became so exceedingly talented that they were able to render things with verisimilitude. Instead, it's that the knowledge base improved radically. After the Renaissance, artists who had access to good information and worked hard to master their craft were able to learn things and draw in ways that their predecessors had never been able to. Rather than just absorbing a set of local symbols, these artists had methods for analyzing and drawing anything they came upon. And, as we'll learn, they also developed methods for constructing naturalistic-looking images from their imaginations.

Challenges in Learning to Draw
Of course, talent plays a role in making art, but it's a much less important one than most people tend to think. In fact, it's difficult to tell how much talent someone has before he or she has put in a considerable amount of work, primarily because it's difficult to draw much if you have scant knowledge. Acquiring knowledge and putting it into practice are the two essential keys to finding out how well you draw. And in this quest, one of the most important elements is the willingness to put in a substantial amount of work. Students who engage at this level will improve significantly.

As you practice drawing, don't avoid working on what you're not naturally good at. You may feel comfortable with line and pencil but not with value and charcoal, or you may like gesture drawing but not linear perspective. You will do better if you apply yourself fully to everything and, in fact, apply yourself with extra energy to the things that you have less of a knack for.

Learning to draw is endless, like learning to cook, to play music, or to write well. You can be a student of these things for a lifetime, continually learning more. As you struggle to learn new things, the feelings of uncertainty will fade away; after a time, you'll realize that the struggle itself is enjoyable and that your efforts are dependably rewarded. How quickly and nimbly you learn something has little bearing on long-term results. Learn for yourself, at your own pace, and for your own sense of mastery.

Learning to See
When we write, we think of a piece of paper as being flat. But to draw, we have to learn to see it as a depth of space. We want to look at the four edges of the page and see them as the four sides of a window frame. The white surface becomes a depth, like a room or a landscape, that we transform through the use of line, shape, mark, and value to suggest volume and space.

Many artists and professors say that learning to draw is all about learning to see, not seeing things to identify them but seeing them as they actually appear—the proportions, angles, values, and the real play of light and color. That's a much harder kind of seeing. It requires looking analytically and abstractly. In his book *Successful Drawing*, Andrew Loomis wrote, "Drawing is really difficult only to those who do not know what to look for." There's a peculiar paradox here. In order for us to draw things in a naturalistic or realistic way—in proportion—we must learn to see them abstractly.

Simple lines can have multiple and complex meanings. Line creates shape, and shape creates pattern. Shapes can also be arranged to create the illusion of three-dimensional volume. Those volumes can be transformed to appear like things in the world around us.

Drawing across the Centuries

As mentioned at the beginning of the lecture, drawing took a great leap forward during the Renaissance, but that's not to say that human beings weren't making interesting and beautiful drawings long before the 1400s. Anthropologists tell us that modern *Homo sapiens* showed up somewhere between 100,000 and 200,000 years ago. And long before we have any records of writing, numbers, commerce, or nation-states, we have evidence of our ancestors making drawings. The oldest known examples, found in the Blombos Cave in South Africa, go back about 80,000 years or more. They consist of incised lines on pieces of ochre. These ancient incised lines form a pattern, and line and pattern are still very much with us today.

Most drawing we know of—at least as measured in years—is prehistoric and took place in caves. You've likely seen examples that feature mammoths, bison, and horses. The oldest cave drawings date to about 40,000 years ago, and the practice of cave drawing continued in Europe for about 30,000 years. In contrast, people have been drawing on paper for only a little more than 2,000 years. Paper was invented in the 2nd century B.C.E. in Han dynasty China, and its method of manufacture was kept secret from the West until the 8th century C.E.

During the early historical period, just about every culture or civilization on every continent practiced drawing in one form or another; there are stunning examples from every corner of the globe. In fact, many of our earliest written languages have origins in drawing. Chinese, spoken by more than 1 billion people today, has its roots in an ancient picture-based writing system going back more than 3,000 years, and the modern written language retains many picture-based characters.

Stylization

Many people imagine artists standing in front of a still life, a landscape, or a model to make a drawing. But looking directly at something and drawing it is a relatively recent phenomenon, as is the idea of artists making their own kind of art, for that matter.

For most of time, from Blombos until fairly recently, people weren't looking at what they were drawing while they were drawing it. In most cultures, at most times, drawing and the related arts consisted of using a set of more-or-less agreed-upon symbols that stood for things, such as a person, a tree, or an animal. We refer to this as *stylization*. From the historical record, it would appear that much of this stylization was determined by local convention, which also determined what to draw, where to draw, and what materials to use. Thus, the early cave artists in Europe followed a set of conventions regarding subject, materials, and technique. Later artists—Egyptian, Greek, Chinese, and others—followed their own conventions.

Yet despite the fact that art has changed over time and place, there has been a great deal of continuity. As we study drawing, we'll find that artists have been using many of the same principles of good drawing and design for thousands of years. Their command of craft and their use of line, shape, value, and color—to name a few of the factors we will explore—begin to explain why these works have stood out and been cherished by people of diverse backgrounds and beliefs over the centuries.

In this sense, this course is comprehensive. The lessons are firmly based in the game-changing discoveries of the Renaissance, but we will also learn from the work of great artists from a range of cultures covering a broad swath of time, from the ancient to the contemporary.

Suggested Reading

Mendelowitz, *Drawing.*

Stokstad, *Art History.*

An Introduction to Drawing
Lecture 1—Transcript

The ability to draw naturalistically did not come easily to human beings. To get the figure proportionate, believably seated in a chair, the chair on the carpet, and the carpet on the floor; well, that took us collectively tens of thousands of years to figure out. The knowledge and methods we use to do these things today were developed and codified during the Renaissance. And you could argue that they represent the greatest set of technical advances this field has known.

While just about every people and culture has produced beautiful and expressive artworks, discoveries in 15th-century Europe changed drawing forever. Before the Renaissance, no one had figured out how to do anything remotely like this. Here, a Hans Holbein; or this, a watercolor by Thomas Eakins. Bits and pieces had been learned and practiced for a period, but local advances were often swallowed up by time and forgotten.

For example, from about the late 1st century B.C.E. to maybe the 3rd century C.E. some Egyptians had their portraits painted on wooden panels. After the person died, the portrait would be attached to that person's mummy, held in place over the head with cloth wrappings. These portraits are amazingly naturalistic for their time.

There was a great show of these works that are called Fayum portraits, at the Metropolitan Museum in New York back in 2000. I remember stepping into the exhibit and looking into the eyes of these long-gone people, and thinking they looked absolutely contemporary and recognizable—like people I'd just seen on the subway. There's a great deal of knowledge evinced in these portraits. But after about the 3rd century, this kind of naturalism would not appear again for many centuries.

Nothing makes the great Renaissance leap clearer than looking at two Last Suppers, both painted in northern Italy. The first, by Ugolino da Siena, from about between 1325–1330; the second, by Leonardo da Vinci, from the late 1490s. In a brief 160 years—a short period to me relative to the tens of thousands of years our species had been drawing—a group of artists,

Leonardo among them, had figured out how to create a believable and proportionate illusion of three-dimensions on a two-dimensional surface.

If you're like most of my students at the University of Washington, it's likely that when you think about learning to draw, you're thinking about being able to do this: Get the proportions right, get the things to sit on the table, maybe even draw a group of figures like this from your imagination. While all this is often mystified—you know, people talk about artistic genius and the secrets of the masters—an overwhelming amount of this is readily learnable if you get solid information about how to do it, and then practice it to make the ideas and methods your own.

The 19th-century British artist and critic John Ruskin made just this point in his book *The Elements of Drawing*. He wrote:

> I have never yet met a person who could not learn to draw there is a satisfactory and available power in every one to learn drawing just as nearly all persons have the power of learning French, Latin, or arithmetic.

I've found the same thing to be true. The drawing concepts and techniques developed during the Renaissance and used by Leonardo and by Raphael here in his School of Athens are commonly used by cartoonists drawing superheroes, video game designers, and animators. While Plato and Aristotle—depicted in the Raphael—are clearly different from Bart Simpson, the methodology underlying the drawing in these images is surprisingly similar. The knowledge is transformative. My beginning students routinely do drawings that some of the early Renaissance masters, like Ugolino, would have marveled at. If they could travel back in time and meet him, he'd ask, "Ma, come l'hai fatto? Sei proprio un genio. How did you do that? You must be a genius."

My students, most of whom have no prior experience with drawing, would answer, "I took Professor Brody's course; it was pretty good. My drawing really improved, though I had to work a lot harder than I thought I would in an art course." I'm kidding, but my students are able to do sophisticated things after a couple of months. And that's because they get good information, and then work very hard to make the knowledge their own. The hard work part's true. You see, it's not that for tens of thousands of years people were visually challenged and then, suddenly, from the Renaissance to the present, a group of artists—Raphael, Rembrandt, Vermeer, Degas, Eakins, and my students at the University of Washington—were all so exceedingly talented that they were able to render things with a surprising degree of verisimilitude.

It's that the knowledge base improved radically. Post-Renaissance artists who had access to good information and worked hard to master their craft were able to learn things and draw in ways their predecessors had never been able to before. Rather than just absorbing a set of local symbols, these artists had methods for analyzing and drawing anything they came upon. And, as we'll learn, they also developed methods for constructing naturalistic looking images from their imaginations.

While, of course, all the artists I just named were brilliant, they were able to even begin to imagine making the kinds of drawings they did because of a depth of knowledge accompanied by hard work. Leonardo, Eakins, and Van Gogh—among many others—wrote about drawing methods and techniques, and we can consult what they wrote. And they were painstakingly serious about learning their craft.

Even Degas—seemingly one of the most facile artists to have walked the planet—famously said, "I assure you no art was ever less spontaneous than mine. What I do is the result of reflection and study of the old masters. Of inspiration, spontaneity, temperament, I know nothing." So the good news is that all this is very learnable. I suppose the bad news, if you see it that way, is there's a lot to learn and it requires hard work. It's rewarding and engrossing, but there aren't any shortcuts.

All this leads us to the subject of artistic talent. I'm often asked if you can teach someone to be an artist. Oddly enough, the answer is a simple yes. You can learn to become proficient in art making just like other people across the campus where I teach become proficient in law, medicine, engineering, and mathematics. I realize, though, that when people ask this question, what they often mean is: Can you teach someone to be a towering genius, to make a revolutionary contribution to art, to make great art that will be cherished by generations to come? There, the answer is plainly no.

That can't be taught any more than a law student could be taught to be an Oliver Wendell Holmes or an Abraham Lincoln, or a physicist could be taught to be a Galileo or an Einstein. What can be taught and learned in all fields are the skills, concepts, and ideas that will help an individual mine their gifts to their ultimate depths. I've met many people who have an interest in art, but were afraid to even begin to learn how to draw because they had somehow formed the idea they had to be geniuses sprung from nature—that they had to be able to do all kinds of very complex and difficult things without training or practice. Fortunately, that's not the case.

Of course, talent plays a role, but a much less important one than most people tend to think. In fact, it's very hard to tell how much talent someone has before they've put in a considerable amount of work. That's because it's hard to draw much if you have scant knowledge. Acquiring knowledge and putting it into practice are the two essential keys to finding out how well you draw.

After working with hundreds of students over decades, it's become abundantly clear to me that anyone with reasonable intelligence and a good work ethic can learn a tremendous amount and increase their drawing ability exponentially. Perspiration wins over inspiration. In fact, perspiration leads to inspiration. Those who work consistently are generally rewarded with insights and exciting outcomes. As Matisse is reported to have said, "Don't wait for inspiration. It comes while one is working."

So, how long does it take to learn to draw well? The 19th-century Brit, John Ruskin, gives this advice:

> Supposing then that you are ready to take a certain amount of pains, and to bear a little irksomeness and a few disappointments bravely, I can promise you that an hour's practice a day for 6 months, some 150 hours practice, will give you sufficient power of drawing faithfully whatever you want to draw.

That squares with my own experience. At the University of Washington, we're on the quarter system. Courses last about 10 weeks. Intro drawing meets twice a week, for a total of six hours. Students who excel report spending an additional 10 hours a week on homework. Sixteen hours a week total times 10 weeks; 160 hours—close enough to Ruskin's 150. Students who engage at this level improve substantially. And when students see the improvement, they often want to improve even further. They know it's possible. They know it's not genius, but time and effort.

The French Impressionist Camille Pissarro wrote, "It is only by much drawing, drawing everything, drawing unceasingly that one fine day one is very surprised to find it possible to express something in its true spirit." But it's not just a matter of quantity of hours. I've encountered students who were passionate about art but hampered their own progress. They were afraid their creativity and spontaneity might be damaged by too much knowledge. I've never heard of anyone else in any field say this. But let me assure you, I've never seen this happen—not once; only the opposite. There's no piece of knowledge or ability which, in and of itself, can do you any harm. And most will do you good. The worst you'll do is waste some time, paper, and ink.

Another often-related mistake some of my students make is to avoid working on what they're not naturally good at. They feel comfortable with line and pencil, but not with value and charcoal; or they like gesture drawing, but don't like linear perspective; or vice versa. Those who do best, apply themselves fully to everything; and, in fact, apply themselves with extra energy to the things they have less of a knack for. The reason why is simple: All of this knowledge is important. You're better off knowing more—having more craft—rather than less.

Andrew Loomis gave his readers some very good advice in his 1951 book *Successful Drawing*. He wrote, "Since the knowledge is available, why try to struggle along without it? The difficulties of not knowing are always much greater than the effort of learning." The artist Ben Shahn echoed this thought in *The Shape of Content*—a compendium of the Norton Lectures he gave at Harvard in 1956 and 1957. He wrote, "Craft is that discipline which frees the spirit."

I've been developing my knowledge of drawing, my analytic abilities, my eye, and hand for close to 50 years. I dependably learn new things every month—every year. In fact, I've learned many new things, made new connections, in preparing this series of lectures. Learning to draw is pretty endless—like learning to cook, or learning to play music, or write well. You can be a student of these things for a lifetime, continually learning more and more. And those torturous feelings fade away as you struggle with things that you're trying to learn because after a time, you realize the struggle's really fun and there's a significant and gratifying pay-off that dependably comes with the effort.

The careers of two French artists, Edgar Degas and Paul Cézanne, provide a great example. They were contemporaries, born in 1834 and 1839 respectively. Both Cézanne and Degas worked very hard, but they had different artistic aptitude. Here's an early Degas: a portrait of his grandfather, completed when the artist was 23. And here's an early Cézanne: a portrait of the artist's father, which he painted when he was 26.

They were the archetypical tortoise and hare. Out of the gate, Cézanne crawled along clumsily. Degas sprinted to the applause of a cheering crowd. Degas was routinely accepted into the Salon—the most important annual exhibition in Paris. Cézanne? No way. He was shuttled into the Salon des Refusé—the show for the rejected. Admittedly, Degas had been honing his craft longer than Cézanne when they painted these portraits. But overall, it took Cézanne a lot longer to put the pieces together than it did Degas. And I'm not aware of a single Degas that's anywhere as near as awkward as what Cézanne produced during his early years. Nor is there a single Cézanne that can match Degas for what most would call grace or elegance.

That said, Cézanne is commonly regarded as the more important artist. He's often referred to as the father of modern art. Picasso called him the father of us all. His very struggles with proportion, shape, the illusion of volume, and depth of space pushed him to discover new ways of drawing; things that simply would never have occurred to Degas. It pushed him into some revolutionary territory.

Some people get things quicker, others take more time. We don't all synthesize things in precisely the same way. Learn like Cézanne, at your own pace. Be patient, be doggedly persistent, and have a sense of humor about the inevitable struggles of getting things right. How quickly and nimbly someone learns something has little bearing on longer-term results. Learn for yourself, for your own sense of mastery. Work consistently, at your own pace. You'll continually find yourself improving.

I started out by saying that drawing took a leap forward during the Renaissance, but that's not to say that human beings weren't making interesting and beautiful drawings long before the 1400s. Anthropologists tell us that we, modern Homo sapiens, showed-up here somewhere between 100,000–200,000 years ago. And long before we have any records of writing, numbers, commerce, or nation states; we have evidence of our ancestors making drawings.

Broadly defined, drawing's nothing more than marking surfaces, and we've been marking surfaces for a very long time. The oldest known examples go back 80,000 years or more—that would be over 300,000 generations. They were found in the Blombos Cave, about 185 miles east of Cape Town in South Africa. These early drawings were made on chunks of ochre—this one, about three inches long. The ancient incised lines form a pattern, and line and pattern are very much with us today.

So, let's try a first drawing exercise. We'll get to the Renaissance, but why not start out where we, well, started out? We'll retrace what one of our ancestors drew 80,000 years ago at the very southern tip of Africa. You don't need anything fancy—a pencil, eraser, and some paper from your printer will be just fine.

Start with three evenly spaced horizontal lines. Then place a triangle in the center. From the center of the base of this triangle, draw two more. One to the left and another to the right. You want the triangles to cross at the centerline. Repeat the process in the right and left triangles. You want to have five triangles in all resulting in a tessellated pattern.

This is actually quite complex, and it can be read in a number of different ways. It could be a drawing of three triangles overlapping two other triangles, or two triangles overlapping three. Alternately, we could see it as alternating small triangles, or group the small triangles differently to see hourglass shapes. Conversely, we could see it as tessellated diamonds. These last two inversions represent a flipping of what we call positive and negative shape. Shapes that fit together like puzzle pieces. We'll pay a lot of attention to this idea in later lectures. But returning to this drawing now, we could stack a second grouping above the first to create even greater complexity. Give it a try.

The pattern you've drawn contains a fractal. A fractal's a figure where the constituent parts are identical in shape and only vary in scale—here, triangles. This fractal's called the Sierpinski Triangle, named after Waclaw Sierpinski, an early 20th-century Polish mathematician who wrote about it.

We could arrive at that same pattern taking a fractal approach. So, try this, too: Draw a large triangle. On the diagonal sides of the triangle, at the halfway point, draw a horizontal line across the triangle's width. Then from the right and left ends of this horizontal, draw a diagonal to the center of the base of the triangle.

This is a complex form. We can read it as a small downward-facing triangle within a big upward-facing one; or as three small triangles, two on the ground with a third stacked on top; or as four triangles tightly packed together to create a larger one. As you'll soon see, understanding the possible visual meanings of a given set of lines or shapes is an essential part of learning to draw.

Let's take this a step further. Draw a horizontal connecting the halfway points of the diagonal sides of each of the four new internal triangles. Then draw diagonals from the right and left ends of these lines to the center of each of the triangles' bases.

Here's a hint: In the upward-facing triangles draw a downward-facing one; in a downward-facing triangle, an upward-facing one. If you could make small enough lines, you could continue this infinitely. If we draw two more large triangles—downward-facing ones, flanking the original one—and then draw small internal triangles within the new ones, the Blombos Cave pattern reemerges.

And here's something intriguing: We can use some of the same lines in our flat pattern to draw a three-dimensional volume—a prism. We just need to select the right lines and we'll get the illusion of planes in space. Draw along with me here.

So the first thing we want to do is: Erase that top triangle; just take it away. And then some of the internal lines over here on the left side; do the same. And then we'll do the same thing over here on the right. And I'll bring back this line a little bit. And you'll see that hiding inside our flat pattern was a three-dimensional prism. Now if I go into that and make some elliptical marks here, we can transform that geometric structure into something recognizable—a piece of Jarlsberg. And then if we begin to add some value to show the effects of light. Cast shadow. The illusion becomes that much richer.

And of course, we can refine this; rounding our edges, adding more value, and the illusion will just get that much stronger. And that's just what I'll do. Have a little bit of a powder charcoal here with a soft brush. Work that in with another brush. Make a little bite out of the cheese. Make some of the edges a little more rounded, a little more natural. Just adding some more value to the side deprived of light. Work that in. And we might want to bring some value into the light side—go light value. Enhance the darks.

If you drew along with me here, you've already drawn line, shape, pattern, volume, and light and shade. In the coming lessons, we'll be studying all of these subjects in great detail; it's central to what's magical about drawing.

When we write, we think of a piece of paper as being flat. But to draw, we have to learn to see it as a depth of space. We want to look at the four edges of the page and see them as the four sides of a window frame. The white surface becomes a depth—like a room or a landscape—that we transform through the use of line, shape, mark, and value to suggest volume and space. What we just drew reveals something about how we do this—how something flat and abstract can be nudged to create the illusion of dimension and representation on the page. Measurement, pattern, abstraction, and figuration all flow together on a continuum.

Many artists and professors say that learning to draw is all about learning to see. Not seeing things to identify them like that's a person, that's a tree; but to see them as they actually appear. To see the proportions, angles, values, and the real play of light and color; that's much harder. It requires looking analytically and abstractly. In his book, *Successful Drawing*, Andrew Loomis, wrote, "Drawing is really difficult only to those who do not know what to look for." And there's a peculiar paradox here. In order for us to draw things in a naturalistic or realistic way, in proportion, we have to learn to see them abstractly.

If you're seeing a lot more in the humble lines we've been drawing than when you first looked at the little chunk of ochre a couple minutes ago, you're beginning to understand this. You're beginning to learn to read visual language at an abstract level. Simple lines can have multiple and complex meanings. Lines create shapes; shape, pattern. And shapes can also be arranged to create the illusion of three-dimensional volume. Those volumes can be transformed to appear like things in the world around us.

Pattern, itself, has fascinated artists for, well, at least 80,000 years. We'll consider it more fully in a later lecture.

The Blombos cave pattern emerges across history. We find a variation in the 12th- or 13th-century mosaic floor of the Duomo in Terracina, Italy, and as the underlying structure of a 1968 painting by Frank Stella called Mitered Squares. Note the alternating diamond in the center and hourglass shapes on the right and left. So the ancient pattern we just drew has a distinguished lineage, and can boast amazing longevity.

In fact, I was editing this lecture on a flight from Chicago to Seattle and happened to look-up from my laptop; couldn't help snap a shot of the upholstery of the seat back. While drawing has changed over time and place, there's clearly been a lot of continuity and recycling over its long history. It's one of the oldest human activities we have any record of—been going on for at least 80,000 years. To give some perspective, we've been planting and harvesting for about 10,000 and reading/writing for a mere three.

And this is mirrored in an individual life. Drawing or scribbling is among the first things we do long before learning to read, write, add, or subtract. And while many people stop drawing as they move out of childhood, many others—perhaps more than we might initially think—use some form of drawing in their work. Architects, engineers, illustrators, fashion designers, animators, video game designers, and mathematicians may all use some form of drawing in their work. Even in the realm of finance and business, communicating with images, charts, and graphs is routine. Collectively, we're great creators and consumers of visual language.

Most of the drawing we know of, at least measured in years, is prehistoric, and took place in caves. You've likely seen examples that feature mammoth, bison, and horses like this one from Chauvet in France. The oldest cave drawings date back to about 40,000 years ago. It's incredible to think that it took 40,000 years to get from Blombos to the earliest cave drawings, then another 40 to get from those to the present. So they represent the mid-point in our history of drawing.

This practice continued in Europe for about 30,000 years, with some caves being used repeatedly for thousands of years by generations of our Paleolithic ancestors. And there are other examples of early cave drawing from all over the globe—from India and Southeast Asia to North and South America, including some relatively recent 6,000-year-old examples in Tennessee's Cumberland Plateau.

So cave drawing wins the longevity contest—tens of thousands of years of it. In contrast, people have been drawing on paper for a little over 2,000. It was only invented in the 2nd century B.C.E., in Han Dynasty China. And its method of manufacture was kept secret from the West until the 8th century C.E. During the early historical period, just about every culture or civilization on every continent practiced drawing in one form or another. And there are stunning examples from every corner of the globe.

And, in fact, many of our earliest written languages have origins in drawing. Chinese, spoken by over a billion people today, has its roots in an ancient picture-based writing system going back to at least the Shang Dynasty—that's over 3,000 years ago. And the modern written language retains many picture-based characters. The character for person in Mandarin, rén (人), looks like stick figures—like the ones most of us we drew as kids, though without the arms and head. If you want to write crowd, just pile up three rén to get zhòng (众). The character for wood or tree is mù (木), and you can see it depicts deep roots; above it, the ground; and above that, a comparatively short tree trunk. If you want to write forest, draw three trees to get sēn (森).

Many people today imagine artists drawing in front of a still life, a landscape, or a model. But looking directly at something and drawing it is a relatively recent phenomena, as is the idea of an artist making their own kind of art for that matter. For most of time—from Blombos, to the Shang, and up to pretty recently—people weren't looking at what they were drawing while they were drawing it. In most cultures, in most times, drawing and the related arts consisted of using a set of more-or-less agreed-upon symbols, not unlike the Chinese pictographs that stood for things—like a person, a tree, or an animal—and we refer to this as stylization.

And from the historical record, it would appear that a lot was determined by local convention. Not just how to draw something, but also what to draw, where to draw, and what materials to use. Early Homo sapiens drawing in Chauvet likely learned from the older people and the drawings around them. They broadly followed a set of conventions regarding subject matter, materials, and technique. About 3,500 years ago on the island of Crete, a Minoan would have drawn in a markedly different manner. And 500 years later, an Egyptian, well, would have drawn like an Egyptian. A 5th-entury B.C.E. Greek would have followed Attic conventions, and a 12th-century Song dynasty artist, others. And those would be different again for a 12th-century Japanese e-Maki, or picture-scroll, artist. Of course, a 14th-century Christian Siennese would follow a different set of precepts and procedures. And an 18th-century artist from India's Punjab hills, another yet. While it's evident that art has changed over time and place, there's been a lot of continuity.

While these works are stylistically different, there's also a lot that's shared. As we study drawing, we'll find that artists have been employing many of the same principles of good drawing and design for thousands of years. Their command of craft, their use of line, shape, value, and color—to name a few of the factors we'll be exploring—begins to explain why these works have stood out and been cherished by people of diverse backgrounds and beliefs over centuries.

In this sense, this course is comprehensive. The lessons are firmly based in the game-changing discoveries of the Renaissance. But we'll also be learning from the works of great artists from a range of cultures, covering a broad swath of time from the ancient to the contemporary.

Drawing Materials for Line
Lecture 2

This lecture lists the materials we'll use for the projects in Lectures 4 through 19. We'll go into detail about graphite pencils, charcoal, erasers, brushes and ink, and drafting and measuring tools. In addition to these materials, you'll also need to get a pad of 18-x-24-inch white drawing paper and a 9-x-12-inch or 11-x-14-inch sketchbook. We'll close the lecture by discussing how you should set up your drawing area.

Graphite Pencils

Graphite pencils come in varying degrees of hardness, which is controlled by the amount of clay that is mixed with the graphite. With less clay, the graphite is softer; with more clay, it's harder.

The primary scale used for artist-grade pencils is known as the European letter scale. There are 22 steps in this scale:

10B 9B 8B 7B 6B 5B 4B 3B 2B B HB F H 2H 3H 4H 5H 6H 7H 8H 9H 10H

The softest pencil is the 10B, and the hardest is the 10H. Historically, most people doing general drawing have used pencils in the 4B to 2H range. The very hard pencils are generally used for more technical drawing and highly detailed work. That said, it's well worth having a set of all 22 pencils.

A second scale, called the American scale, has five degrees: 1 2 2½ 3 4. Theoretically, the 1 is equivalent to a European B; the 2 to an HB, the 2½ to an F, the 3 to an H, and the 4 to a 2H. Neither the European nor the U.S. scale is standardized; thus, two pencils of the same number from different manufacturers may vary in their degrees of hardness. Not all brands and all qualities are alike either. For this reason, choose a set of pencils from one good manufacturer. Mitsubishi Hi-Uni makes a good complete set.

In addition to using a pencil sharpener, many artists sharpen their pencils using a utility knife and a sanding block, which allows the pencil to be formed into a number of different shapes.

Test your pencils by making a single straight line on a page with each one, noting the pencil you're using. Then, make a series of small lines or scribbles to get an idea of how each pencil is different. Note, too, that the way a pencil behaves is affected by the kind of paper you use.

Mechanical pencils are also great tools. The graphite for these comes in four thicknesses: 0.3 millimeter, 0.5 millimeter, 0.7 millimeter, and 0.9 millimeter. The graphite used for mechanical pencils ranges from about 4B to 4H.

Charcoal

Along with graphite, charcoal is among the most common drawing materials. It comes in four basic forms: vine or willow, compressed, charcoal pencils, and charcoal powder. For our line drawings, we'll use vine or willow, which tends to be the most forgiving, that is, the easiest to erase.

This charcoal is called vine or willow because it's commonly made by charring pieces of vines or willow in kilns. Because no binder is used—it's just cooked wood—it turns to powder easily. That makes it easy to erase, but then, it's also easy to rub away a morning's work with a careless swipe of your hand.

Vine and willow generally come in four grades: extra soft, soft, medium, and hard. They also come in a variety of shapes and sizes, from thin to thick, from cylindrical to rectangular, and even in chunks. For line, the medium and hard cylindrical sticks work well.

Erasers

Some artists avoid erasing; they want a pristine surface, and heavy erasing can modify the surface texture of the paper. Many other artists embrace erasure. Matisse, for example, made erasing very much a part of his drawing. In this course, erasing will be necessary for many of our projects.

Different erasers modify or erase what you draw in different ways. The factors involved here include erasing power, precision, ability to handle large areas, amount of smearing, and residual marks made by the eraser itself. It's probably best to start with three erasers: a kneaded, a Pink Pearl, and a pencil-type eraser.

Using the kneaded eraser doesn't result in any crumbs, and in fact, the adhesive quality of this eraser can be used to lift crumbs off the page. It's also possible to modify the shape of a kneaded eraser. This eraser works well with vine charcoal and graphite and can be used to modify the darkness of a given line or area of value by gently pulling it across that section of the drawing.

The Pink Pearl eraser has a distinctive wedge shape and a sharp, knifelike edge. If you draw a line that's too thick, you can use a Pink Pearl fairly precisely to make the line thinner. To maintain that sharp edge, trim the eraser with a sharp knife. Pencil-type erasers are also useful for making precise erasures. Again, try your erasers with different types of pencils, charcoal, and paper.

Brush and Ink
Two brushes will work well for drawing line: a small one, about 1/16 to 1/8 inch at the top of the ferrule (the metal piece that holds the hairs together), and another about 3/8 to 5/8 inches long. These types of brushes are made from animal hair or synthetic materials. The most expensive are labeled sable, though they're generally made using mink or weasel hair. For our purposes, synthetic sables, at a fraction of the cost, are fine.

When you buy your brush, it may feel a bit stiff. Many manufacturers dip the hairs in light glue to help maintain the brush's shape. Before you use a new brush, run it under warm water. Gently massage the hairs to remove the glue, then dry the brush.

Your brush should come with a small plastic cap. After you use the brush, rinse it, dry it, and replace the cap to keep the brush from getting damaged. It's difficult to control line or mark if the brush's shape becomes irregular.

Speedball Super Black is a good-quality deep-black ink. To avoid knocking over the bottle of ink when you're drawing, pour some of it into a small cup. Experiment with the brush and ink by making a thin line. It can be helpful to brace your hand against the page so that you're not putting all the weight of your hand onto the brush. Then, try to make a thicker line. Make sure the brush is adequately charged and apply a little more pressure. Next, try creating a discontinuous line, allowing the brush to kind of skip along. Also, experiment with drying out the brush to get lines of varying darkness.

Drafting and Measuring Tools

For basic drafting and measuring tools, you need a clear, gridded, 18-inch ruler; a T-square; and a 14- to 16-inch clear triangle. You also need a transparent grid and a viewfinder, which you can make yourself. The transparent grid is a sheet of clear film with a 1-inch-square grid on it. The viewfinder consists of two L-shaped pieces of cardboard that have been calibrated in line increments. You'll use this to help frame and compose your drawings.

The simplest way to make a grid is to go online and find a site that lets you generate and download custom graph paper. Enter the desired dimensions and print or photocopy the grid onto clear transparency film.

For the viewfinder, you'll need a piece of mat board or heavy cardboard that's at least 12 x 14 inches. First, lightly rule a 2-inch border around the rectangle with a well-sharpened 2H pencil. Next, using your utility knife and straightedge, cut out the center rectangle and put it aside. Turn the frame horizontally. From the upper left corner, measure 12 inches toward the right and make a vertical line. From the bottom right corner, measure 12 inches to the left and make a similar vertical line. Cut along both lines with your utility knife; you should have right angles that are 12 inches in either direction. With your 2H pencil and ruler, calibrate both right angles along their inner edges, measuring out from the 90-degree angle along each arm. Make a thin, light line at each 1-inch interval; then, number the inches. Hold the viewfinder together with two clips.

Setting Up to Draw

If you're making small drawings—about 12 to 15 inches—you can easily draw on a table or with your drawing board supported on your knees and against the table's edge. For larger drawings, if you lay the paper flat on a table, the page will be in a foreshortened position; it will look like a trapezoid instead of a rectangle. As you can imagine, this makes controlling shapes and proportions on the page more difficult. For this reason, larger drawings should be supported more or less vertically, using an easel.

Set up the easel so that the center of the page is about at the height of your collar bone. Both the page and easel should be at about 90 degrees to your line of sight. You should be at a distance of about 18 to 24 inches from the page to allow you to see as much of it as possible without moving your eyes or head. You should also have 5 to 8 feet of back-up room behind so that you can step back periodically and look at your drawing from a greater distance.

When you're working on still lifes, you'll need a second table positioned against a wall for your objects. An average-height table, about 30 inches, with a plain top is best. For many of our projects, white will be ideal for both the table and the wall behind. If your table and wall are not white, you can cover them with a large sheet of white paper or foam core.

When drawing from observation, it's good practice to put the easel or drawing board parallel to and just to the left or right of what you're drawing. Ideally, you want to be able to view your drawing and the subject at the same time without swiveling your head. When you back up, you want to be able to see both at once in the same planar orientation.

As we'll see, when drawing from observation, it's useful to be able to draw from different heights. Having a chair or easel that can be lowered or raised is helpful for this purpose.

Finally, you'll want sufficient light in the room so that you can see light lines and marks on the page. But make sure that the light doesn't throw glare or cast shadow on the page, both of which can be distracting.

Suggested Reading

Cennini, *The Craftsman's Handbook*.

Guptill, *Rendering in Pencil*, chapters 1–3.

Mendelowitz, Faber, and Wakeman, *A Guide to Drawing*, "Beginner's Media," pp. 17–35, and "Dry Media," pp. 184–207.

Drawing Materials for Line
Lecture 2—Transcript

I'd like to talk about the materials we'll be using for the projects involving line. We'll also talk about how to set-up to draw. One of the great things about drawing is that the materials are relatively inexpensive. You can set yourself up with professional quality drawing tools for a very modest sum. For many of the projects you'll need 18 × 24 inch white drawing paper, so get a pad. A smaller sketchbook will also be useful. Something that's in the 9 × 12 or 11 × 14 range would work very well.

To get started, we'll be making a test sheet using graphite, charcoal, and ink. So you need a couple sheets of 18 × 24 inch white paper and a drawing board large enough to accommodate the paper. Put two sheets of paper on your board. The under sheet's a buffer; it adds a little more give to the surface. It also protects your drawing in case there are any irregularities or dirt on the board itself.

Except for the buffer sheet, you don't want to put any other sheets of paper underneath the sheet you're drawing on because it's easy to emboss lines on the sheets underneath. If you put value over an area with embossed lines, you'll get white lines where you've embossed, and that can ruin a drawing. You may want to attach the paper to the board with some clips or tape as you need to.

Let's start with pencils. Though we commonly call these lead pencils, they're actually made of graphite mixed with clay. The root of the word "graphite" comes from ancient Greek; it means to write or draw—same root as graph or graffiti, which are literally little drawings. The first large deposit of graphite was found in England by the mid-16th century. Later, people figured out how to turn it into a powder, then reform it into a solid shape and encase it in wood. Graphite pencils come in varying degrees of hardness, and that's controlled by the amount of clay that gets mixed with the graphite—less clay, softer; more clay, harder. The primary scale used for artist grade pencils is known as a European Letter Scale—10B's the softest and darkest, 10H is the hardest and lightest.

The Numbering system's pretty straightforward; we have 22 pencils in all. And starting over here at the 10B, we go down to 10, 9, 8, 7, 6, 5, 4, down to a single B. Then we climb up on the other side—the hard pencils—from H, 2H, all the way up to that 10H. Between the Bs and the Hs, we have an HB; and between the HB and the H, we have an anomaly—an F. Different ranges have existed at different times, and different manufacturers make different ranges. Some manufacturers only make an 8B–9H. Looking back at some text from the mid-20th century, it seemed like the common range then was from 6B–9H.

One of the first things you want to do, just as I've done here on my page, is to take out all your pencils. Go from the softest to the hardest; make a single line. Note, of course, what pencil you're using. Make a straight line, then make a series of small lines, a little area of value, some scribbles—whatever you want to try—just to get an idea of what each of your pencils does, and how they're different.

The way the pencil behaves is also going to interact with the kind of paper you're using, and they're going to look different on different papers. Historically, most people just doing general drawing have used from about 4B–2H. The very high H pencils are used for drafting, and illustration, and technical drawing, and for very fine detail. But because pencils are so inexpensive, it's great to have the whole range and to experiment with all of them.

This is that European scale, going from 10B–10H. But, of course, you're familiar with the famous No. 2 pencil, and that's part of the American scale; and that one has five degrees, going from a 1, 2, 2.5, 3, and a 4—although you don't see the 3s and the 4s very much. Over here, I have a 1 and a 2. Technically the 1 is an equivalent to a B, the 2 to an HB, the 2.5 to an F, the 3 to an H, and the 4 to a 2H; but neither the European or U.S. scale is standardized. So if you have two pencils of the same number but from different manufacturers—let's say you have two 2B pencils—one may well be softer than the other; that's pretty common. And not all brands and not all qualities are alike either. So what a good idea is to get yourself a whole set of pencils from one good manufacturer, and that way at least they'll correspond to each other across that manufacturer's scale.

Of course, there are all kinds of pencils—like this one over here—which isn't part of either scale. But all these pencils are great; they can all be used. Look around your house, see what kind of pencils you have, gather them all together, and begin to make some marks with them in addition to the ones you make with your full set. And let's just make a couple marks here. Here we are with this No. 1 pencil, which is supposedly equivalent to a B, and I'll put it right under my B over here—and it's just a little bit lighter; a little bit harder. Here's my No. 2, which is supposedly like an HB. And it, too, is just a bit lighter than the HB that I've used from this set. We'll take this—which is just called a jet black, extra smooth—and make a line with that as well. And you can see that's a very robust dark pencil, even more so than my 10B.

One thing we want to talk about is sharpening our pencils. And, of course, we can use a standard pencil sharpener to sharpen a pencil, and it gives us a nice fine point, and that's very good for a lot of drawing, and certainly useful for writing. But artists sharpen their pencils in a variety of ways, and the two tools we call upon are a utility knife and a sanding block. And what we can do is we can taper the pencil in a number of ways. I'm going to take this No. 1 pencil here, and what we're going to do is we're going to expose a lot more of the graphite than we normal would with a regular pencil sharpener.

What I'm doing is I'm holding the utility knife in my right hand. And I'm just keeping it steady in my right hand, but I'm pushing it forward with the thumb of my left hand, and I'm trying to cut not at too deep a diagonal. I want to remove the wood without gouging the graphite itself. I can use the utility knife to begin to shape the graphite to a gradual point. I'm rotating the pencil in my left hand as I'm scraping with the utility knife in my right. I can combine that with using my sanding block to get a very long exposed piece of graphite. So now, I cannot only get a nice thin line using the point, but I can also get a much thicker line using that side plane.

A variation on that is to take that sanding block and to make a wedge shape—kind of a chisel shape—on the pencil. Now I have my edge where I can make a nice, very thin line; and just by twisting the pencil—turning the pencil—I can now move from thin to thick, and back again. A variation on that is to take that wedge shape and to blunt it, and this way I can get a continuously thicker line—as thick as the width of the graphite itself.

What I'd like you to do is to start with your cheap pencils, just some pencils you have kicking around your drawers of your house, and you'll want to practice sharpening them. Bring them to different kinds of points, and then play with them on your paper. Once you've figured out a good way to sharpen them, what you want to do is take two of your good pencils—I have a 6B here, and a 6H, which I've sharpened into the wedge shape—and then you can take these and see how they'll behave differently. Here we are with a 6B on the wedge, back to the point; on the wedge, to the point; on the wedge, to the point. And you'll want to see how that plays out. So that was the 6B. Here we are with the 6H, a much harder pencil, and I'm on the wedge—on the wedge, back to the point. And so you'll find with a box of pencils, you can get a great, great variety of line.

As you whittle down your pencils, they get smaller and smaller, of course, and a good tool to have—and you might want to get a couple of these—are pencil extenders. Very simply, the small pencil will fit into the extender and it just gives you more life out of your pencil.

Another great took are mechanical pencils. They come in four different thicknesses of lead. We call them lead, again, it's still graphite. We have a .3mm, .5mm, .7mm, and a .9mm. The leads that they make for these come from about 4B to 4H, so not as extensive as with the graphite pencils.

The way these work is—we'll have the .3mm here—is that you generally take off the eraser end and deposit the leads, which are about two inches long, into the pencil and then click them forward. Here I have a .3mm— that's a very small lead—with a 2H, which is on the hard side; and we'll make a line with it. Nice and light; thin. Now let's try that .5mm with an HB lead, so this is a little thicker and a little darker. Next, a .7mm; a little thicker yet with B lead. And finally, a .9mm with a 2B led; thickest and darkest of the group. These will all be useful when we get into perspective and more technical drawing.

A related tool is the lead holder; and these take leads from 6B to 6H, and they're longer, and they generally come in tubes or containers—something like this. This, unlike the mechanical pencils, these generally insert from the front end. These we sharpen with something called a lead pointer. So using the lead pointer, we can bring the lead to a fine point. Let's make a line with it. I have a 2B lead here. And we can also use our sanding block to bring it to a wedge shape. This way I can get a fine line with the edge of the wedge, and as I rotate, I can get that much thicker line; and I can move back and forth between the two. So try all your graphite tools. Make lines of various lightness, thickness, and darkness; try sharpening in various ways; and test them all out.

Along with graphite, charcoal's among the most common drawing materials.

It comes in four basic forms: vine or willow, compressed, charcoal pencil, and charcoal powder. For our line drawings, we'll be using vine and willow. We'll talk about the others later as we begin to get into value. Vine or willow's the most forgiving; easiest to erase. It's called vine or willow because it's commonly made from pieces of grape or other vines, or pieces of willow.

One of the first western books on art materials, *Il Libro dell'Arte—The Book of Art*—was written in late 14th-century Italy by Cennino Cennini. And he gives us a recipe for making charcoal:

> Take a nice dry willow stick and make some slips of it the length of the palm of your hand. Divide these pieces like match sticks. Then take a brand new casserole and put in enough to fill-up the casserole.

He goes on to tell us to wrap it up tightly and take it to the baker's at the end of the day, after he's all finished work, then leave it in his oven until morning.

The idea here is to let the wood char at the right temperature and for the right amount of time; and it has to cook in the absence of oxygen, hence the tight wrapping—oxygen gets in and you get ash instead of charcoal. Today, artist's charcoal is made in kilns. Since there's no binder, just cooked wood, it turns to powder pretty easily. On the one hand, that makes it very forgiving—it's among the easiest materials to erase. But it's highly fugitive on the other—easy to rub away a morning's work with a careless swipe of the hand.

In fact, Cennini tells us, "Take a feather—chicken or goose, as may be—and sweep the charcoal off what you have drawn. That drawing will disappear."

Vine and willow generally come in four grades: extra soft, soft, medium, and hard. They also come in a variety of shapes and sizes from thin to thick, from cylindrical to rectangular, and even chunks. For line, the cylindrical sticks work very well.

So, here we have four grades of that cylindrical vine and willow charcoal. We have an extra soft, we have a soft, we have a medium, and we have a hard. Let's take a look and see what kinds of lines they give us.

We'll start with the extra soft. If we want to get a thin line, we can use that edge—that rounded edge. And if we want to get a thicker line, we can just use some more pressure—that's very common; it's very brittle stuff. And if you put pressure on it, especially when it's very long, it can break. So that's our extra soft. Here's our soft. We'll put some more pressure on that, again, breaking.

Here's our medium, and you can see I've sharpened this to a point; and we can use the edge of it to get something thicker, and we can move from one to the other so it can get a real variety. And the way this sharpens; very easily. Just put it in your pencil sharpener, and we get a point. And the hard. Again, we can sharpen; get a nice point. And we can use the side edge to get thicker lines as well.

Just as with our pencils, we'll wear our charcoal down, so this charcoal holder is another great tool. We can take even our very small little slips of charcoal and still get some real use out of them.

Next up, erasers. Some artists avoid erasing; they want a pristine surface, and heavy erasing can modify the surface texture of your paper. Many other artists embrace erasure. Matisse, for example, made erasing very much a part of his drawing. So, there's an aesthetic consideration here. For this course, erasing's a necessary part of many of the projects, so don't be timid with your erasers. I like to have every eraser I can find. Unlike collecting vintage automobiles, collecting erasers is a very affordable, if less romantic, pastime.

Different erasers modify or erase what we draw in different ways; they all have strengths and weaknesses. The factors involved include: erasing power, precision, ability to handle large areas, amount of smearing, and residual marks made by the eraser itself.

I'd suggest getting three different erasers to start: a kneaded, a pink pearl, and a pencil type eraser. The kneaded is a great eraser. It can erase and won't give us any crumbs at all. In fact, here I have some eraser crumbs. We can use its adhesive quality to actually lift the crumbs off of our page. As you can see, we can modify its shape. So sometimes, when I want to get in and just get a small amount of something, I can make a little shape on my eraser so I just get exactly what I want. It's terrific—this is our vine charcoal here— very good for the vine charcoal; takes it right off.

With other things, one of the great capabilities of this is that it really acts like a volume switch. Let's say I don't want to take it all away, but I just want to make that gray a bit lighter; I can lightly tap it, and I can lighten my gray. Similarly, with the graphite—if I take a look at some graphite over here, and I think it's just too dark; if I just tap with the kneaded eraser, I take the volume down. The other thing, as we knead it, it becomes self-cleaning. So that's one of the great qualities of this, it does something that a lot of other erasers do not.

Our next eraser is the pink pearl. It has that distinctive wedge shape, and it's very useful because it has a sharp, knife-like edge. So if I have some line where the line is too thick, I can use that in a fairly precise way to make my line thinner. Over time, that knife-like edge is going to wear down. So what we're going to want to do is have a good kitchen knife—a sharp knife— available. And if we take these erasers that have worn down, and we can just cut into them and return to a nice knife-like edge.

Next are these pencil type erasers. Again, very useful for making more precise type of erasures. I want to thin out a line; I can really almost draw with the eraser, tapering my line as I need to.

Another useful tool is the Chamois cloth. While not an eraser—if we remember, Cennino Cennini tells us that take that feather and you can wipe away the charcoal—if I take this and just wipe the charcoal, a lot of it will go away. So it can be used also as an erasing tool.

There are many other vinyl and rubber erasers; you'll find them all at your art stores. There, in fact, are electric erasers, and there are erasers which will fit on the back of your pencils. All of these are very useful, and they'll interact with different materials. Each one will interact with different materials and papers in different ways.

One of the things I'd like you to do is to take your erasers and try them with your different materials—with your different types of graphite; 10B–10H, any other pencils you have around, and with your charcoal—and experiment with your erasers, and see what they'll do.

You'll notice that as I've been erasing, I have all of these eraser crumbs; and we're going to want to get rid of that as we work. One of the easiest ways is simply to lift up your page, and we're going to take it over the garbage can and just shake it off. And some of it will come off, but some of it will still adhere to our page. So what we're going to want to do here, as we noted, we could use that kneaded eraser to take up some of it. We could also just lightly blow and sometimes that will get rid of the erasure.

Then we have various types of brushes we can use to get rid of the erasure. Sometimes you'll want something rather pointed where I could really get in, in a delicate way. A one-inch chip brush, or a two-inch chip brush, can also work pretty well, and we want to flick up and away so we don't spread the material off our paper. And of course, as we get into some perspective drawing, we may want to use a larger brush—a drafting brush.

Next, let's talk about ink. You'll want a deep black—a good one is Speedball Super Black. For line, a small brush about $1/16$–$1/8$ of an inch at the top of the ferrule—that's the metal piece that holds the hairs together—and about $3/8$ to $5/8$ inches long works very well. These types of brushes are either made from animal hair or from synthetic material. The most expensive are labeled sable, though they're generally made using mink or weasel hair. For our purposes, synthetic sables at a fraction of the cost will be just fine.

When you buy your brush, it may feel a bit stiff. Many manufacturers dip the hair in light glue to help maintain the brush's shape. Before you use a new brush, run it under warm water, gently massage the hairs to remove the glue, dry the brush, and you're set. Your brush should come with a small plastic cap; hold onto it. After you use your brush, rinse it, dry it, and replace the cap. This keeps the brush from getting damaged. It's very difficult to control line or mark if the brush's shape becomes irregular.

So the first thing you want to do is to take your ink and pour a little off into a cup. You run the risk of knocking the whole thing over and making a mess if you just use the ink right out of the bottle. This way we can contain any problems.

First thing, I'd like you to try and do is to make a thin line. It helps if you brace your hand against the page so you're not putting all the weight of your hand onto the brush.

Then try and make a thicker line. And, again, we just need to make sure the brush is adequately charged, and we'll apply a little more pressure. You can see that the range of mark—the range of line thickness—we can get with a little brush like this, is pretty extraordinary.

We can also go from thin to thick to thin again just by changing that pressure. And we can expand the range by having a couple brushes. These are even fairly similar in size. I can still get a fairly thin line with one of this size, and I can get something really quite robust as well.

Another thing you want to try is creating a discontinuous line. We'll let the brush kind of skip along, and we'll have an even greater quality of lightness when it's discontinuous.

Another thing you can try is drying out the brush so that rather than getting a full black, or even a dark gray, we can get a very, very light gray—a real whisper. I'm going to take out a little more ink here. And as we pull more and more ink out of the brush; well there I've gone—I don't know if you can even see that—very, very, very faint, faint gray.

Use the rest of the page that you have here to experiment, make some different kinds of lines, use your graphite, your charcoal, your erasers, and ink, and see all the different kinds of lines that you can come up with.

Next, let's look at our drafting and measuring tools. A gridded, clear 18-inch ruler, like this 18-inch C-Thru Graph Ruler is very useful. Line up a grid line on the ruler with the vertical edge of your page, and you can draw a good horizontal. Line up a grid line with the horizontal edge of your page, and you can draw a vertical.

For greater accuracy, we use a T-Square. Make sure the edges of your page are parallel to the edges of your drawing board. Place the T against the vertical edge of the drawing board to draw a horizontal line. Place the T on the top of the drawing board to draw a vertical line. Put the T-square back in the horizontal position. Take out your clear triangle—one that's 14–16 inches will work best. Put the base of the triangle on the T-square. Now you can easily draw verticals. Move it out of the way to draw horizontals with your T-square. This will be a time-saver when we get into linear perspective.

I'll be using what's called a parallel straight edge drawing board instead of the T-square. It's an option to investigate if you get into a lot of technical drawing.

As you begin to generate a lot of lines, the graphite can rub-off on these tools. If this happens, your tools will begin to spread a gray mist over your drawing; so keep an eye on this. If your tools begin to get dirty, wash them with a small amount of light soap and warm water. Dry them well, and you'll be ready to continue drawing.

The last tools in this category you'll make yourself. They include a transparent grid and a viewfinder. The transparent grid's a sheet of clear film with a one-inch square grid on it. The viewfinders are L-shaped pieces of cardboard you'll use to help you frame and compose your drawings.

Let's start with that grid. The simplest way to make one is to go online. You'll find a number of sites that let you generate custom graph paper and download it. Just search custom graph paper. You'll be able to enter the dimensions and print this or photocopy it onto clear transparency film. You could also draw one with your ruler and T-Square, or on a program like Photoshop; then, similarly, copy or print onto transparency film.

For the viewfinder, you'll need a piece of mat board or heavy cardboard that's at least 12 × 14 inches.

First, lightly rule a two-inch border around the rectangle with a well-sharpened 2H pencil. If you have a ruler like this, which is exactly two inches wide, you can line it up with the mat board's edge and trace.

Next, using your utility knife and straight edge, cut out the center rectangle and put it aside. Make sure you do this on some kind of safe surface—a clean kitchen cutting board will work fine.

Turn the frame horizontally. From the upper left corner, measure 12 inches toward the right and make a vertical line. From the bottom right corner, measure 12 inches to the left and make a similar vertical line. Cut along both lines with your utility knife and you should have right angles, which are 12 inches in either direction.

With your 2H pencil and ruler, calibrate both right angles along their inner edges measuring out from the 90-degree angle along each arm. Make a thin, light line at each one-inch interval, then, number your inches.

You'll also need two clips to hold your viewfinder together.

There are a couple miscellaneous items that will be useful, including masking tape, a compass, some push-pins, and a box or carrying case for your materials.

Our final topic's setting-up your work area. If you're making small drawings–say, not more than 12–15 inches in any direction—you can easily draw on a table, or with your drawing board supported on your knees against the table's edge. Then arrange your materials and supplies on the table so they're conveniently at hand. Larger drawings need to be supported more or less vertically. An easel's a logical choice.

Here's the reason. If we lay the paper flat on a table, the page is in a foreshortened position. It will look like a trapezoid instead of a rectangle. As you can imagine, this makes controlling shapes and proportions on the page more difficult. Ideally, you want to set up so that the center of the page is at about at the height of your clavicle—your collarbone. That's a default position. Of course, you can raise it and lower it as needed, even rotate your drawing to make working on a given section more comfortable or natural.

You also want the easel to be at about 90 degrees to your line of sight, and you want to be 18–24 inches from the page. This will, of course, depend on your arm length, but one of the goals is to draw at a distance from the page that allows you to see as much of the page as possible without moving your eyes or head.

When drawing at an easel, many people set up their materials on a table to their side at a 90-degree angle to the easel; on the right for righties, on the left for lefties. Having backup room behind you is a real help, five to eight feet's ideal. That's so that you can walk back periodically and look at your drawing from a greater distance. It's much easier to see how the various parts of the drawing are relating with a bit of distance.

When we're working on still-life problems, drawing from observation, you want a second table positioned against a wall for your objects. An average height table about 30 inches, with a plain top is best—something without any distracting wood grain or pattern. A plain wall's best, too. For many of our projects, white will be ideal for both. If your table and wall aren't white, you can cover them with a large sheet of white paper or foam core.

When drawing from observation, it's good practice to put the easel or drawing board parallel to, and just to the left or right of what you're drawing. Ideally, you want to be able to view your drawing and the subject at the same time without swiveling your head. When you backup you want to be able to see both at once in the same planar orientation.

As we'll see, when drawing from observation, it's very useful to be able to draw from different heights. These different views can be dramatic and can make our compositions and drawings much more interesting. Having a chair that can be lowered or raised, that's a real benefit. Having an easel with a similar range is equally useful. Even having a small low stool and a sturdy box or step-ladder to stand on can all be great additions.

You'll also want sufficient light in the room so that you can see light lines and marks on your page, but you want to make sure that the light isn't throwing glare or cast shadow on your page—both can be distracting. You're going to also need some still-life objects. You'll be able to use many things you likely have in your home. We'll talk about specifics in the lessons ahead. We'll also be doing some self-portraits, so a full-length movable mirror will be extremely useful.

These materials will get us started. We'll talk about additional materials in future lectures as we need them.

Drawing Fundamentals and First Exercises
Lecture 3

M any people have the idea that artists stand in front of a subject and draw what they see, but in fact, most of the drawing you have likely seen is the result of some mix of observation, construction, and abstraction. *Drawing from observation* means drawing what we see before us. *Construction* refers to methods for drawing that rely on building what we draw using shapes, geometric solids, and linear perspective. *Abstraction* refers to the way we bring abstract visual thinking to bear on the drawing decisions we make. An example would be thinking about how we divide a drawing—essentially a rectangle—into two horizontal sub-rectangles to signify a tabletop and a wall in a still life or the land and sky in a landscape. We'll learn more about these aspects of drawing as we move through the six sections of this course: (1) introductory materials; (2) line and formal language; (3) linear perspective; (4) value, texture, and color; (5) the figure; and (6) advanced approaches and projects. This lecture offers an overview of the course.

Drawing as a Language

Drawing is a language. Thus, studying drawing can be similar to studying a new language. We start by learning about different kinds of line—comparable to learning a new alphabet. Next, we use line to draw shape, just as we use letters to form words. Then, we use shape to construct drawings of individual objects—like forming words into sentences. And we draw multiple objects together in coherent compositions—similar to organizing sentences into paragraphs.

In drawing, our grammatical parts are line, shape, volume, mark, value, and color, among other elements. If we want to make sophisticated drawings, we must understand how these pieces function in the visual realm.

Examples Used in the Course

One art historical cliché describes the history of art as a series of advances through tumultuous breaks from the ignorance or overbearing restrictions of past conventions. There's also much ink dedicated to showing how one culture's art is markedly different from that of another. No doubt, art has certainly changed across time and place, but at the same time, there has also been a great degree of continuity in the language of art across the continents and over the millennia of drawing practice.

The reason that many diverse people have used similar visual strategies is that our eyes and brains—our hardware and software—have remained pretty much the same for a long period. Thus, a large portion of the underlying visual mechanics of making drawings has remained fairly consistent. This is one of the reasons that we can look at art made by people who lived very different lives from our own and find the things they made evocative, potent, and beautiful. At a certain level, we "get it" because these works were crafted to speak to beings wired like ourselves.

Looking at examples of artworks from a range of periods, cultures, and geographic locations, we'll see that artists in different times and places have used similar visual strategies and techniques. Because their work has stood the test of time and local bias, it's reasonable to suspect that the visual ideas they've employed are good ones.

Analyzing Drawings
Looking at drawings is as important to an aspiring draftsperson as listening to music, tasting food, or watching a game is to an aspiring musician, chef, or athlete. But it's also crucial to make the shift to active analysis. Many of us drive cars, but our relationship with them ends there. Someone who loves cars and wants to understand them deeply takes cars apart and puts them back together again. To be a real student of drawing means that your relationship with drawing must become analytical. You must take drawings apart, reverse engineer them, and reconstruct them.

How to Use These Lectures
Each lecture in this course is about 30 minutes long, but it will generally take you much longer than that to complete the drawing projects in the lectures. For this reason, you may want to stop and start the lectures as you draw. Of course, you can also watch each lecture all the way through once, then go back and replay it to do the exercises. Because one-on-one feedback is

helpful in learning to draw, you may also want to watch the lectures with a family member or a small group of friends who are also interested in learning to draw. This activity will allow you to offer one another feedback and constructive criticism on your drawings.

Topics to Be Discussed
You can think of these 36 lectures as divided into six conceptual sections. The first includes introductory materials. The second focuses on line and introduces formal language or drawing's grammar. The third section provides an overview of linear perspective. The fourth bring us back to our discussion of formal language to cover value, texture, and color. The fifth section focuses on the figure. And the final section details advanced approaches and projects. In general, the progression of topics in these sections will be as follows:

- Contour, construction, and cross-contour line

- Aggregate shape

- Object-ground relations

- Positive and negative shape

- Composition

- Gestural line

- Proportion

- Principles for creating the illusion of three-dimensional space on a two-dimensional surface

- Linear perspective

- Value

- Mark and texture

- Color theory, properties, and palettes

- The human figure, canons of proportions, and artistic anatomy

- Advanced concepts and projects.

There is a natural progression in this sequence of study, from concentrating more on acquiring knowledge, skill, and technique to thinking about how to use skills in reference to specific content related to your own interests. The goal at the beginning is mastery of the breadth of accumulated knowledge. As you advance, you'll be able to apply this knowledge and skill to your own individual creative vision.

Take your time as you move through the course. If you do, you'll find each new piece building on what you've learned in prior lessons, and you'll be on your way to developing a depth of knowledge regarding many of the ways in which drawings are conceived and made. Whether you choose to fully work through all the problems or not, simply developing a conceptual understanding of the ways in which artists think and pursue their work will fundamentally change the way you see both art and the world around you.

Suggested Reading

J. Paul Getty Museum, *Formal Analysis*.

Kennedy Center, *Formal Visual Analysis*.

Pumphrey, *The Elements of Art*, pp. 55–61.

Drawing Fundamentals and First Exercises
Lecture 3—Transcript

These lectures incorporate what—after four decades of study, studio work, and teaching—I've found to be the most important and useful things to know about drawing. Knowing what I do now, it's what I'd have wanted someone to teach me when I was starting out. Many people have the idea that artists stand in front of a model, a still life, or landscape and draw what they see. But in fact, most of the art you've likely seen—drawing, paintings, and the like—was arrived at through some mix of what I'd refer to as observation, construction, and abstraction.

Drawing from observation means drawing what we see before us. Construction, that refers to the methods for drawing that rely on building what we draw using shapes, geometric solids, and linear perspective. We'll be combining both approaches. Abstraction refers to the way we can bring abstract visual thinking to bear on the drawing decisions we make. An example would be thinking about how we divide a drawing—essentially a rectangle—into two horizontal sub-rectangles to signify a floor plane and a wall plane in an interior, or a tabletop and wall in a still life, or land and sky in a landscape, or water and sky in a landscape or seascape.

The subject matter's clearly different in each of these works, and they're stylistically different, too. But all four depend on a similar abstract compositional strategy. Much of what we call the formal language, or the grammar of drawing, operates at this kind of abstract level; even though the content's descriptive, and the work might be even be classified as realist.

To draw a bottle in a still life or a figure in a room, we're really not, in a sense, drawing a bottle or a figure at all; we're simply drawing lines. But if we get the right lines in the right places, the still life or figure emerges. That means the lines have to be of a certain type and begin, end, and meet at specific points. In fact, even to draw the simple triangular pattern in the first lecture, you had to draw specific kinds of lines—lines that were horizontal and diagonal, and some had to be parallel. Drawing these kinds of lines, and having them meet at specific points, involves measuring. We'll be calling on these skills throughout the course, so practicing all this is a good place to start.

There's an entry in Leonardo's journals titled: *De' Giochi che debono fare I disegnaitori*—*The Games that People Who Draw Should Play*. He begins by saying, "You should always practice such things as may be of use, giving your eye good practice in judging accurately." He goes on to describe a competitive measuring game where one person draws a straight line on a wall. Then all the others, standing at the same distance from the wall, try to gauge the line's length. Whoever closest wins.

Here are several games or first exercises I'd like you to try. They all benefit eye-hand coordination and will help you when drawing everything from a still life, to a landscape, to the figure. In that sense, they're pretty serious games.

Try drawing a horizontal line. And then try finding the half-measure. Then the quarters. Then the eighths. Then try and draw a line that's parallel to the first line you just drew. And then you can try doing that vertically as well— parallel vertical lines. And try diagonals, too.

Here's another great first exercise: Give yourself a point. And then another point. And just connect them with a straight line. You can kind of trace over lightly what we call phantom drawing—just moving the pencil back and forth to get an idea of the angle. You can even leave little traces of graphite as you go. And then when you feel like you have an idea about where that line is going, let the pencil touch the page and pull your line across.

Let's try another one. We'll just add another dot. Again, the same thing— tracing back and forth over the line, over the direction. And as you gain confidence, make the line.

And let's do one more. Make another diagonal. Give yourself another point. Trace back and forth over the page. Leave small amounts of graphite. And then make your line.

Another exercise is making curved lines. So, so far we've made verticals, horizontals, and diagonals. We can give ourselves two marks along a line segment. Find the center point. And then try and find an even curve going from one to the other. Follow the same process. When you feel comfortable, make the line.

Here's another exercise: Give yourself a vertical. Then cross it with a horizontal. And then draw the 45s through the center—all this is great aiming practice. And then try and take an even curve around the whole thing.

We've been drawing horizontal, vertical, diagonal, and curvilineal lines. When we draw with line, those are our major directions; those are the major types of lines we'll be using. If we practice those kinds of lines, we'll be in good shape to do a lot of different kinds of drawing.

I'll make a curved line segment, then another. A vertical, another. Horizontal. Diagonal. Another diagonal.

If we can associate lines with measure, we can begin to draw all kinds of complex things: diagonal, diagonal, horizontal. And I think you can see where this is going. I'll draw a figure standing in a room. And what you'll find is that all the lines I use are either horizontal, vertical, diagonal, and curvilineal lines. Once you've tried this with your graphite, try it with your other materials, too—charcoal, pen and ink—just drawing lines. And I can draw a rug on the floor with a pattern, it's just made up of diagonal and horizontal lines.

To draw a light fixture on a ceiling, all I need is some: curvilineal line here grouped into an ovoid, two verticals, and another curvilineal line segment. A curtain on a window—nothing more than some horizontals, and some curvilineal line segments.

One of our powerful tools is overlap. If I show that the curtain is securely overlapping the wall, we'll feel that it's in front and the wall's behind. At the bottom of the curtains, now I'm drawing cross contours—and we'll learn about those in a coming lesson. They help give us a sense of three dimensionality when we're drawing with line.

We can take flat things and make them feel three-dimensional by adding planes. I can take the flat shape of the painting on the wall and make it dimensional by giving it a plane too. We can take those simple shapes and make slight adaptations to make them more resemble things like an arm, a leg, a breast. Taper them a little more. Round a little here; more angular there—small adaptations to some very regular shapes.

You'll learn to control the viewer's eye and create focal areas and focal points by creating hierarchies of value. All else being equal. Where there's higher contrast, well, that's where our eyes going to go first.

I think you'll find that studying drawing's a lot like studying a language. We just started with some lines; they're like letters of the alphabet. And, as you see, we can use them to draw figures and all kinds of other things—just like letters forming words, verbs and nouns, adjectives and adverbs. And soon we'll be constructing sentences and paragraphs—whole compositions. In this way, the lectures build cumulatively in a step-by-step fashion with each new idea or concept building on the previous ones.

We don't think much about the underlying grammatical structure of the sentences we create and hear as we go through a typical language-saturated day. One exception, of course, is when we're speaking a foreign language—one that we're not too familiar with yet. And we think, "Oh yeah, the verb needs to go over here. And I need this termination to agree with my pronoun; and right, the indirect object gets shuttled over there." But as you begin to master the language, all this becomes more and more automatic and natural.

Similarly, if you're learning to play a musical instrument, at first you're hyper-conscious of which finger goes where. But after some practice, you think much less about the mechanics and more about the music itself.

You'll likely find the same thing here. A whole lot of what we call instinct, or having even a feel for something, is often really an instance of deeply engrained learning. Einstein once said, "Intuition is nothing but the outcome of earlier intellectual experience." In drawing, our grammatical parts are line, shape, volume, mark, value, color—amongst a number of others. If we want to begin to make sophisticated drawings, we have to begin to understand how these pieces function in the visual realm.

The approach is pretty simple. I'll describe and explain a new concept or technique, I'll situate it in its historical context, and illustrate it with visual examples. These will include my own drawings and diagrams, additional ones created by the very talented team here at The Great Courses, examples from my students, and masterworks from a range of periods and traditions in the history of art.

One art historical cliché described that history as a series of advances through tumultuous breaks from the ignorance or overbearing restrictions of the past conventions. There's also a lot of ink dedicated to showing how one culture's art is markedly different from that of another. No doubt, art has certainly changed with time and place. But at the same time, I think you'll find—as you move through these lectures—that there's also been a great degree of continuity in drawing's language across all the continents and over millennia of drawing practice.

Earlier, I showed this watercolor by Thomas Eakins—a 19th-century American. I used it as an example of the way which artists compose. In this case, the drawing's shape—a rectangle—is divided into two sub-rectangles; a lower one for water, and an upper one for sky. I could equally have chosen a 13th-century Chinese example to demonstrate the same point. This is titled, *Mountain Market, Clear with Rising Mist* by Xià Guī. Again, the rectangle's divided in half. The lower rectangle contains the near landscape; the upper, the mountains receding in the distance and sky.

I'd suggest the reason why many diverse people have employed similar visual strategies is because our eyes and brains—our hardware and software—have remained pretty much the same for a very long period. So, a fair portion of the underlying visual mechanics of making drawings has remained pretty consistent. It's one of the reasons why we can look at art made by people who lived very different lives from our own and find the things they made evocative, potent, and beautiful. At a certain level, we get it because these works were crafted to speak to beings who were wired just like ourselves.

I've made it a point in my teaching at the university, and in these lectures here, to include examples of artworks from a range of periods, cultures, and geographic locations. My thinking has been that if artists cumulatively— in different times and places—have used the same strategy or technique for millennia, and their work has stood the test of time and local bias; it's reasonable to suspect that the visual idea's a good one and has some real staying power. The examples I use also vary in terms of material or media, too. Of course, I've called upon all types of drawings from graphite, to charcoal, to pen or brush and ink—obviously so. But I've also included examples from directly related fields—from art practices which are direct extensions of drawing per se, like painting and printmaking.

In the first lecture, I defined drawing as marking surfaces. With that in mind, I've included the incised piece of ochre from the Blombos Cave; as well as painted ceramics; Chinese brush paintings on silk; and, in a more contemporary vein, examples from comics and animation. As I noted in the first lecture, drawing has been and is going on all around us in many shapes and forms. In choosing each example, my main criteria has been that it effectively illustrates the visual point being made.

Looking at drawing is as important to an aspiring draftsperson as listening to music, tasting food, or watching the game is to an aspiring musician, chef, or athlete. But it's crucial to make the shift to active analysis. I drive a car, but it ends there. Someone who loves cars wants to understand them deeply; takes a car apart and puts it back together again—or better yet, several cars. To be a real student of drawing means that your relationship with drawing has to become analytical. We have to take drawings apart, reverse engineer them, and put them back together again.

I'll be helping you develop the abilities needed to understand how a given drawing has been made and why it's been made the way it has. If you can begin to learn how to do this on your own, you'll be well on your way to becoming a successful draftsperson and autodidact. Studying examples is very important. Many are available online for download; others, in books on drawing. Build your own image library so that you can consult them as you draw.

As I noted earlier, I've supplemented the examples of artworks by professional artists to include numerous examples by my students. Of course, I've chosen very good and excellent examples, but my students do very good and excellent work on a regular basis. These examples will give you a clear visual take on possible responses to a given drawing problem. They should also serve as encouragement and inspiration. What we're doing here is absolutely doable. People just like you learn to draw all the time.

Each lecture is about 30 minutes long. It'll generally take you much longer than that to complete the drawing projects I'll describe, so you may want to stop and start the lectures at intervals. That said, if you want to watch the whole thing through and just listen, and then go back and replay the videos doing the exercises a second time; wouldn't be doing yourself any harm.

In learning to draw, one-on-one feedback can be really helpful. So if you have a family member; or a friend; or even better, a couple friends who are also interested in learning to draw, you'd likely find it useful to work together. You might want to watch the lessons together, or perhaps meet once a week to get together to critique each other's drawings. It can also keep you motivated. Getting together with others to talk about art and drawing can also be a lot of fun.

Whether or not you pursue art beyond this course, I think you'll find that studying drawing will change the way you experience your own visual perception. It will literally change the way you see the world, and significantly change the way you'll be able to appreciate the paintings and drawings you see in museums and galleries.

The 36 lectures that make up this course run about 18 hours; but, as I noted, the drawing projects are another matter. It could well take someone eight months to over a year to work through all the exercises and assignments. People are routinely surprised at all the things artists actually consider when they draw. While they may have some inkling that proportion and light are important topics, they generally have little exposure to ideas about negative shape, line weight, or the use of value as a compositional tool.

And some students are impatient to get to certain topics, like shading or the figure. So I'd like to take about 15 minutes and lay out before you the progression followed in this course. This way, you'll get a sense of how the parts connect and begin to appreciate how each piece is important to the whole endeavor.

You can think about the lectures as divided into six conceptual sections. The first contains introductory materials. The second focuses on line, and introduces formal language or drawing's grammar. The third section provides an overview of linear perspective. The fourth brings us back to finish our discussion of formal language while covering value, texture, and color. The fifth section focuses on the figure. And the final section details advanced approaches and projects.

We've actually already started your study if you drew along with me earlier. Line's foundational, and it's actually quite complex. There are many kinds of line, each with different utilities and expressive potentials. At first, we'll speak about two types of line: contour, and construction line. We'll see how together, they can help us accurately draw simple shapes. And we'll use these simple shapes to draw everyday objects like the kinds of things found in still lives—like this pitcher here. We'll learn how by adding a third type of line—cross contour; a line in the inside of the shape—we can create the illusion of volume and three-dimensions in the objects we draw.

You're probably already seeing how the drawing exercises we did earlier will pay off. To draw the pitcher and the block, we have to draw horizontal, vertical, diagonal, and curving lines. The lines have to relate to one another in terms of measure and meet at specific locations if we want to create the shapes we need. So keep practicing those lines; they're fundamental to everything we'll do. We'll talk about different types of shapes, including aggregate shape. Now that's a kind of shape that holds all our objects together compositionally in relation to the shape of the drawing itself.

It will also help us control proportions because it serves as the container for the objects we'll be drawing. We'll also learn about object-ground relations—essentially, how all the main objects or subjects in a drawing or painting relate to even larger shapes we call the ground shapes, and you'll learn how these shapes construct the shape of the drawing itself. Next, you'll learn about shapes between things, what we call negative shapes. You'll see how they hold a composition together, and also how they can help you maintain accurate proportions.

Once you understand negative shapes, you'll have a whole new appreciation for many great 19th- and 20th-century artists—from Bonnard to Picasso, from Matisse to Morandi. Having covered these materials, we'll be primed for a detailed investigation of composition. We'll talk about the different types of dynamics in the rectangle, and the latent internal structures of rectangles or armatures. And we'll learn how a range of artists have used these geometric relationships to compose still lives, landscapes, and figure drawings.

This is a drawing by the American artist Richard Diebenkorn. You can see how many of the visual elements hew to specific divisions or measures in the drawing's rectangle—things like the horizontal, vertical, and diagonal halves and quarters; and then their subdivisions. And you're going to apply these compositional strategies you've learned to drawings both from observation and from your imagination.

As we're digging into composition, we'll learn about a fourth type of line: gestural line. Here's an example by Rembrandt. Note the speed with which it was drawn. Gesture's a powerful tool that does the work of contour, cross contour, and construction line all at once. And you'll learn how to use this direct, all-encompassing, kind of line—gestural line—to work through compositional ideas with great rapidity without having to draw every object in all its detail. And we'll speak about the many ways in which line qualities can be evocative and expressive

After delving into line and composition, we'll address the crucial problem of proportion. We'll learn how, during the Renaissance, artists began to develop specific tools and methods for solving these problems. We'll learn to use the gridded velo of the Renaissance polymath *Alberti*, depicted here in a woodcut by Albrecht Dürer; we'll use it to draw a deep interior space. And I think you'll be surprised how the proportions and angles all become understandable. And we'll study many other measuring techniques, including how to measure difficult angles using the metaphor of clock hands.

Following proportions, we'll study the principles that govern the creation of the illusion of three-dimensional space on that flat page. We'll study the many ways in which artists as diverse as Leonardo and Van Gogh controlled this in their drawings and paintings—using diagonal lines, oblique planes, and geometric volumes, to name a few.

At this point, if you've been working diligently, you'll have a lot of the knowledge you'll need to be able to tackle many complex drawing problems. You'll be able to challenge yourself with complex interior spaces. You'll also draw a master study focusing on line weight, proportion, volume, and space.

And using what you've learned about line, composition, proportion, and spatial illusion; you'll be able to draw figures in complex interiors from observation, including a self-portrait—just as students do in my Intro Drawing course at the University of Washington.

All these drawings are made with lines—horizontals, verticals, diagonals, and curved line segments. You'll be applying these skills you hone in drawing exercises like the ones we did earlier with these kinds of drawings. All the concepts and methods we'll use to establish proportion and the illusion of depth in these projects are referred to as empirical perspective.

Following our study of empirical perspective, we'll study linear perspective; it's a really powerful tool. Taken together, empirical and linear perspective enabled artists to create images of astonishing verisimilitude—well beyond anything, human beings had been able to accomplish prior to their use. The use of perspective is ubiquitous; it's at the heart of so much of the visual material we consume—from high art, to animation, to video games.

We'll start out with some exercises. We'll build a solid, believable, and complex image without reference to observed reality. We'll draw a building in a landscape, and then we'll draw furniture and objects in the interior of the building as if we had x-ray vision. Using one-point perspective, we'll create a scaled gridded room. If we imagine that each tile equals one square foot, we'll be able to measure distance in the three-dimensional space of the drawing. We'll also learn how we can create pattern and make those patterns recede in perspectival space. Once you've understood these basic principles, you'll be able to use all this knowledge—along with what we'd covered earlier—to draw your own inventions from you imagination

Next, we'll really up the complexity with discussions of value, texture, and color. In one of the first lectures on value, we'll see how artists conceive a value—steps of light to dark as a scale, just like a musical scale. Then we'll see how artists use different ranges of value to expressive effect in their work. Here, a drawing on the light end of the scale. Here, a much more robust use of contrasting values. And we'll learn how, with each value palette—light, robust, or even just black and white—we can create a convincing illusion of light, space, and volume.

As well as understanding the compositional implications of using value, you'll learn how you can create focal areas and focal points by controlling relative value contrasts. And you'll be able to apply everything you learn about value to drawing from observation—things like still-lives, interiors, the head, and the figure. We'll also extend our study of value to see how it interfaces with linear perspective, and you'll learn how to project the shadows of basic forms. This will give you the tools you need to begin to draw in light and shade from your imagination. Once you understand basic forms, you'll be able to turn them into everyday objects and draw still-lives and other kinds of drawings from your imaginations, too.

While we can apply value in a relatively smooth way, there's a whole world to be discovered in mark and texture. We'll study hatching and cross-hatching, and you'll apply it to your own drawings. And we'll investigate other ways artists have used mark for centuries, both in the East and in the West. And we'll also see how contemporary artists use mark making to great effect today.

Following mark making and texture, you'll learn about color. We'll study the basics of color theory, and learn about color properties. We'll also look at the relationship among the colors and various versions of the color wheel. More practically, we'll learn about the affects of light and color on three-dimensional form in space. We'll see how artists use all these ideas and think about color in terms of palettes. These are groupings, or limitations of color that help us create qualities of light and mood.

For example, here, in this Vermeer, we find a fairly neutral orange-blue complimentary system. While in this Wayne Thiebaud, we see a much more saturated yellow-violet system that's hinged on the three primary colors: red, yellow, and blue. The moods are clearly different, but in both we get the illusion of form in light—of space and volume. And we'll learn how we can create form in light in various moods. Just like composers can inflect melodies in different keys or through different types of orchestration.

As we did with value, we'll learn how we can use color compositionally to create a visual hierarchy with focal areas and focal points. You'll see how you can apply all these ideas to your own drawing to create different qualities of mood, light, and form. You'll apply these ideas to draw both from your imagination and from observation.

In the next group of lectures, we'll zoom in on the human figure; and we'll approach the figure in several different ways, which are geared to help you draw figures both from observation and from your imagination. We'll start with an examination of canons of proportions, and you'll learn how to build a figure out of a set of measures related to the parts of the body. We'll relate this to a study of the major bones in the body, and draw figures uniting a canon of proportions with what you'll learn about the skeletal system. We'll go through the major muscle groups as well, and you'll use what you've learned to draw a self-portrait in three views, as well as figures from your imagination. We'll also talk about some specialized drawing problems, like how to approach the foreshortened figure. And we'll relate what we've learned about the figure to what we'd studied earlier, including our study of perspective—to draw figures from the imagination in imagined environments.

The last two lectures, 35 and 36, extend into some more advanced concepts and projects. We'll consider changes that affected art in the late 19th century, including visual ideas that led to greater abstraction. And other forms of figuration that depend on synthesizing abstraction with multiple points of view and imaginative interpolations—moving into areas involving fantasy and personal subject matter from the imagination, and from observation. We'll close with a discussion and a set of projects that are designed to help you begin to identify the kind of art you want to make, and some thoughts on how to go about this.

It took me about 15 minutes to outline the exercises and projects associated with this course. As I noted earlier, it could easily take a year or more to work through all this; it's equivalent to what you'd cover at a university in four academic quarters. The projects suggested in the final two lectures could extend well-beyond that.

There's a natural progression in this sequence of study—from concentrating more on acquiring knowledge, skill, and technique; and then thinking more about how to use it in reference to specific content related to your own interests. The goal at the beginning is mastery of the breadth of accumulated knowledge. As you advance, you'll be able to apply this knowledge and skill to your own individual creative vision. So take it slow; one piece at a time. If you do, you'll find each new piece building on what you've learned in prior lessons and you'll be on your way to developing a depth of knowledge regarding many of the ways in which drawings are conceived of and made.

Whether you choose to fully work through all the problems or not, just developing a conceptual understanding of the ways in which artists think and pursue their work will fundamentally change the way you see both art and the world around you.

Line and Shape: Line and Aggregate Shape
Lecture 4

As we learned in the first lecture, people have been drawing lines and shapes for a very long time—at least 80,000 years. This is also the way most of us started drawing as children. Because it seems to come so naturally, drawing lines and shapes is a logical place to begin. In this lecture, we'll start by learning about two kinds of line: contour line and construction line. Then, we'll see how we can use these to draw simple shapes. By combining contour line, construction line, and shape, we can draw all kinds of things, including the kinds of objects commonly found in still lifes. We'll conclude the lecture by discussing a special kind of shape: aggregate shape. We'll see how we can use this to organize the various shapes associated with objects in a drawing.

Contour and Construction Lines

Contour lines are often used to describe the outer edges of objects or to outline shapes. An example might be drawing a circle by putting your pencil on the page, following the circle's edge, and returning to the point of origin.

Construction lines (also called *diagrammatic lines*) are like scaffolding at a construction site. The scaffolding helps the workers build the building, but as the project moves toward completion, it's removed. In drawing, a construction line might be a centerline that helps you ensure the object you're drawing doesn't lean in one direction or the other. Artists may also use construction lines to figure out relative spacing and sizes in a drawing, but such lines are usually erased from completed drawings. Both construction lines and construction shapes help build more complex objects.

Simple Shapes

As you begin to develop a vocabulary of shapes, you can put them to use to draw objects. For example, you can draw a wine bottle—an object commonly found in still lifes—using a centerline and four simple shapes: a large rectangle for the body of the bottle; a triangle for the "shoulders"; a smaller, thinner, vertical rectangle for the neck; and a much smaller horizontal rectangle for the collar. You would then erase the centerline and soften the hard corners of the construction shapes to finish the bottle.

Practicing with Still-Life Objects

Many things in our homes can be constructed using simple shapes, such as circles, ovals, rectangles, and triangles, especially when they're in an upright and frontal or profile view. Gather a few simple objects, such as a vase, a candlestick, a coffee mug, and a wine glass. Put one object at a time on your still-life table and analyze it. What constituent shapes could it be constructed with? Draw a centerline and construct each object using shapes. Check at each step for symmetricality and proportion. Also try drawing some other objects, such as a house, car, bicycle, or furniture. Once you understand the basic principle of using construction lines, contour lines, and shape building blocks, try drawing from your imagination, too.

Aggregate Shape

So far, we've seen how contour can be used to make shape, and we've seen how we can use contour and shape, with the aid of construction lines and shapes, to draw a wide range of things, both from observation and from the imagination. Often though, we're not just drawing a single thing but groups of things, such as objects and fruit in a still life or groups of trees and other elements in a landscape. In these cases, another kind of construction shape, *aggregate shape*, is useful. Aggregate shape is essentially the container for the objects in a drawing.

Suggested Reading

Guptill, *Rendering in Pencil*, chapter 7, "Object Drawing in Outline."

Pumphrey, *The Elements of Art*, chapter 6, "Line and Dot," and "Shape," pp. 90–131.

Sale and Betti, *Drawing*, "Shape," pp. 99–106.

Smagula, *Creative Drawing*, chapter 4, "Line" pp. 84–87.

Line and Shape: Line and Aggregate Shape
Lecture 4–Transcript

As we learned in the first lecture, people have been drawing lines and shapes for a very long time, at least 80,000 years. It's also the way most of us started drawing as kids. It comes pretty naturally. So it's a logical place to begin.

We'll start by learning about two kinds of line—contour line and construction line. Then, we'll see how we can use them to draw simple shapes. By combining contour, and construction line and shape we can draw all kinds of things. Including the kinds of things commonly found in still lives. We'll finish-up by talking about a special kind of shape, aggregate shape, and how we can use it to help us organize the various shapes associated with objects in a drawing.

You'll need: pencils; erasers; sharpening tools; a t-square, triangle, or ruler; and a drawing board. We'll also use a bunch of paper. So, $8\frac{1}{2} \times 11$-inch printer paper or a similar sized sketchbook would be fine. You'll also need a table positioned against a wall and some objects–a simple bottle, like a wine bottle, among them. Other useful objects would be things like a pitcher, a vase, candlesticks, coffee mugs, wine glasses, and the like.

This is one of the drawings we looked at in the first lecture. It's by the great 19th-century American artist and teacher, Thomas Eakins. It's a study for his 1873 watercolor, *John Biglin in a Single Scull*. This drawing uses many types of lines including the two we're discussing here, contour and construction line.

We'll start with contour. I'd like you to draw three shapes: a circle, a rectangle, and a triangle. Do it now.

To draw the circle most of you probably put your pencil's tip on the page and made a more or less continuous line. You started at a certain point and then without crossing back over the line you've drawn, you returned to that point of origin along a continuous curve.

Most of that would constitute a reasonable set of instructions for making a shape of any kind—put your pencil's tip on your page, don't lift the pencil from the page, draw a line in any or all directions, don't cross over any line you've drawn, and then, return to that point of origin. The kind of line you've used here is called contour. It's often used to describe the outer edge of something.

In Eakins' drawing of John Biglin, a lot of the figure is defined by contour. Note the line starting at the top of the head, the one that continues along the back of the skull. It's not much different than a portion of the circle you just drew.

The long line describing Biglin's back and the lines, which define the top edges of his arms those are also contours. And, as you may have already noticed, the reflection on the water contains a lot of contour too.

Contour is the primary type of line we use to outline shapes. And, it's the type of line you just used to draw your circle, rectangle, and triangle.

We also find construction line in Eakins' drawing. It's also referred to as diagrammatic line. I'm sure you noticed the many ruled radiating lines on the river's surface. You may have guessed that these are perspectival construction lines.

Eakins uses them to better understand the plane of the surface of the water. These lines will also help him figure out the relative spacing and relative size of any ripples or wavelets he introduces on the water's surface. The lines help Eakins draw the things he wants to draw. But, the lines themselves aren't going to make it into the final watercolor.

Construction lines are often like scaffolding at a construction site. It helps the workers build the building, but as the project moves toward completion, it's removed.

Going back to Eakins' drawing, you've also likely noticed the strong central vertical. That drawing is actually made on two pieces of paper joined in the center. And this may have been reiterated with line as well. In any case, this vertical helps Eakins pin the rower dead center in the page. And, this central construction line helps him keep the reflection vertically aligned with the subject reflected. It's like a guide, like the lines painted on the highway that tell you where to steer your car.

We also use construction shapes. Those are shapes that help us draw something. Some people use construction lines and shapes instinctively. And, in fact, you may have used them to draw your circle.

Drawing a decent circle isn't easy. But, try it starting with a construction shape—a square. Cross the diagonals then extend a vertical and a horizontal through the center point to the square's edges. You could also add a diamond by connecting the center points of the square's sides. These are all construction lines and shapes.

Now, like Eakins, you know where to locate your subject. Right here, inside your construction shape. And you've given yourself five guide points–four along the perimeter and one in the center.

If you pass through each of the four outside points, like in a connect-the-dots drawing, while staying equidistant from the center point you'll have given yourself a real leg up in getting a good circle.

You'll also notice you have four distinct quadrants as you draw your circle, and you can compare the curvature in each one. You can measure the curvature against each of the diagonals of the internal diamond too. Now most of us tend to do better in one quadrant than another. So now, we can compare them and bring each quadrant up to the quality of the best one. You may find it helpful to rotate your paper as you draw.

We're going to be using construction lines and basic shapes to build more complex things. So, try drawing a circle using a square and construction lines now. If you'd like, use your ruler or T-square. Then, draw your subject, the circle, freehand. You'll note that Eakins did just that.

One hint: Draw the construction lines light and thin. Try a well-pointed 2H or 4H pencil. Then use an HB or 2B for the circle itself.

Now you're ready to draw more shapes.

Start with a right triangle. Then, two right triangles back-to-back. Then, that same shape without the center line. Now, make another with its mirror image, and you get a diamond. Flip it on its side you'll to get a parallelogram. Return to the diamond construction. But, point the triangle down, the lower up, and you get an hourglass. Back to the triangle: Chop off its top, and you get a trapezoid. Stack these, a hexagon. You could invert it, and then you'd get an hourglass variation. Take a circle, half it, you get a hemisphere. Condense a circle to get an ellipse, ovoid, or spheroid. And invert the sides to get a curvilinear hourglass variation. We're beginning to develop a vocabulary of shapes. And we can put them to use to draw objects.

People have been using shapes in just this way for a long time. This is a page from the sketchbook of a 13th-century Frenchman named Villard de Honnecourt. Part of the inscription reads, "Here begins the method of representation as taught by the art of geometry."

So, let's adopt this method. We'll start with an object often found in still lives–a wine bottle. We'll draw it from our imaginations, upright and seen straight on. Like many things seen this way, it's also bilaterally symmetrical.

Imagine from this point of view we can construct it using four simple shapes: a large rectangle for the body; a triangle for the shoulders; a small, thinner, vertical rectangle for the neck; and a much smaller horizontal rectangle for the collar.

Four shapes total—three rectangles and a triangle. Following Eakins' example, we'll start with the centerline, and that will help us control the shape's symmetry. Make your center line however you like, whatever size. And then, also, give yourself a horizontal to represent the width of the body. But then, put aside your straight edge. Then what we're going to do is we draw a rectangle for the body.

And then, take a look at it and make any adjustments you need to. Then our next shape will be a triangle for the shoulders. And then, we'll take that, and we'll turn it into a trapezoid and make a rectangle for our neck. Then you can refine your line as needed. Use the kneaded eraser to take away some of the erasure. Then we'll add a final horizontal rectangle for the collar.

Now, we can erase our centerline, we can erase some of our construction shape, erase what we don't need. Then we can soften the hard corners, a little erasing there. And then we can just round through a little bit—rounding at the shoulders, rounding a bit at the collar, at the top of the bottle and on the other side. And then we'll just round a bit at the bottom—at the base—of the bottle. And erase what we don't want, and we're done.

Now, you might ask, "Why not draw a bottle starting at one point and moving around its edge—just outline it like the way many of you drew your initial circle."

Here's the problem. When most people just follow the edge of an object, they run into a routine problem. The object is out of whack. It leans to the left or to the right, and the left and right sides don't really correspond. While this can be expressive, if we want a naturalistic result, using a centerline and constructing with shape can really help.

Instead, by drawing the shape on a centerline we draw the top, and the bottom, and the sides of the object, or portion of the object, in one fell swoop. So, it's easier to see and control the proportions, the widths and the heights. And, we'll be much more aware if there's a right-left alignment problem, or if the object's tilting off a true vertical. Drawing with construction lines and building-block shapes helps us see all of this more clearly. And, crucially, we haven't invested in precious details. We're just making simple shapes, which are easily judged, edited, and erased.

We just drew a bottle from the imagination. Let's try it now from observation. We'll be doing this often, relating imagination or construction to observation. Both are very important ways of drawing. You'll need a simple bottle. More or less, like the one we just drew, put it on your table and draw it using the same constructive method we just used. Don't worry about the label, the bottle's contents, or any other details, just the centerline and shapes.

We have three goals here: We want the bottle to be truly vertical, no leaning; truly symmetrical, no bulges; and, proportionate to the bottle you're looking at. Take it step-by-step and take it slow.

Leonardo Da Vinci's, *Trattato della Pittura* or *Treatise on Painting*, is a compilation that was put together by one of his students, Francesco Melzi. This is back in the mid-16th century. In this treatise, Leonardo gives this advice to new students. "*Ti ricordo che impari prima la diligenza che la prestezza,*" "I remind you to first learn diligence, not speed".

So, take the time to get each step right before going on to the next. Start with a centerline. Then a rectangle for the body of the object, it's just four lines. Check them–make sure you're centered on that centerline. Then, look at the height to width proportions. Make sure they correspond to the proportions of the bottle's body. If not, erase and correct, just four lines.

Understanding the width to height proportions may take time at first. But, you'll get better with practice. You're developing a new skill. You're seeing how you can measure with your eye. When you're satisfied with your first shape, add a truncated triangle or trapezoid for the shoulders—three new lines. At each step, check for symmetry and proportion.

Now, the thin neck, three more lines. Add a rectangle for the collar. Now a final check for symmetry and proportion.

Part of learning to see involves analyzing what we're seeing, and breaking complex things down into understandable pieces. In this case, simple constituent shapes.

While the end goal of drawing is often expression, it has its distinctly quantitative side. Especially if we want the result to be naturalistic, relative proportions, angles, and distances all have to be carefully determined.

As we'll become abundantly clear in coming lectures, a lot of this relates to measure of one kind or another. We put something down. We look analytically, measuring size, placement, degree of symmetry and a host of other variables. Then we edit, correct, and adjust. Many would say that drawing is not so much an action as a process. Part of that process involves coming to a visual understanding of what we're seeing or imagining and drawing. With that in mind, let's up the ante and use our vocabulary of shapes to construct some more challenging subjects.

This is a still life, a 1996 pencil drawing by the contemporary American artist, William Bailey. And, it's like the Eakins, complex. But, using what we've learned about drawing construction lines and shapes we'll be able to get a pretty good handle on how we might begin to go about drawing the kind of objects we see in this still life.

And don't worry if things don't come out as precisely as you'd like at first. I've been drawing for decades and often feel the same way. I'll often use my erasers as often as my pencils, if not more. If you can tolerate a bit of awkwardness and summon your patience and persistence, you'll see real improvement. This is just the first step. Stick with it and practice, you'll see your ability develop. And in the coming lectures, we'll be studying specific methods for getting all those proportions to correspond with what we see.

Let's draw the central pitcher. First, we'll draw a light vertical center construction line. You might want to use a straight edge, like Eakins. But, draw the rest freehand. Look at the pitcher. What shape is that body? Not much more than a slowly tapering trapezoid. So, draw a similar trapezoid on your centerline—four lines. Then eyeball the result, first in reference to the centerline. Is your shape centered and bilaterally symmetrical? If not, adjust. Now, compare the shape to Bailey's. Does it have similar height-to-width proportions? Are the diagonals of the sides similar in angle? Adjust again. Take it slow. It's only four lines.

Next, the spout, what shape is it? Not much more than a small triangle. Two lines, really. Then, check the placement and scale. Are the lines in the right place? Are they the right length and diagonal? If they aren't, erase and change anything that looks off.

We'll tackle the handle in two pieces using construction shapes. First, we'll draw an oval for the top part and a downward-pointing triangle for the bottom. And if we've gotten our shapes about right, the handle should more or less fall into place. Again, eyeball the results and adjust as needed.

When you're satisfied erase the construction lines, then slightly round some of the angular edges to make it feel more naturalistic. Last, we'll add two light lines for the rim at the top and bottom of the pitcher.

Let's follow the same procedure with the elaborate vase on the right. No worries, we can boil it down to six simple shapes. And we'll build it, like a skyscraper, from bottom to top. Once again, we'll start with that centerline. Then, a rectangle for the rounded bottom portion—four lines. This, in part, will be a guide shape. You want to hinge this rectangle on the centerline and make sure it captures the height to width proportions of the bottom shape. Take a moment to eyeball it, then make any corrections you need to.

Next, round-out the sides. It's more or less like drawing a smiley-face, smile upended. Many people also turn their paper as they draw. It's often easier to draw certain things in one position rather than another. So, you could try that too. On top of the bottom rectangle we'll add a really small rectangle. And on top of that a section of a hemisphere with a flat bottom. Eyeball your first three shapes for proportion then adjust. We'll cap the hemisphere with a triangle. These last three shapes taken together should look like a top. The fifth shape's another rectangle–a slim, vertical one. The sixth and final shape will be a downward pointing triangle. Check the proportions and all the shapes' alignments with the centerline. Using the top three shapes as a guide draw the slightly curving sides of the vase. Then, erase the construction lines and round some of the angles. Last, you could add those decorative stripes.

If it didn't come out quite the way you'd like, don't worry, this is a beginning. Try it a couple times and it will improve. And it would be a great exercise to draw each of the remaining objects in the still life using the same method.

Many things in our homes can be constructed using simple shapes like circles, ovals, rectangles, and triangles—especially when they're in an upright and frontal or profile view.

I asked you all at the beginning of the lecture to gather up some objects. Like a pitcher, a vase, a candlestick, a coffee mug, or a wine glass. Put one odd object on your still life table. Analyze it. What constituent shapes could it be constructed with? Give yourself a centerline and build your object. Check at each step for symmetricality and proportion, just like we did earlier.

Many other things can be drawn the same way. Houses, cars, bicycles, furniture, fruit, vegetables, even the human figure, all of these could be analyzed and drawn using these ideas. So, try drawing the things around you. Once you understand the basic principle of using construction lines, and contour and shape building blocks, try drawing from your imagination too.

This has its parallel in writing. We can construct all the words in most languages with a finite set of letters. Even Chinese, which is pictographic, has a finite set of visual units called radicals—214 in all. In drawing, we can construct just about all the things in the world around us with a finite set of shapes.

And, we can combine observation with imagination and improvisation. You could start with a bottle, using it as a model. Draw the body and shoulders just as you see them. But, you could make the neck much longer or shorter, or make the body wider. So, we can move from observation, to construction, to invention. Before moving on with the rest of the lecture, you could take some time to draw now to practice and experiment with these approaches.

So far, we've seen how contour can be used to make shape. And, we've seen how we can use contour and shape, with the aid of construction lines and shapes, to draw a wide range of things—both from observation and from the imagination. Often, though, we're not just drawing a single thing, we're drawing groups of things. Like objects and fruit in a still life, or groups of trees or other elements in a landscape, or a group of people in a room. In each case, another kind of construction shape, aggregate shape, can really help us out.

One of the most common problems beginning drawing students encounter is that they run out of paper in one direction or another. They can't fit all the objects in the still life in their drawing. Or, even with a single figure, they ran out of room for the legs and the feet, or the neck and the head, or both. They fall off the page. Another common problem is that the objects don't relate well to one another or to the shape of the drawing itself. And this is absolutely avoidable if we adjust our procedure.

When most artists draw, they're not only thinking about the individual objects or figures. They're thinking about how those things get organized. To begin to think this way it helps to start with a large encompassing shape instead of starting with a detail, or a part of an object or figure.

Earlier, we looked at this Greek Amphora. There are four unique figures. But, they're conceived of collectively. They form an aggregate shape. As much as each figure has a shape identity, the group does as well.

Traveling 1600 years forward in time, let's take another look at those "Court Ladies Preparing Newly Woven Silk."

Here, too, the figures form an overall grouping—a wide rectangle that rhymes in shape with the central rectangle of the scroll itself. Within that, we find sub-groupings. The four figures on the right and the four on the left each form a rectangular grouping.

And we can conceive of the three central figures, with the addition of the small child on the left, as forming a house-shaped grouping–a rectangle topped by a triangle. The small child under the stretched silk actually links the central and left groups. We could also say that the far left figure in the right grouping helps link that group to the central one, because she's facing in towards them.

Let's jump ahead another 200-plus years to Renaissance Italy. Leonardo's "Last Supper" is surprisingly similar to the "Song Dynasty Court Ladies," in that, the figures form a long rectangular grouping, with clear sub-groupings. Reading left to right we can see this as a rectangular group of six, a triangle of one, and a rectangle of six. Or, we could also see it as a group of three, another three, a one, a three, and a final three.

And, in the 16th century, Holbein, well, he's thinking similarly. We get a large rectangular grouping. This time it could be subdivided as a large trapezoid receding into space, and a smaller rectangle or pentagon of sorts.

Moving forward a century or so, we find Rembrandt. You'll note that most of the crowd forms an aggregate rectangle with smaller rectangles on the upper right and the lower left. There are also sub-groupings of interlocking rectangles and triangles.

And here's a drawing from Rembrandt's contemporary, the French, Nicholas Poussin. The figures on the ground group into a wide rectangle, the figures above into a squarer one, as do the figures between the columns of a large building in the back.

Traveling to the 18th century to India, the "Two Lovers" form an aggregate triangle. Next, to 20th-century Bologna, this is a still life by Giorgio Morandi—known very much as an artist's artist. His still life forms an aggregate rectangle, here, a vertical one.

And let's return to the Bailey. The objects are grouped, more or less, into a long rectangle. We could also view that shape as a rectangle framed by two right triangles—a trapezoid really—or as two overlapping trapezoids.

One of the things that make all these works so interesting to look at is the way we see a variety of patterns of interconnected groupings and sub-groupings. What they all share is that they unite the disparate individual elements. This provides connection and solidity. It creates an abstract structure of shape that makes visual sense in the drawing.

I've chosen a wide range of examples to make the point that this isn't about a style or type of art. It's a fundamental visual principle. We started out with the problem of falling off the page, not having enough room to fit the things intended in the drawing. Starting with aggregate shapes helps to preclude this and it establishes strong relationships among the shapes, among the things that we want to draw.

So let's try it now.

You'll need: a pencil, an eraser, and a sheet of 8½ × 11-inch paper. We'll combine this new idea with what we've already learned. We'll start with a large aggregate shape to locate three objects in the page. Then, use construction lines, contour, and building-block shapes to construct the objects themselves.

This is what we're going to draw. There's nothing inherently special about it. It's simply a means to understand a set of procedures.

We'll start with the aggregate shape–a wedge shape, taller than it's wide. We'll place it a bit off-centered to the right, and with more white of the page below than above. We'll work from the back forward.

So, we'll start with the pitcher by drawing a tall-ish trapezoid in the lower right quadrant of the aggregate shape. We want to extend a bit beyond the horizontal and vertical halves of the aggregate shape and its placement. Take some time to get it in the right place. Next, add a centerline, then adjust the trapezoid.

Now, we'll add the upper trapezoid—an inverted one—and a triangle for the spout. Then the handle, let it extend to the aggregate shape's edge. Do this freehand, or if you prefer, use a construction shape like we did earlier.

Next, the bottle, we'll draw it using four shapes. First, the base, aligned with the aggregate shape on the left, and a bit above it horizontally. Note the relationship of the height of this rectangle relative to the pitcher. It's just a bit shorter.

Now, we'll add a centerline and adjust, then a trapezoid for the shoulders, a gently tapering neck and a cap extending to the aggregate shape's border. We'll add a thin line under the cap for the collar.

Now, let's turn to the bowl. We'll start with a trapezoid for the body. Note its location, just above the bottom border of the aggregate shape. The top's above the half of the bottle's base. Also, note how far it extends right and left. When you think you've got it about right, add a center line and adjust as needed.

Starting about halfway down the trapezoid on either side we'll draw a curve extending to the center point of the base, then a partial trapezoid for the bowl's base. Add a couple of decorative stripes and we're almost there.

So the first thing we'll do is to erase the aggregate shape. And then, we'll want to imagine it in space, so we'll take our pencil and draw on a couple of lines to represent the point where the tabletop is sitting against the wall. That will place it into space.

Now we have a bunch of erasing to do. Why don't we start with those centerlines, we can get rid of those. In some of the tight places, I'll use my kneaded eraser. And we can get rid some of the other construction lines and shapes—internal shapes. And, we can also get rid of the pieces that are being overlapped. And, we might want to do a little more erasing, especially at some of those angled edges, sharp edges, places where we want to round.

And then, we can go back in with our pencil and begin to do some of our round and making things a little more natural. And where we've lost some line we'll just reiterate as needed. And we're pretty much done.

Here's what I'd like you to do next: Gather up the drawings of individual objects you did earlier. Look through them. Imagine how three to five of the objects could be drawn together to form an aggregate shape. Then, draw the imagined aggregate shape in your page. Using your earlier drawings as a reference, build your objects into that shape.

After you've done this, try it from observation. Set-up three to five still life objects on your table to form that aggregate shape. Draw the shape on your page. Then use building-block shapes and centerlines and construct your drawing.

Next, we'll further explore how the shapes and objects we draw relate to the page.

Line and Shape: Volume and Figure-Ground
Lecture 5

In this lecture, we'll learn about a third kind of line, cross-contour, and we'll see how it's related to an oblique shape. We'll also learn how oblique shapes are related to geometric solids. We can use this new knowledge to make the objects we draw appear three-dimensional. Related to aggregate shape, we'll introduce the concept of figure-ground relationships, which will help us structure our drawings in a more sophisticated way.

Cross-Contour Lines and Geometric Solids

Cross-contour lines are those that exist inside contours. They magically transform flat shapes into volumetric solids. Consider, for example, a hexagon drawn with contour. By introducing three interior lines—cross-contours—we transform the hexagon into a three-dimensional cube.

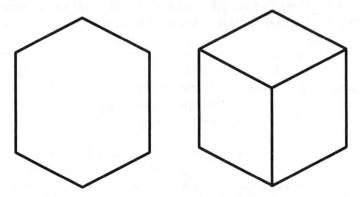

Foreshortened Shapes

By drawing cross-contours like the one in the example above, we create a new kind of shape: *oblique* or *foreshortened shape*. Such shapes are ambiguous. They can appear flat, but they can also express a recession in space. Thus, they're useful for creating the illusion of three dimensions on a two-dimensional surface.

Integrating Contour and Cross-Contour

In the schematic drawing of the cube, the cross-contour and contours were presented as separate. And, at times, they may well be used that way. But it's also common to integrate them, to flow from contour into cross-contour.

As noted earlier, at a certain level, we're not really drawing still-life objects or people; we're just drawing lines, and we have to decide where each line begins and ends. We move from the edge of the form, the contour, to the interior of the form, the cross-contour, and vice versa. We let the lines create clear overlaps to show what's in front and what's behind. This is one of the most elegant ways of creating the illusion of three-dimensional volume. Much of the "art" here involves making subtle choices about how this is done.

Drawing Ellipses

The things we see around us that are circular, such as plates, bowls, clocks, tires, and so on, are rarely seen from a vantage point where they appear truly circular. The only view in which these objects actually appear circular is when they're seen straight on, as in looking straight down at a plate. In all other views, we see them as foreshortened circles, or ellipses.

Drawing ellipses is challenging, and given that so many of the things we want to draw involve ellipses, it's a good idea to practice this skill.

When you're drawing ellipses, there are a couple things to check for. First, every ellipse can be thought of as having a horizontal and a vertical centerline.

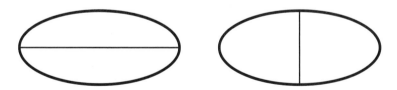

These are referred to as the *major* or *long axis* and the *minor* or *short axis*. A true ellipse is symmetrical on either side of each axis. Thus, using centerlines can help when checking for symmetry.

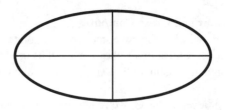

You should also make sure that the ends of the long axis are continuously rounded, rather than almond-shaped, and that the long curve is not flattened.

Figure-Ground Relationships

Before we draw more complex still lifes, we need to tackle the concept of figure-ground relationships. In a drawing, the *figure* generally refers to the aggregate grouping or shape of the individual things or objects that we would commonly identify as the subject of the drawing. The *ground* is often what's defined by the larger divisions of the rectangle that sets the stage for the figure or aggregate shape. We might say that *ground* refers to the shape of what some people commonly think of as the background. But it's much more than that. It's the construct of the environment in front, to the sides, and in back of the figure.

In the Eakins painting, the rower and scull are the figure, and the surrounding landscape is the ground. The ground, which is synonymous with the composition's rectangle, consists of two sub-rectangles, with the top rectangle being just slightly smaller. Again, rectangles create the shape of the drawing itself.

Here, we've used a horizontal line to divide the rectangles describing the ground shapes, but we want to avoid thinking about this as just a line. It's useful to think about it in two seemingly contradictory ways at the same time.

Here's a rectangle divided by a line:

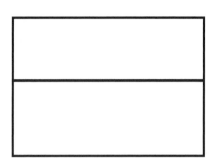

We can choose to see this as purely flat—as two rectangles meeting to form a larger one—or we could read it as expressing dimension; it could be a floor meeting a wall. This is just how we want to think about the ground. First, it is flat, made of large, flat shapes meeting to create the drawing's overall shape. Second, we want to think about the ground as being three-dimensional. Think about it as perpendicular, or right-angle, planes that meet back in space in one of the deepest parts of the drawing.

In a landscape, the major ground shapes or planes would refer to land and sky; in a seascape, to sea and sky; in a still life, to table and wall; and in an interior, to floor and wall. In terms of the underlying grammar of drawing, all these situations are similar.

Suggested Reading

Chaet, *The Art of Drawing*, "Figure-Ground," pp. 22–26.

Curtis, *Drawing from Observation*, chapter 10, "Cross-Contour."

Norling, *Perspective Made Easy*, chapter 14, "Practical Uses of Cylinders in Drawing," pp. 131–142.

Rockman, *Drawing Essentials*, "Different Kinds and Functions of Line," pp. 59–65.

Smagula, *Creative Drawing*, chapter 4, "Line," pp. 88–90.

Line and Shape: Volume and Figure-Ground
Lecture 5—Transcript

Now we'll learn about a third kind of line, cross contour. We'll see how it's related to a special kind of shape, oblique shape, and we'll learn how oblique shapes are related to geometric solids. We'll use this new knowledge to make the objects we draw appear three-dimensional. Related to aggregate shape, we'll introduce the concept of figure-ground relationships, which will help us structure our drawings in a more sophisticated way.

You'll need some pencils, erasers, and some smaller paper. 8½ × 11-inch printer paper or a medium-size sketchbook would be fine. You'll also need two sheets of 18 × 24-inch white paper and a couple sticks of vine charcoal. You'll also be using your still life table and 8–10 simple objects, things like we used in the last lecture.

The drawings we've made so far have been pretty flat, and this limitation leads us to consider our next type of line, cross contour. These are lines that exist inside the contours. They magically transform flat shape into volumetric solids.

Here's a hexagon. It's drawn with contour. Six lines. By introducing three interior lines, cross contour, we transform it into a 3D cube. Here, seen from above. Here's an identical hexagon. To draw a cube seen from below, we change the cross contours, now we're looking up at our cube.

And this will work with curvilinear forms as well. Draw a modified rectangle, one with a curving top and bottom. Add a single curved line. This creates a top plane, and you've got a cylinder seen from above. Invert the cross contour to create a cylinder seen from below.

Remember this figure from the first lecture? The beginnings of our piece of Jarlsberg. The internal line is a cross contour. Take it away, you get a flat shape, a trapezoid.

Let's draw a circle. Now add a curved line along the horizontal axis and we've transformed it into a sphere. Draw another over its vertical axis and the illusion is that much more pronounced.

By drawing our cross contours, we've also created a new kind of shape, oblique or foreshortened shape. These shapes are ambiguous. They can appear flat, but they can also express a recession in space. So they're very useful in creating the illusion of three dimensions on a two-dimensional surface. In fact, before the advent of linear perspective in 15th-century Europe, artists all over the world routinely used these kinds of shapes to express spatial depth.

This 12th-century scroll is attributed to the Song Dynasty court of Emperor Huizong. The drawing is fairly flat, but you can see how certain shapes— parallelograms and an ovoid—have been used to make certain planes pitch back into space.

Let's go back to that block we just drew and take it apart. It consists of two parallelograms with a diamond crown. Try drawing these shapes. They each represent a plane, which in the real world would be a rectangle, all 90-degree angles. But when these planes turn away from us in space, they change shape and appear like the shapes we've just drawn.

Draw a trapezoid. It behaves similarly. Add three lines below, and it's the top of a block. Draw another. Add three lines above, and it's the floor of a room.

Here's the essential idea, take a rectangle, like a floor tile. Hold it up at eye level, perpendicular to your line of sight, it's a rectangle. But as we tilt it, even slightly back away from us, it becomes a trapezoid. Tilt it a bit more, and it becomes an ever-slighter trapezoid until it loses dimension and becomes a straight line. As it tilts away, the base of the trapezoid remains unchanged. The angles of the diagonals become more acute and the height gradually diminishes to zero.

You could make your own flipbook animation of a tile falling backwards in the corner of a sketchbook. Start out on the first page with a square in an upright position. On each subsequent page, draw the same base in the same place, but successively diminish the trapezoid until it becomes a single line. Then do the inverse. Flip the book and you'll see the tile fall back and then rise up to its original position.

Triangles also share this quality, and that's not surprising because a trapezoid is a triangle minus the pointed tip. If we imagine a straight road on a level surface going back in space to the horizon, it will appear as a triangle, though in reality, seen from above, it's a very elongated rectangle.

What's the common element? What do parallelograms, diamonds, trapezoids, and triangles have in common? Diagonals. Shapes with diagonals have a greater propensity to suggest spatial depth.

Even a cylinder can be thought of in this way. Start with a block. The top's a curving version of the diamond. The bottom similarly reinterprets the diagonals of the left and right parallelograms.

Let's return to the block you drew. Imagine it's a gift box. Now, wrap it with a ribbon moving across the center of each surface in two directions. Now, draw a cylinder. Wrap a ribbon around its center, then cross it vertically and pull the line over the cylinder's top. Draw another circle. This time, wrap it with stripes like a beach ball, first seen from above, then seen from below, then from the right, and then from the left.

Flat shapes, oblique shapes, and geometric volumes, they're all related like members of a family, a very important family. Paul Cézanne famously said, "Treat nature by the cylinder, the sphere, and the cone." Because by learning to draw basic shapes and volumes, we're well on our way to being able to draw many of the things around us.

In the beginning, there were two primary shapes, a rectangle, and a circle. It's a flat world. Early reproduction is asexual. The rectangle and circle divide to produce more rectangles and circles. But through random genetic mutation, we begin to see a new generation emerge, foreshortened shapes that push into space. First, a rectangle emerges, but, with inward pointing sides, the trapezoid is born. Then others with both sides angling to the right or left, parallelograms are born. Next, one of these emerges, point down, the diamond joins the clan. Then, a further mutation, a rectangle divides along a diagonal to produce the first triangles. Further mutations produce further triangular variety. Some, closed-close, acute; others, opened-wide, oblique; others, with two equal sides, isosceles; others, with three, equilateral. While all this is happening the circle has given birth to an infinite variety of ellipses, ovoids, and spheroids.

In the next generation, we arrive at sexual reproduction, and that produces three-dimensional volume. A rectangle mates with a parallelogram to produce a block. A diamond with a parallelogram, another. Triangles mate to produce three-sided pyramids while others mate with a parallelogram to produce a four-sided one. Another such mating produces a prism. A circle mates with an ellipse to produce a sphere, a block with an ellipse to produce a cylinder, and a triangle with an ellipse to create a cone, and the basic family's complete.

With what we've learned so far in mind, let's take a look at how artists use all this. Holbein's drawing of *The Family of Thomas More* is a great place to start. It's a tour de force example of the use of contour, cross contour, and foreshortened shape. Look at the footrest on the floor. The top's constructed just like a block, nine lines, and three planes. Its shape is hexagonal, six lines with three internal lines, cross contours, creating the volume. Alternately, we could see this constructed of three shapes, three parallelograms, one large, and two small.

Note the line representing Thomas More's headband. It moves around his forehead, lending volume to his head. Seen with his chin, it's structurally not much more than a cylinder. Also, note the cross contours on More's feet, which turn the otherwise flat shapes into volumetric shoes. The curved lines creating the collars of the three kneeling women transform their necks from flat shapes into three-dimensional volumes. Cylinder and neck, same idea.

And let's take a closer look at the woman in the foreground. We get a powerful sense of volume in her body, in her neck, chest, shoulders, abdomen, arms, and down through her folded legs. The volume is expressed by the wealth of cross contours along both the horizontal and vertical axes.

In my schematic drawings of the block and cylinder, the cross contour and contours were presented as separate and at times, they may well be used that way. But it's very common to integrate them, to flow from contour into cross contour. As I noted in an earlier lecture, at a certain level we're not really drawing still life objects or people at all. We're just drawing lines, and we have to decide where each line begins and where it ends.

We'll move from the edge of the form, the contour, to the interior of the form, the cross contour, and vice-versa. We let the lines create clear overlaps to show what's in front and what's behind. This is one of the most elegant ways of creating the illusion of three-dimensional volume. Much of the art here involves making subtle choices about how this is done.

Let's return to the central kneeling woman, to her right shoulder. There's no continuous outline here. Instead, we move from the contour, the top of the shoulder, to the inside of the form. And this repeats six times as we move from the shoulder all the way down to the forearm.

If we look at the woman's bonnet on the far left, we see the same thing. We move from the right, across the top of the bonnet in contour, and then turn diagonally down. The line becomes a cross contour much like the lines we drew earlier over our circles to transform them into spheres.

Freeze the image of this drawing or download a high-res version from the web. Then trace over the play of contour to cross counter with your finger. It will give you a heightened sense of what Holbein was doing—put you in his shoes.

Good ideas tend to be widespread. Here's a detail from a wall painting from Shŭishénmiào, *The Water God's Temple in Shānxī, China*. It was painted in 1324, a world away and over 200 years before Holbein made his drawing. But it's actually constructed of contour and cross contour. Note the sinuous line flowing vertically down from the kneeling official's shoulders all the way down to his feet. The sensation of volume is enhanced by all the cross contours moving at an angle to the vertical one, much the same idea as in Holbein's kneeling woman.

And here's that beautiful 18th-century drawing from India's Punjab Hills. It's titled *Two Lovers Sitting on a Dais with a Water Pipe*. Note the series of cross contours wrapping around from the underside of the man's thigh, as well as the ones riding over the top ridges of his flowing robe. There are many more throughout the drawing. It's also worth noting the elaborate still life objects and the tables and pillows. They're all fashioned out of flat and oblique shapes—triangles, trapezoids, and parallelograms—as well as volumetric solids—modified blocks, cylinders, and spheres—all drawn with contour and cross contour.

Earlier, we looked at Eakins' drawing of John Biglin to understand something about contour and construction line, but he's using cross contour, too. Start with the sweatband tied around Biglin's head. Not at all unlike the hat in the Holbein—really convincing, three-dimensional—but when you look closely, you realize there's hardly any shading, but we do see several lines. I count nine. These are cross contours operating inside the contour, crossing over the three-dimensional form of his head to describe its planar structure.

There are many more cross contours in the drawing. The arm and elbow get a lot of their volume from the small interior lines. At the shoulder, the opening of Biglin's t-shirt gives Eakins a great opportunity for a powerful cross contour moving over the deltoid and creating volume there. On the far shoulder, five cross contours pitch it into three-dimensionality.

And you may have noticed the several cross contours on the oar. Eakins even goes so far as to draw these as if he had x-ray vision, continuing the cross contour into the interior of the oar's long handle. We call this drawing-through. It's a useful technique for helping us fully imagine three-dimensional form on a two-dimensional surface.

Let's take a look at a more recent example, a 1916 *Portrait of Guillaume Apollinaire* by Picasso. Apollinaire was one of the most famous poets of the early 20th century. He's generally credited with being the first person to use the term surrealism. At the time the drawing was made, Apollinaire had just returned to Paris from the front. It was World War I, and he'd been wounded in the head by a piece of shrapnel.

Like Eakins and Holbein, Picasso uses a cross contour, here describing the bandage under Apollinaire's hat, to express the head's volume. This cross contour is reiterated by the lines in the hat itself. We can also see cross contours in the shoulders, chest, and throughout the rest of the figure, all create volume. In fact, the long line going down the front of his jacket and intersecting with the belt as it travels down and along his thigh is behaving the same way as the long serpentine line in the government official's robe in the Chinese temple painting. Six hundred years and continents apart, but the visual grammar is much the same.

Let's take a look at the elaborate chair legs. They're formed of modified spheres, like donuts and tapering cones, all using cross contours to communicate three-dimensional form.

Let's draw another bottle, but this time we'll incorporate what we've learned about volume with what we learned in the last lecture about line and shape. Like we did before, we'll start with a light centerline and some shapes, a rectangle for the bottle's body, a trapezoid for the shoulders, and a slim rectangle for the neck. We'll deal with the collar later. Here's the new part. We're going to turn the shapes into volumes. The rectangle, we're going to turn into cylinder, the trapezoid into a truncated cone, and the slim rectangle into a cylinder. For our collar, we'll go in and just draw a slight bulging cylinder. We can then go in and begin to erase some of our construction lines, edit symmetricality. We can imagine the foil wrapping, using the cross contour we have as a guide. Do a little bite of rounding. Take advantage of the label as another cross contour. Remembering Holbein's Shoe, we might add some more internal cross contours, just to express dimensionality. And we can just edit our curvature to make things feel more natural.

Now, I'd like you to try this from observation. Put a bottle on your still life table and draw following the same steps we used to draw this one from our imagination. Start with a centerline, then shape, then volume. Then try some of the other objects you have. Take them one at a time. As we did in the last lecture, after you've drawn from observation, try combining observation with imagination and improvisation. Don't worry if in the first shot things don't come out as perfectly as you'd like, there's no magic trick, it's a matter of concentration and repetition. This part of drawing is like practicing piano, guitar, or violin.

To draw the bottle, we had to draw a number of ellipses. The things we see around us which are circular, measurably 360—like plates, bowls, clocks, garbage cans, wheels, tires and the like—are rarely seen from a vantage point where they appear circular. The only view in which these object actually appear circular is when they're seen straight-on, like looking straight down at a plate. In all the other views, we see them as foreshortened circles or ellipses.

Drawing ellipses is challenging, and given that so many of the things we want to draw involve ellipses, it's a good idea to practice drawing them. Here are two great exercises.

For the first, go online and do an image search for bowls and drinking glasses. Print out a number of these images. With a dark pen or marker, just trace over the ellipses. Another good key word to search is tire dumps. You'll get whole fields of ellipses in a range of orientations. Print some out and trace over these, too. These exercises will give you visual references for many different ellipses seen from a variety of points of view.

For the second exercise, you'll need a tall, clear glass or vase, a simple cylindrical one is best. Put the vase on a piece of paper on your table. Tape the piece of paper to the table, then trace the shape of the vase's base on the paper. It's ideal if you can position yourself so your eye level is at about the vase's mid-point. You can test this by holding your pencil horizontally in front of your eyes. Push the pencil straight out away from you so that you can see its relationship to the vase.

Now, make a careful line drawing of the vase. Start with its aggregate shape, it's more-or-less some kind of rectangle. Establish its basic height to width proportions. All you need are two vertical and two horizontal lines. Note the back edge of the table. Drawing this is going to help the vase sit down.

Next, concentrate your efforts on the ellipses of the top and the base of the vase. Since it's clear glass, you'll be able to see the interior of the ellipses.

Now, fill the vase with water to about an inch or two from the top. Place the vase back on the table using the outline you drew of its base to return it to the same location. Now, draw the new ellipse of the water level.

Next, pour off an inch or two of water. Then draw the new ellipse. Repeat this until you've emptied the vase. What you'll find is that the ellipse at eye level is nothing more than a horizontal line, as you move away from eye level, either up or down, the ellipses become wider and wider.

Here are a couple things to check for. Every ellipse can be thought of as having a horizontal and a vertical centerline. These are referred to as the major or long axis, and the minor or short axis. A true ellipse is symmetrical on either side of each axis, so using centerlines can help when checking for symmetry.

You can also trace over an ellipse you've drawn using tracing paper, then flip the tracing paper over on top of the original drawing. This is going to reveal discrepancies in symmetricality.

There are two other things to look for. One is the rounding at the ends of the long axis. Many people take the two curving lines and have them meet at a point, like an almond-shape. It should be continuously rounded. Another common mistake is flattening out the long curvature, so make these three checks as you do this exercise: Check for symmetricality in relation to the axes; check the rounding at the ends of the long axis; and check for flattening on the long curve.

We're just about ready to draw a more complex still life, but before we do, we need to tackle a new concept, figure-ground relationships.

The first part, the figure, is related to the idea of aggregate shape and it's pretty easy to understand though ground is what a lot of people new to drawing often miss. In fact, as a student, it took me some time to appreciate just how important this concept is to constructing a sophisticated drawing, painting, or design. But once you become aware of the idea, it'll begin to make a big difference in the way you conceive of a drawing.

It's by no means a totally foreign concept. A simple business card has a figure-ground relationship. The words, numbers, and logo are the figure, the color of the card stock the ground.

A page of a legal pad could be considered a figure-ground drawing, though admittedly, not a compelling one. The ruled lines are the figure and the yellow page is the ground but if I write several sentences on the page, the words become the figure and the lined pad becomes the ground so there's a relative aspect to all this.

In a drawing, the figure generally refers to the aggregate grouping or shape of the individual things or objects that we'd commonly identify as the subject of the drawing. In the William Bailey still life, for instance, the 11 still life objects taken together form the figure. Here, the figure is synonymous with our aggregate shape, and this can often be the case.

The ground is often what's defined by the larger divisions of the rectangle which set the stage for the figure or aggregate shape. You could say that the ground refers to the shape of what some people commonly think of as the background, but it's actually more than that. It's the construct of the environment in front, to the sides, and in back of the figure.

In the William Bailey still life, it would correspond to the two planes of the table and the one plane of the wall, three rectangles in all, which in combination make up the shape of the drawing itself.

Here's another way to think about it. Imagine setting up this still life. The multiple objects are the figure. If you were then to remove all the objects, everything left there, the table and wall, would be the ground. Though, if then we made a drawing of the table, it would be the object and the wall would be the ground. Like I said, it's relative.

In the Eakins, the rower and scull are the figure, the surrounding landscape the ground, and we find much the same thing as we did in the Bailey. The ground, synonymous with the composition's rectangle, consists of sub-rectangles, two this time, with the top rectangle being just slightly smaller.

In the Indian drawing, the man and woman are the primary figure. Combined with the still life on the floor, they form an extended aggregate figure, and the floor and the wall form the ground. And we find a very similar structure as in the Bailey and the Eakins. Large shapes, again, rectangles, create the shape of the drawing itself.

In these illustrations, I've used a horizontal line to divide the rectangles describing the ground shapes. But we want to avoid thinking about this as just a line. It's useful to think about it in two seemingly contradictory ways at the same time.

Here's a rectangle divided by a line. We can choose to see this as purely flat, as two rectangles meeting to form a larger one. Or we could read it as expressing dimension. It could be a floor meeting a wall. And this is just how we want to think about our ground. First, we want to think about it as flat, made of large flat shapes meeting to create the drawing's overall shape.

Second, we want to think about the ground as being three-dimensional. We want to think about it as planes, often perpendicular planes, right angle planes, that often meet back in space in one of the deepest parts of the drawing.

In a landscape, the major ground shapes or planes would refer to land and sky; in a seascape, sea and sky; in a still life, table and wall; and in an interior, floor and wall. In terms of the underlying grammar of drawing, all these situations are very similar.

So let's put all these new ideas together in a still life, which we'll draw from our imagination. We'll use aggregate shape and object-ground relations to structure the drawing, and we'll use cross contours and geometric solids to create volumetric objects.

Turn your 18 × 24-inch page horizontally, what we call the landscape position. And let's use our vine or willow charcoal. We'll start out light and thin, drawing construction lines and construction shapes.

The first thing to draw is the format shape of the drawing. Here it's going to be 16 × 18 inches. Next, divide this with a horizontal line to create the two large ground shapes that represent the table top and the wall. I've put this at about seven and a quarter inches above the format's border. Then, draw an aggregate shape. I've used an equilateral triangle, more-or-less in the center of the page.

Now, using centerlines and simple shapes, we'll lay out three objects. Just off center, start with a carafe, a variation of the bottle you just drew. A rectangle for the base, a trapezoid for the shoulders, short edge up, and one more for the neck, short edge down, extending almost to the top of the aggregate shape. In front of this, on the right, add a pitcher. You know how to do this, a trapezoid for the body, touching the aggregate shape boundary, triangle for the spout, and an ovoid and triangle as guides for the handle. The handle can extend a bit beyond the aggregate shape. In front on the left, add a bowl, a trapezoid for the body, and another slim one for the base.

Now, check the shapes using centerlines and make any adjustments you need to. Then, just like we did with the bottle earlier, turn your shapes into volumes using ellipses. And use what you learned from the ellipse exercise. Imagine you're looking down at the still life as if you're standing looking at it on your table. The lower ellipses will be wider, the higher ones thinner.

Everyone knows the stereotype of the tormented artist. Remember, he's not tormented because of an existential dilemma. He's tormented because it's really hard to draw a decent ellipse. But with patience and practice, we're infinitely capable of moving ever closer to that ideal ellipse on the horizon.

Now, you can erase some of the construction lines, and you can also do some editing and rounding to make things more proportionate and natural.

You could also put some liquid in the carafe, and then add some stripes on some of the objects, as well as other incidental interior lines, all examples of cross contours being used to bring out more volume. But let's add something different, something less regular. Let's add two pears, one on the right and the other one on the left.

So, we can do it with a couple basic shapes. We'll start with a circle and a triangle, and we'll modify them a little bit. And we'll have this one seen from the back. We'll erase part of the bowl we won't see. And we can move from our cross contour to our contour—make it a little more angular, a little more pear-like. And if we're overlapping the triangular portion, it will be as if these pear's going back in space. And if we let the stem of the pear be overlapped by the tip, similarly give us that projection, and we can create a small divot.

And on the right, we can do the same thing. We'll start with a circle and a triangle, and then we'll modify them, a little rounder over here. And this time, we can change the spatial reading by letting the triangle overlap the circle. And this time, the tip of the pear will be projecting forward. So we have contour moving to cross contour, contour moving to cross contour. We'll erase what we don't see. Clear overlap, and in the front, we'll have the stem overlapping the tip of the pear, the opposite of what we did earlier. And we can introduce a couple other little cross contours in here.

Here's a variation you could try right now. A still life like the one we just drew, but this time working inversely. Begin in the center of a new page so you have room to expand. Start with individual objects and move up the food chain to arrive at some kind of aggregate figure shape. Then add a horizontal line to express the edge where the table meets the wall. Then draw your two ground shapes to create the shape of the drawing itself. You generally want the lines that are representing the border of the drawing to be light and thin.

Next, try this from observation. Set-up some objects on your still life table arranged to bring out different kinds of aggregate groupings. Then draw following the same set of steps we've used here.

You can play with these concepts in many ways. You can draw from observation, from your imagination and from your prior drawings of individual objects. The more you practice, the more it will become your own.

Line and Shape: Positive and Negative Shape
Lecture 6

This lecture concerns another important kind of shape: negative shape, also referred to as inter-shape. When artfully considered, negative shape, like figure-ground relations, makes the things we draw and the composition itself much more powerful. In addition, it's a useful tool for helping to establish accurate proportions. In this lecture, we'll also learn to use our viewfinders. We'll see how, when drawing observationally, we can analyze shape, select what we draw, and determine the shape of a drawing using this device.

Negative Shape and Format Shape

When artists draw, they're not just drawing shapes to represent things. They also consider and draw shapes that represent the spaces between things—shapes to represent where things are not. Artists are preoccupied with the relationships between the "stuff"—the objects they want to represent—and the "non-stuff," the three-dimensional space within which the stuff exists.

In drawing, all the stuff of the world obviously becomes shape. But the non-stuff—the three-dimensional space existing between the stuff—becomes specific and expressive shape, as well. We call these shapes *negative shapes*.

Format Shape

When you draw a shape—a positive—on the page, you actually get at least two shapes—the positive and its accompanying negative. Often, depending on the first shape and its relationship to the page, you may get many more negatives.

In the two-dimensional visual arts, positive and negative shapes together create the overall structure and shape of the drawing, painting, print, or photograph. We refer to this final shape—the shape of the artwork itself—as the *format shape*.

Using the Viewfinder and Practicing Drawing Negative Shapes

Below are a few tips for using the viewfinder correctly:

- First, stay in one place, in a fixed position. If you move backward or forward or from side to side, even slightly, you'll see a different framing, which translates to a different image.

- Hold the viewfinder at a constant distance from your head. The easiest way to do this is to make sure that your arm is always fully extended.

- Hold the viewfinder perpendicular to your line of vision, which is generally perpendicular to the floor. If you don't, the opening will not be a true rectangle but a trapezoid.

- Finally, close one eye—always the same eye.

When doing the negative shape exercise, keep these tips in mind:

- Use one sheet of paper, such as basic printer paper, for each drawing. Center your format shape in the page and outline it with a 2H or 4H pencil. This allows you to modify the format on any side if it will benefit the drawing.

- Turn your page in sympathy with the drawing's shape. If the framing is horizontal, turn your page horizontally. If vertical, turn the page vertically.

- Think of drawing from observation as choosing and framing. Try to choose and frame visual situations that will yield a drawing with strong and interesting negative shapes.

- Think about what you choose to draw. Spend some time walking around with your viewfinder just framing things as you see them around your home. Look for compelling negatives.

- Plants often have interesting shapes between their stems, leaves, and flowers. If you draw outdoors, look at the spaces between trees. In a single tree, notice the spaces between the limbs.

- Try to set up still lifes purposefully to bring out the negatives.

- Once you've finished a couple of drawings, take a step back and ask yourself: Do your lines convincingly create negative shape? When you cover the positives, do the negatives come out forcefully? Are the large inter-shapes or negative shapes being used to build the composition and assert the rectangular format itself? Are the large negative shapes active?

Skill Building

The concepts we've learned so far are all connected:

- We can make shapes out of contour line.

- We can create the illusion of volume using cross-contour, oblique shapes, and geometric solids.

- We can construct objects using contour, shape, cross-contour, oblique shapes, and geometric solids, often with the use of construction lines.

- We can organize the objects in our drawing using aggregate shapes. Aggregate shapes help us create visual groupings. They contain and place what it is we want to draw within the drawing's shape.

- We can conceive of the space around the main objects or subject as large, flat shapes—ground shapes. These shapes form the shape of the drawing itself.

- We can conceive of yet another kind of shape that expresses the distances and spaces between things: negative shape. Our drawings will benefit when the negative shapes are as tangible and compelling as the objects themselves. Negative shapes are also useful for checking the proportions of the positives, or the objects.

- The positives and negative fit together like puzzle pieces to create the shape of the drawing—the format shape.

Suggested Reading

Curtis, *Drawing from Observation*, chapter 6, "Positive/Negative Shape."

Pumphrey, *The Elements of Art*, "Ground," pp. 40–43.

Sale and Betti, *Drawing*, "Positive and Negative Space," pp. 107–115.

Line and Shape: Positive and Negative Shape
Lecture 6—Transcript

This lecture concerns another very important kind of shape—negative shape. It's also referred to as interspace. When artfully considered, negative shape, like object/ground relations, makes the things we draw and the composition itself, much more powerful. In addition, it's a great tool that helps us establish accurate proportions.

In this lecture, we'll learn to use our viewfinders. We'll see how, when drawing observationally, we can analyze shape, select what we draw, and determine the shape of our drawing, using this device. And, as will become abundantly clear, this last shape I mentioned, the shape of our drawing, is in and of itself, a really important one.

The drawing materials we'll need are: pencils, erasers, sharpening tools, viewfinders and clips, and some 8½ × 11 inch printer paper or a medium-size notebook. We'll also be using eight to ten simple objects like those we used in the last two lectures. Pitchers, vases, candlesticks, teacups, wine glasses—all that stuff works fine. Among the objects, make sure you have two tallish bottles, like those used for wine or olive oil, and two small to medium-size bowls. Make sure one bottle is taller and of a somewhat different shape than the other. It will also be best if one bowl is a little taller than the other. A group like this one would work very well.

We started out by drawing objects, and, of course, drawing objects is important, but the obvious stuff is only half the story. So I want to disabuse you of a commonly held and unsophisticated idea about how you go about making a drawing. It goes like this. You look at your objects or subject, like some bottles on a table, a barn in a field, or a group of people at the beach. You copy it. Outline it. Put in the details, maybe some shading. Put in a background. Throw in some artistic feeling, and voilà, a masterpiece.

It's actually much more complex than that, as you've already come to see. In addition to the obvious objects, we have to think about, we also have to consider abstract shapes and volumes, aggregate shapes, and object-ground relationships. One of the reasons the ground is so important is that every square inch of the format, that would be the drawing's shape, is important. It has to be considered.

An architect can't just think about the building itself. He or she has to think about how a particular building relates to a particular site. The building has to be considered relative to a whole set of factors like the shape of the site, its topography, the climate, and many others. We, similarly, have to think about how what we put on the page sits in relationship to the drawing's environment. At a minimum, we have to consider the edges of the page. That's our maximum building site. You may have already intuited that when working with your aggregate shapes, sensing that they have to relate to the drawing's shape, but there's more to it than that. When artists draw, they're not just drawing shapes to represent things, or even groups of things. They're also considering and drawing shapes, which represent the spaces between things, shapes to represent where things are not. And that's because they're preoccupied with the relationship between the stuff, the objects they want to represent, and the non-stuff, the three-dimensional space within which all the stuff exists.

In drawing, all the stuff of the world obviously becomes shape, but the non-stuff, the three-dimensional space existing between the stuff, becomes specific and expressive shape as well. We call these shapes negative shapes. We could make the analogy to music here. Composers and improvisers are just as concerned with rests, the measured amounts of times where no sound event occurs, as with the notes themselves. The spaces help create the sensation of a musical phrase. Without considering the rests, the notes would become a jumble.

Returning to drawing, let's say I have a rectangular piece of paper, and using contour, I draw another rectangle centered in it. The minute I've drawn the internal rectangle, I've transformed the remaining part of the page into a shape, a frame. And, of course, this drawing is ambiguous. It could be a drawing of a white label on a white wall, or it could be a drawing of a white cardboard frame, like your viewfinder, held in front of that same white wall. This is an illustration of object/ground ambiguity. The object could be a white label on the wall as ground, or, alternately, the object could be a white frame, in front of a white wall as ground.

Let's look at this in a little more depth using a more complex shape—a figure. Me. We'll get the camera to zoom in so that the top of the frame touches the top of my head, the sides of the frame touch my elbows, and the bottom of the frame touches my toes. I'm a shape, and my shape meeting the frame automatically creates seven other shapes. Altogether, eight shapes that fit together like a jigsaw puzzle to create the image.

Our preponderancy to want to see the figure is so great that I'd like to line up the negatives so you can get a good look at them and understand that each one is a unique shape. If we pull the frame out, the negatives are a little harder to discern, but they're there none-the-less. What's inescapable is that by making a shape, any shape, within the drawing's shape or format, we get other shapes automatically. And if you're not aware of all the shapes you're making in a drawing, you're at a disadvantage.

So let me rephrase something I said in an earlier lecture. I offered this set of directions for making a shape using contour line: Put your pencil's tip on your page; don't lift the pencil from the page; draw a line in any or all directions; don't cross over any line you've drawn; return to the point of origin.

And, indeed, you will make a shape, but as we now know, in relation to the format shape, you actually get at least two shapes, and often, depending on the object and its relationship to the format, many more.

And here it's worth dipping into a bit of Daoism. Chapter 11 of the *Dàodéjīng*, a 6th-century B.C.E collection of the teachings of Laozi, is called "wúyòng." It means "worthless." It's a very clever take on the importance of the negative. The writer tells us that the usefulness of a clay pot depends on its empty interior. That the windows and doors are only of use because they contain empty space, and that it's the space between the walls that defines the usefulness of a room.

Good artists are clearly aware of all this, just as composers and improvisers are keenly aware of the relationship between notes, or other sound events, and rests which separate those sounds. The positive and negative fit snugly together, like pieces of a puzzle, to create, in one case, the overall shape of the drawing, in the other, the overall structure of time in a musical composition.

In both, taking all the positives and negatives together gives us the full shape of the work in question. In the two-dimensional visual arts, positive and negative shapes together structure the overall shape of the drawing, painting, print, or photograph. And we refer to this final shape, the shape of the artwork itself, as the format shape. We're now ready to move beyond these abstractions and look at some examples.

So, let's return to Eakins' watercolor. Now I know, to the uninitiated, it may look like he was just faithfully representing what he saw, but he's doing a lot more than that. First, we'll zoom in on the figure, just like we did with me. Let's look at the shape between his arm, chest, and knee, or the shape under his bent knee, or the shape between his hand, oar, leg, and the boat. And when we zoom out, we see the larger negative shapes are just as thoughtfully considered. Look at the big shape starting on the right of the page, climbing in steps along the top of the boat, moving up to his back, neck, and head, moving back to the right along the edges where the water meets the land.

The shapes between things, the negative shapes, are highly rendered. In other words, they're not left over after drawing the objects, after drawing the figure, or the boat, or even the reflection, but, they're drawn with as much calculation as the figure itself.

I want to take a look at a couple other examples from different places and times. I want to make it clear that this is not about a style, or even a type of art. It's an underlying principle, which diverse peoples have been using all over the world for millennia. Why? Because you get better results if you pay attention to this.

Here's our 2,500 plus year-old Greek amphora. You can see how carefully each of the shapes that exist between the dancers are weighed and defined. They're given as much attention as the dancers themselves. Here are our Court Ladies from 12th-century China. Look at the shape between this woman's sleeve, dress and the fabric she's holding. Or this, between the woman's head and the wooden tool she holds. And the larger shapes function the same way. Look at the large shape in the upper right corner. The negative made by the two women on the right as they relate to the edges of the format shape. Or the shape that occurs between the woman in the blue dress and the green carpet. All very specifically tailored shape.

And here's the Poussin. Note the tautness of the many shapes on the ground plane between the figures and the figures' shadows, as well as the large wedge-shaped negatives in the sky above the central building. Here you'll get a sense of how being able to see the negative becomes even more important when we work with value. If I want a light building to emerge from a darker sky, I have to be able to form the negative shape around it, draw the negative shape. And, if I want a pillar to emerge from the darkness behind it, I have to draw the dark negative abutting it. To make light positives emerge, as Poussin does here, you have to draw the negatives.

In the Punjab Hills drawing, we find a similar attention to negative shape. Note the shape between the man's profile and arm. Or the shape between the two lovers themselves, and as we zoom-out, this becomes part of the large negative shape of the screen that sits behind them.

And here's a 1910 drawing by Egon Schiele, titled, *Schiele With Nude Model Before the Mirror*. Note the large central negatives between the model's side and arm and reflected hip. Then note the ones formed by the format shape, starting on the upper right—format shape to hat and shoulder, format shape to underarm, rib cage, hip and down the leg. Next, the triangular shape between the model's legs. Then, the one between her leg, the reflection of her leg, and Schiele's foot. Next, the rectangular one between their reflected legs. Then, the skinny right triangle formed by Schiele's leg, arm, and the edge of the page, and lastly, the very large shape straddling all three figures and closed by the page's edges.

Jumping to the late 20th century in California, we have an example from Richard Diebenkorn. It's a figure drawing done from observation. If we glued that drawing to a piece of masonite, we could neatly cut it up into a set of interlocking puzzle-pieces.

In much of the late 19th century, and throughout the 20th century, many artists, both in Europe and in the U.S., were very interested in ambiguous depictions of space. People like Bonnard, Vuillard, Cezanne, Picasso, Matisse, and Philip Pearlstein, to name a few, all played with this in their paintings, drawings, and prints. And a lot of this interest in ambiguous depictions of space, centered on the play between positive and negative shape. Pretty natural. Remember, earlier, we noted how a drawing of a label on a wall could flip to become a drawing of a frame in front of a wall.

One of the peculiarities of drawing, and of the page, is that what's in front and what's behind, can easily shift back and forth before our eyes. And crafty draftsmen can, and do, lean on their drawings so that they do just this. We're going to talk about all this at much greater length towards the end of this course. But, the drawing we looked at earlier by Giorgio Morandi typifies this approach. You can see how he's set things up so that there's a rhyming of shape between the two bottles on the right and their negative. And the bottles on the far left and the right dematerialize into the back wall. Or, we could see this as the back wall advancing into the objects. And, of course, this drawing and the visual idea examined here, relate directly to what we did in our first drawing, the reconstruction of the 80,000 year-old incised piece of ochre from Blombos Cave. Shape sits against shape. Positive to negative. And, as we saw in the first lecture, the positive to negative structure can be made to flip back and forth. The essential idea here is that the positives and negative shapes taken together form the shape of the whole drawing.

Morandi's drawing provides a good segue to our next drawing project. It involves using some simple still life objects to begin drawing positives, and their accompanying negatives. We'll need the four objects I mentioned at the top of the lecture—two bottles and two bowls. Make sure one bottle is taller and of a somewhat different shape than the other, and that one of the bowls is a little taller than the other one, too. I'd like you to line your bottles up so that they're pretty close to, and equidistant from, the wall. Then, take your tall bowl and put it underneath your shorter bottle, and balance your shorter bowl on top of your taller bottle. Best if both constructions are about the same height. Now, I'd like you to make sure that you have about two to three inches separating the two structures. That would be at their closest point. It should look something like this. The next step is to frame your still life in your viewfinder. Position yourself so that you're looking straight on. The table's back edge should appear as a true horizontal. It should be parallel to the top and bottom edges of the viewfinder. Also, make sure there's some space, some wall and table, above and below the objects. You also want some space between the objects on the right and left sides like this. Once you've got this successfully framed, clip your viewfinder together. Then, lightly, with a 2H pencil, trace the shape of the format in the center of your page.

Now, before we get further into the drawing, I want to give you some tips on how to use the viewfinder. First, you have to stay in one place in a fixed position, just like with a camera. If you move backward or forward, or from side to side, even slightly, you'll see a different framing each time. That means a different image. You also need to hold the viewfinder at a constant distance from your head. It's easiest to make sure your arm is always fully extended. That way, always the same distance. And you have to hold the viewfinder perpendicular to your line of vision. That's generally perpendicular to the floor. If you don't, the opening will not be a true rectangle. It's going to be a trapezoid. Last, close one eye. Always the same eye.

Now, I'd like you to draw two light centerlines, one for each of the two stacked-object groupings. Do this with a lighter pencil. Say, an H or 2H. Look out through the viewfinder and try to gauge where the centerline of each object would register in relationship to that top horizontal of the viewfinder itself. Then, make your vertical lines in relation to the line representing the top of the viewfinder that you traced on your page. Don't worry if it's not perfect. Dive in and make the best guess you can. We have to start someplace.

Now, analyze the objects in term of constituent shape. Then, draw the bottles and bowls as they appear through the viewfinder relative to your centerlines. Use contour to draw simple shapes to construct the objects. And don't bother with any details. If there're labels, or lettering, ignore them. And don't bother with any shading. It's just going to get in the way. We only want to use contour line and shape. When you need to, erase and correct your lines as you go along. All of this takes repetition and practice. It doesn't have to be perfect the first time. Anyway, it's just cheap paper and a bit of graphite. There's really nothing much at stake. It's a good idea to always keep Degas' advice in mind. "You must do over the same subject ten times, a hundred times." And, you know, he was Degas.

When you feel your proportions are about right, you're ready for the next step. Take your viewfinder and place it on top of your drawing. Close it vertically so that you're cropping the tops and bottoms of both sets of stacked objects. Now, with a 2H pencil, trace the new format shape on top of the existing drawing. Then remove the viewfinder.

You should see five shapes. Starting from the left, alternating positive and negative, and fitting together like pieces of a jigsaw puzzle. To make the negatives more present, take a 2B pencil and trace over your three negative shapes. Make sure to draw the whole shape. On the right and left, it should include portions of the vertical edges of the format shape itself. In all three, it will include the horizontal portions of the format shape. Next, on a separate piece of paper, copy each of the negative shapes. Don't worry about their position relative to one another. Just try to make a real study of each one. The goal is to draw each negative shape intentionally.

On a new sheet of paper, redraw the negatives in their proper scale and position. You can analyze them and build them out of their constituent sub-shapes. If your negatives are proportionate and in the right locations, magically, you'll see the positives reemerge, even though you weren't drawing them at all.

Now, let's take the whole thing again, but this time draw the negatives from the get-go. To switch things up a bit, let's move our right stack to the left and the left stack to the right. Also, take the taller bowl and put it on top of the shorter bottle. Take the shorter bowl and put it underneath the taller bottle. But, this time I'd like you to frame the still life in your viewfinder so that there's room on the right and left sides of the stacked objects. But, the top and bottom of the objects are cropped. Just enough to clearly bring out those five shapes—two positives and three negatives.

Now, on a new sheet of paper, lightly, with a 2H pencil, trace the shape of your viewfinder centered in your page. Look out through your viewfinder and analyze the three negatives. What kind of shapes are they? If you want to add a step here, make a study of each negative. On a separate sheet of paper, break each one down into its constituent shapes. This is a bit more difficult than what we've done before because these shapes are less regular and less symmetrical than a bottle or bowl. Either way, analyze what you're looking at. When you feel you have a grasp of it, take out an HB or 2B pencil and begin to draw your three negatives as they appear in your viewfinder.

Remember, each negative shape will be made of at least four line segments. Make sure you go over the vertical and/or the horizontal edges of the format shape itself to draw the complete negative. Once you've done this, check your proportions. Are the heights to widths of each negative about right? Compare the three negatives. Are they all drawn to the same scale? Lastly, do the objects, your bottles and bowls, emerge in their correct scales? It's very common for things to be off. No worries, just erase and make your shapes wider or thinner as needed, and use the negatives to help do this.

In coming lectures, we'll talk at length about the methods we use to arrive at accurate proportions, and negative shape is one of them. If we're trying to get the positive to come out accurately, we can use the negatives to check and correct them. Similarly, when drawing the negatives, we can use the positives to do the same. But the negatives, oddly, tend to be easier to see clearly. That's because we know we don't know what they look like, at least before we actually study them. With objects, like bowls, bottles, or people, we have preconceived ideas about what they look like. With negative shapes, we have no preconceptions. We can't, because they're not things. They're just shapes and each one is different. So, we know we really have to analyze this. And this helps us trick ourselves into seeing clearly, seeing without bias. As they say, learning to draw is all about learning to see.

The overriding notion here is that the positives and negatives fit together like jigsaw pieces. Each exactly cut to fit the other. In the aggregate, they extend to the boundaries of the puzzle itself to create the drawing's shape. It's also like that yin-yang symbol. The two large shapes precisely meet and create the larger circular shape of the symbol itself.

Let's return to our drawing project. Our next step is to do the inverse of what we did earlier. We'll open up the viewfinder to make the vertical opening larger so that we can now see the tops and bottoms of our stacked objects. Again, with a 2H pencil, we'll trace the new format shape on top of our existing drawing. Then, with the 2B pencil, we'll draw both a top and a bottom negative shape. On the top shape, we'll reiterate the bottom line just above the existing one, doubling it, so that we get clear shape delineations. We'll do the same thing with the lower shape, but here, reiterating the top line for the same reason. Once you've done this, you could try these variations. Though, for variety, you might want to get some more objects— candlesticks, vases, pitchers and the like.

For one variation, we could include the horizontal edge where the table meets the wall. And you might want to do this first with the viewfinder adjusted so that you're cropping both the tops and the bottoms of the objects. When you do this, double the line representing the edge where the table meets the wall. It will help you distinguish between the bottom shapes that represent the table, and the top shapes that represent the wall, doing this will give you six negatives instead of three. Then, open up the viewfinder and add the top and bottom shapes, just like we did in the previous drawing.

Next, you could repeat this, again, maybe changing the objects. But, this time, start with the viewfinder in the open position. You'll get two large negative shapes, though these can be a little harder to see at first. After doing these exercises, you'll likely be seeing negative shapes all over your house or office because negative shapes are all around us. Wherever you have a space between one object and another, you have a negative shape. The more you study them, frame them and draw them, the more they'll become an everyday part of the way you see and draw. And, after doing the preliminary exercise we've talked about, that's just what you want to do.

Here are some notes you might find useful as you work through your own drawings as homework projects.

Use one page for each drawing. Basic printer paper works great for this. Center your format shape in the page and outline it with a 2H or 4H pencil, a hard pencil. This will allow you to modify the format if it will benefit the drawing.

Turn your page in sympathy with the drawing's shape. If the framing is horizontal, turn your page horizontally, if vertical, then vertically.

Think of the drawing from observation as choosing and framing. Try to choose and frame visual situations that will yield a drawing with strong and interesting negative shapes.

Think about what you choose to draw. Art teachers often assign drawings of folding chairs because interesting and complex negative shapes emerge between the legs, and from many points of view.

But, actually, what you can draw is pretty unlimited. So spend some time walking around with your viewfinder just framing things as you see them in your bedroom, kitchen, office, bathroom, or other room. Plants often have very interesting shapes between their stems, between leaves, and between flowers. If you draw outdoors, look at the spaces between trees, and in a single tree between the limbs themselves. Also, as we did here, try setting things up purposely to bring out the negatives. Part of drawing is finding the right thing to draw for a given project. By looking analytically, you'll be educating your eye. Once you've finished a couple drawings take a step back, and give yourself a self-critique.

Here are some good questions to ask yourself: Are your lines convincingly creating negative shapes? When you cover the positives, do the negatives come out forcefully? Are the large inter-shapes or negative shapes being used to build the composition and assert the rectangular format itself? Are the large negative shapes active?

Here are some excellent examples of negative shape drawings from my students at the University of Washington. In the first example, you can see how one bottle has been stacked on top of another object, and the negatives are beginning to emerge. You can also see that their horizontal lines within the negatives. These are sub divisions to try to analyze the negative. In the next drawing, you can see the negatives emerging even more strongly. The first one has a wider section at the top and narrows to the bottom, and the bottle begins to emerge between those two shapes. In the next example, we have a lamp, which is emerging very strongly. But, if you really look at the drawing carefully, you'll see that it's made of four negative shapes, and we can peel those shapes away, and let's just line them up so we can see each of those shapes clearly. And here's an even more complex lamp, a lamp with four heads. The lamp seems to come very much to the fore, the object comes very much to the fore, but again, let's peel those negative shapes away and just line them up so we can see that the drawing is really clearly made of those negatives.

At first, they trick you. You think the person has drawn the object. But when you crop the positives, you see that what has been drawn has indeed been the negative itself.

Let's sum up what we've learned. It's all connected. We can make shapes out of contour line. We can create the illusion of volume using cross contour, oblique shapes, and geometric solids. We can construct objects using contour, shape, cross contour, oblique shapes, and geometric solids often with the use of construction lines. We can organize the objects in our drawing using aggregate shapes. Aggregate shapes help us create visual groupings. They contain in place what it is we want to draw within the drawing's shape. We can conceive of the space around the main objects or subject as large flat shapes, ground shapes. These shapes form the shape of the drawing itself. We can conceive of yet another kind of shape, which expresses the distances and spaces between things. We call these negative shapes. Our drawings are going to benefit when the negative shapes are as tangible and compelling as the objects themselves. And those negative shapes are also useful for checking the proportions of the positives, the objects.

Composition: The Format and Its Armature
Lecture 7

W e've been working our way up in degrees of complexity. We started at the microcosmic level with line. We then moved on to shape, then a single object, then several objects. Next, we turned shape into volume and drew multiple volumetric objects, considering aggregate shape and object-ground relations. Finally, we learned about positive and negative shape. These last ideas took us well beyond drawing isolated objects and gave us a more sophisticated idea about how the parts of a drawing relate. Though we didn't name it, we were starting to talk about composition, which is really nothing more than organization—organizing parts of a drawing into a coherent whole. In this lecture, we'll talk about the underlying structure of rectangles because that's the shape of most of the drawings we make. Artists refer to this structure as the *armature*.

Drawing the Armature
Most drawings have a rectangular shape made of constituent shapes that relate to the rectangle. Drawings benefit when all the internal shapes have a relationship with the shape of the drawing itself.

To understand the rectangle a bit more, put a sheet of paper on your drawing board in the landscape position. Then, draw a rectangle that's 9 x 12 inches in the center of the page.

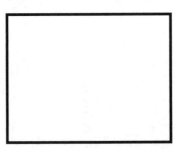

Start by connecting opposite corners with diagonal lines.

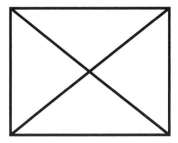

The intersection of these two lines creates the center of the rectangle, which suggests two more lines: a horizontal and a vertical through the center point.

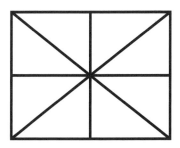

From here, we have many potential points to connect: the diagonals of the vertical halves, the diagonals of the horizontal halves, and the diagonals of the four quadrants. Ultimately, these lines create what artists call the rectangle's *armature*.

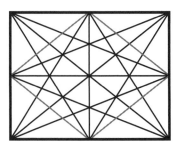

Some artists envision a more scaled-back version of the armature, and others, a more complex version. And of course, not all artists draw armatures in their rectangles, but doing so in a range of different rectangles is useful, especially if you pay attention to the shapes and relationships that emerge as you add each new line. Drawing armatures is a great way to develop sensitivity to the underlying structure of the format's shape.

Ratios in Rectangles

The essential character of every rectangle is defined by the relationship of its verticality to horizontality. That relationship can be expressed by a ratio. A rectangle with a 1:1 ratio is a square; it feels solid and stable. A rectangle with a ratio of 1:2 feels expansive and panoramic.

You may have heard of something called the golden rectangle, which is based on the golden ratio. It goes back more than 2,000 years to the Greek mathematician Euclid, who was among the first to define it. The ratio itself is 1.618 and is represented by the Greek letter φ (phi).

In the golden rectangle, the relationship of the height (b) to the overall width (c) is the same as the relationship of a to the height, a being the remainder if we subtract the height from the width. Mathematically, this is written as: $a/b = b/c$, or $0.618/1 = 1/1.618$. To put it more succinctly: a is to b as b is to c.

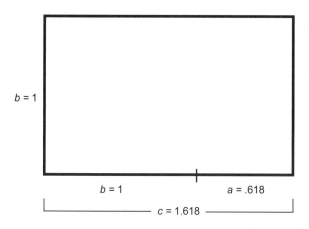

$b = 1$

$b = 1$ $a = .618$

$c = 1.618$

Many have studied the golden rectangle in significant architectural and artistic works, from the Parthenon in Athens to Hagia Sophia in Istanbul, from Leonardo's *Mona Lisa* to Mondrian's abstract paintings. But scholars disagree about the extent to which artists have relied on it. After exploring it, you should decide for yourself whether it's in any way special to you.

Suggested Reading

Aristides, *Classical Painting Atelier*, chapter 2, "Composition," pp. 19–43.

Curtis, *Drawing from Observation*, chapter 9, "The Golden Mean," pp. 93–114.

Hamm, *Drawing Scenery*, "Introduction to the Basics of Scenery Drawing," pp. 1–15.

Loomis, *Creative Illustration*, pp. 27–28, 35–39, and 47.

Pumphrey, *The Elements of Art*, "Format," pp. 40–49.

Rockman, *Drawing Essentials*, "The Golden Section," pp. 39–45.

Composition: The Format and Its Armature
Lecture 7—Transcript

We've been working our way up in degrees of complexity. We started at the microcosmic level with line, then shape, then a single object, then several. Then we turned shape into volume, and drew multiple volumetric objects considering aggregate shape and object/ground relations. Finally, we learned about the positive and negative shape. These last ideas took us well beyond drawing isolated objects, and gave us a more sophisticated idea about how the parts of a drawing relate. Though we didn't name it, we were really starting to talk about composition.

Composition's nothing more than organizing. It's about organizing parts in a coherent whole. The Italian word "disegnare" means both "to draw" and "to design," and the two are intimately connected.

In 1890, in a work titled *The Definition of Neo-Traditionalism*, the French artist, Maurice Denis, wrote "We should remember that a picture—before being a war horse, a nude woman, or telling some other story—is essentially a flat surface covered with colors arranged in a particular order."

He's saying "Sure, you see a war horse or a nude woman, but artists can't just think about horses and nudes. Artists have to consider the abstract stuff, the formal elements—line, shape, volume, and color—and how they're organized."

In this lecture, we'll talk about the underlying structure of rectangles because that's the shape of most of the drawings we make. Artists refer to this as the armature.

For this lecture, you'll need: pencils, erasers, a ruler, your t-square, triangle, compass, a sheet of 18 × 24-inch paper. Most drawings have a shape—generally, a rectangle—and it's made of constituent shapes that relate to that rectangle. That follows from what we learned about aggregate shape and negative shape. Drawings benefit when all the internal shapes have a relationship with the shape of the drawing itself. These relationships have a fair amount to do with geometry because our starting point, a rectangle, it's a geometric shape.

Even if we're drawing figures like Eakins or Diebenkorn, we have to make sense of them in terms of the abstract geometry of the rectangle. You can see how both are organized in relation to halves, quarters, diagonals, and other significant measures of the rectangle. We'll see in coming lectures how artists across a great swath of history, culture, and artistic convention have routinely composed in just this way.

Many of the great artists of the Renaissance, like Leonardo and Dürer, were fascinated by abstract geometry and its application to drawing. In fact, you could say that drawing's very nature is abstract. The English word "abstract" comes from the Latin "abs trahere." "Abs" is a preposition meaning "from." "Trahere" is a verb that has several meanings, including "to draw." "Abs trahere," or "to abstract," is literally "to draw out from."

If you've studied a Romance language, you'll likely note that "trahere" looks an awful lot like a verb—an infinitive. We have a root, "trah," and then a Romance verb termination, "ere." The root, "trah," survives in modern Italian. "Tratto" means *line*, and "ritratto" means *portrait*. There's a connection between "trah" and "draw," both four letters with the same two central letters—r and a—and they sound alike: trah, draw, trah, draw.

Both first letters—t and d—are sister sounds. We make them very similarly; try it: T, D, T, D. For T, the tongue's slightly more forward when it hits the roof of the mouth. In phonetics, they're both called alveolars; means the tip of the tongue flicks against the alveolar ridge. That would be the gums, just behind the teeth.

Similarly, the final letters of "trah" and "draw"—h and w—are also related. Again, give it a try: H, W, H, W. These are referred to as approximants. Both demonstrate smooth airflow. So taking our root and swapping out t for d and h for w, "trah" is "draw."

In English, "to abstract" retains its "abs trahere" meaning of "to draw out from." An abstract of an article refers to the main idea or ideas drawn out from the article as a whole. A track, like one you might run on, is like a line drawn on the earth.

A related word, "tract," as in "a tract of land," is a piece of land that's been abstracted or drawn out and set apart from all the surrounding land. That tract itself could be created with a tractor. In this sense, a tractor's just a big drawing tool. And artists have indeed drawn with tractors and similar tools, marking the surface of the earth at a large scale. You may have seen images of James Turrell's *Roden Crater*, or works like this one—*Spiral Jetty* by Robert Smithson.

Many people, when they hear the word abstract, immediately think about a kind of art—Jackson Pollock or Willem De Kooning—and, of course, abstraction does have this meaning, too. But here, we're not talking about a kind of art, but about concepts that apply to all kinds of art.

Both Eakins and Diebenkorn are abstracting. They're pulling out a particular rectangle's worth of visual event, and they're organizing it relative to a given rectangle—the drawing's shape. And as you've done, they're using abstract shapes to draw with, to create large ground shapes, aggregate shapes, and as building blocks to construct the things in their drawing. So our challenge, to paraphrase Maurice Denis, is to arrange things on a flat surface—generally a rectangle—in an order that makes visual sense.

Every rectangle, even before we make a mark on it, has a latent visual structure buried just beneath the surface, and this structure affects the way our eyes traverse the blank page.

Take a piece of paper and put two dots on it. Your eyes go back and forth between them. We're drawn to connect them on a linear path. If I add a third dot, you'll likely connect them as a shape—here, a triangle.

It's just what many ancient peoples did looking up at the night sky. They saw points of light, stars, and connected them, seeing lines and shapes. That's our operating system at work. We're wired to connect the dots, and this has direct bearing on composition.

Let's get into this a bit. Put a sheet of paper on your drawing board in the landscape position; then draw a rectangle that's 9 × 12 inches in the center of your page. Take a hard look at your rectangle. Are there any points to connect? Is there a line implied by the rectangle itself? You're probably getting the idea.

You could connect the corners with a diagonal. The way our eyes react to the rectangle's corners is similar to the way they react to two random dots on a page—or stars in the night sky. Our eyes will move automatically from corner to corner on an otherwise blank page.

Our next implicit line is the other diagonal, so draw that, too. The intersection of these two lines has created a new point—the center of the rectangle. It's an important and strategic location. While it doesn't give us two points to connect, it does suggest two more lines: the first, a horizontal through the center point; the second, a vertical through the same point. These two lines, in a way, echo or rhyme with the four lines of the rectangle itself. The central horizontal echoes the top and the bottom. The central vertical, the right and the left sides.

Now your choices really open up. So many potential points to connect. Let's start with four diagonals—the diagonals of the vertical halves. These create two large intersecting triangles. Each one's flanked by a set of right triangles pointing in opposite directions. It also creates a symmetrical diamond pattern reminiscent of the Blombos Cave etched piece of ochre.

Let's add another four diagonals—those of the horizontal halves—and a final set, the diagonals of the four quadrants. These create a large diamond in the rectangle. Artists refer to this as the rectangle's armature. Some artists envision a more scaled-back version—others, a more complex version.

We'll be adding a couple more layers of complexity. But just as it is, I find this figure fascinating to look at. While ostensibly flat, it also begins to appear three-dimensional, like a faceted transparent crystal or diamond.

It's worth noting we really didn't invent anything here. We're just listening to the rectangle, doing its bidding. Not only is this figure distilled from the rectangle, but it gives us a lot of information about the rectangle.

Notice these points of intersection. They're intersections of the diagonals of the vertical and horizontal halves. They indicate our vertical and horizontal quarters. Let's draw those in. The rectangle now has two underlying grids. We already had a grid giving us the rectangle's quadrants. We now have an additional grid on the quarter. We've divided the rectangle into 16 equal sub-rectangles—4 columns and 4 rows. There's a fractal quality to this.

There are a couple more interesting points of intersection. There's the three-way intersection of the diagonals of the rectangle, the diagonal of the vertical half, and the diagonal of the horizontal half. This reveals the rectangle's vertical and horizontal thirds. Let's add these in, too. This gives us a grid of thirds.

Here's another—all the two-line intersections of the diagonals of the vertical and horizontal halves. These reveal the rectangle's horizontal and vertical fifths. Let's add this grid, too. We now have four layered grids: a 2 × 2 with 4 units, a 3 × 3 with 9 units, a 4 × 4 with 16, and a 5 × 5 with 25. All together, we get this.

There's a clear correlation with music here, in particular, rhythm. We can think about the page like a musical measure. It could be left empty, divided in two, in three, four, or five, and in many other ways that compound on these simple divisions. As in music, we could juxtapose these divisions creating complex visual polyrhythms.

The Mandarin word "huà" means *painting* or *drawing*. The modern character looks like this: It depicts a rectangle framed inside a rectangle with divisions at the horizontal and vertical halves. There are also stresses at about the quarters. In many ways, this character is like the horizontal and vertical aspects of the armature we've constructed and a blueprint for a common compositional strategy.

That Chinese has such a wonderfully distilled character like huà isn't wholly surprising. An attribute of good Chinese handwriting is that the strokes for each character balance within an imaginary square. Whether the character consists of 3 or 30 strokes, the strokes have to relate to that square.

When learning to write Chinese, students practice their characters within a square grid. There are several types, but a very common one looks like this. Familiar, isn't it?

As we've discussed, written Chinese is a pictorial-based language. How do you practice making pictures? Well, it's a good idea to do it in relationship to the major stresses, or armature, of the rectangle. Those would be the horizontal, vertical, and diagonal halves.

When you look at Chinese characters, you can see how they're organized around the major stresses, or major thoroughfares, in the rectangle. Some characters are quite simple and symmetrical, while others are quite complex and asymmetrical. But the characters, little drawings really, are composed in relationship to that imagined rectangle and its armature.

Coming back to our rectangle, it's worth noting that all we did was follow some simple procedures—a game of connect the dots—and we've learned a lot about our rectangle's measures—halves, thirds, quarters, fifths—and we did all this without a ruler.

We could go on like this infinitely. We now have scores of points that could be connected. We also have all the new rectangles in our four sets of grids. That would be 54 rectangles. Each one of these has all the same relationships that we found in our primary rectangle. So if we could draw small enough lines, this could proceed fractally and infinitely.

You might want to take this further to see what kinds of relationships you can bring out. There's a great deal of complexity in all this. I find I can stare at these figures for a long time; all kinds of interesting visual meanings emerge. I can read lines and flat shapes on the surface, or I can read darker lines as coming forward in space, and lighter ones moving behind, receding into the distance. I can read the lines as constructing planes twisting in space, as well as 3D crystalline structures.

One of the ways I've come to think about the armature is that it reveals that not all paths through the rectangle are equal. There are the equivalent of eight-lane superhighways, four-lane local roads, humble dirt trails, and open fields. Developing a sense of the rhythm of the landscape of the page is central to composing well.

I'm not claiming that all artists have drawn armatures in their rectangles. Some fine artists develop a feel for composing by looking at other artists' work, paying close attention to the compositional strategies that are deployed. We'll be doing this, too.

But drawing the armature in a range of different rectangles is useful, especially if you pay attention to the shapes and relationships that emerge as you add each new line. It's a great way to develop a sensitivity to the underlying structure of the format's shape.

The essential character of every rectangle is defined by the relationship of its verticality to its horizontality. That relationship can be expressed by a ratio. A rectangle with a 1:1 ratio it's a square. It feels very solid and stable. A rectangle with a ratio of 1:2 feels different, expansive, panoramic. Simply rotating this shape so that it's now 2:1, produces a rectangle that feels much less stable than either the square or the 1:2 rectangle; no doubt this has to do with the way we experience gravity.

The rectangle you just drew is 9 × 12 inches—a 3:4 ratio. A next step is to experiment with different ones. Try a 1:3, a 1:4, a 2:3, and a 2:5, and then rotate them 90 degrees; note how they feel in their portrait orientation. Getting to know rectangles is like playing scales and arpeggios for a musician. You begin to develop a feel for the terrain and the measure among the intervals.

There's one rectangle you've likely heard of: the golden rectangle. It's based on the golden ratio, also known as the extreme and mean ratio, the golden section, the golden mean, and the divine proportion. It's had a long history.

The idea that there are certain ratios or proportions that are beautiful or harmonious goes back at least 2,500 years to the Greek mathematician and philosopher Pythagoras. A couple hundred years later, his countryman and fellow mathematician, Euclid, was among the first to define the golden ratio.

You'll remember, many of the Renaissance heavyweights were enamored of geometry, and both Pythagoras and Euclid are thought by some art historians to be among the figures in Raphael's *School of Athens*. Some scholars identify the figure wielding the compass as Euclid. Pythagoras's and Euclid's ideas about measure and proportion would turn out to be very important to 15th-century Italians like Raphael and his contemporaries.

Many ideas about ideal proportions made their way to 15th-century Italy via the 1st-century B.C.E. Roman architect and writer, Vitruvius. He authored *De Architectura*, translated as *The Ten Books of Architecture*. In it, he wrote about many things, including pulleys, water clocks, and surveying instruments. But he also coined what have come to be known as the Vitruvian Virtues. He describes how a structure should be *utìlitas*, *firmitas*, and *venustas*—utilitarian, solid, and beautiful. He related this last virtue, beauty, to proportion, and he applied this not only to architecture, but also to the human figure.

Fourteen hundred years later, Leonardo da Vinci would pick up on this and make his famous drawing based on Vitruvius's ideals of measure and beauty. It's no accident that Leonardo became familiar with Vitruvius. His writings were rediscovered in Florence in the early 1400s and deeply influenced a number of Italians of the period. Notable among them was Leon Battista Alberti, who wrote his own book on architecture, modeled on Vitruvius's, *De Re Aedificatoria—On the Art of Building*. Alberti also wrote a seminal treatise on painting, titled *De Pictura*. We'll speak about that book when we delve into proportion.

Alberti's contemporary, Luca Pacioli, was a friar, a mathematician, and one of the first to develop systems of accounting—a true Renaissance man. He wrote a text called *De Divina Proportione—The Divine Proportion*. This text concerned itself with artistic proportion and the golden ratio in particular. Both he and Leonardo, at the time, were enjoying the patronage of Ludovico

Sforza, the Duke of Milan. Pacioli asked Leonardo to illustrate his text, and the two collaborated on the project.

Many people have studied the golden section in significant architectural and artistic works—from the Parthenon in Athens to Hagia Sophia in Istanbul, from Leonardo's *Mona Lisa* to Mondrian's abstract paintings—and there's some consensus among scholars and some disagreement about how much artists have indeed relied on it.

There's even a paper, written in 2008, titled "Golden Section and the Art of Painting," by a Romanian scientist, Agata Olariu. In it, she claims to have measured and tabulated the ratios of the rectangles of 565 paintings by Caravaggio, Cézanne, Delacroix, Goya, Rembrandt, Van Gogh, and others. She reports that the average rectangle used by these artists was far from a golden ratio rectangle. In fact, she reports that very few of the rectangles used by the artists in her sample were golden.

In any case, it's so famous that I'd be remiss if I didn't explain how to construct it, and I'll leave you to decide for yourself if it's in any way special.

Let's start with that ratio—Euclid's ratio. The basic idea is this: We have a line segment made of two constituent line segments of unequal length. And here's the key: The ratio of the shorter line segment to the longer line segment must be the same as the ratio of the longer line segment to the entire line segment.

I know that's a bit dense, so let me repeat it. The ratio of the shorter line segment to the longer line segment must be the same as the ratio of the longer line segment to the entire line segment.

To do this, make a line segment. Using the segment as a base, draw a square. From the center of the base, draw a diagonal to the upper corner of the square. Here we've gone to the right. Now take a compass, and put the point on the center of the base, and draw a portion of a circle from the upper corner of the square to a point where it would intersect with the base; then extend your base to intersect with your circle. The ratio of your two line segments is now a golden ratio.

The ratio itself is 1.618, and it's represented by the Greek letter φ. This is in honor of the 5th-century B.C.E. sculptor and architect Phidias, who's thought by some to have used it in his Parthenon statues.

Now onto our golden rectangle. We'll retain the height of the square, and construct a new rectangle on the golden ratio base. That's it. So this is our 1.618 rectangle, meaning the height is 1 to a width of 1.618. What makes this rectangle special? We want to keep Maurice Denis's idea about composition in mind. Things have to be "arranged in a particular order." And this may sound a bit odd, but we're trying to find an organizing principle for the relationship of the vertical to the horizontal aspect of the rectangle. That relationship defines the rectangle. We want them to relate. We want them to feel like they belong together.

A jacket and a pair of pants are clearly different things, but we can make them relate, make them feel like they belong together, when we, literally, make them from the same cloth. We get a suit.

The vertical and horizontal could be identical twins. That's a very strong relationship. It produces a square. But some might say squares are too predictable, not interesting enough. So we could design a rectangle where one measure was clearly related to the other measure, but not identical.

For instance, one side could be a given length, and the other could be 1½ times as long or 1¼ times as long, which, incidentally, according to the Romanian scientist, is the most popular ratio for rectangles used by the artists she sampled. Over 400 of the 568 rectangles exhibited ratios around 1:1.25. That would look like this. In the golden rectangle, there's a real relationship, but it's somewhat complex.

The height, b's relationship to the overall width, c, is the same as a's relationship to the height, b. And a is the remainder if we subtract the height, b, from the total width c. So they're intimately connected. Here's the math: a divided by b, which is 0.618 divided by 1, is equal to b divided by c, or 1 divided by 1.618. The quotients are identical—0.618. Put more succinctly, a is to b as b is to c.

Another permutation is the root rectangle. It's constructed similarly to the golden rectangle, but instead of drawing the diagonal from the center point of the base of the square, we draw it from one of the lower corners.

Let's try it. Draw a square. From the lower left corner, draw a diagonal to the upper right corner. Place the compass point on the lower corner, and draw a portion of a circle from the upper corner of the square to a point where it would intersect the base. Extend the base to intersect the curve. Retain the height of the square, and construct a new rectangle on the longer base. That's a root two rectangle. Repeat this procedure on the new rectangle to produce a root three rectangle, and repeat it again for a root four rectangle.

If you're interested in making circular drawings—we call them tondos—or elliptically shaped drawings, the same ideas can apply. As we've noted, the circle has a strong relationship with the square, and many of the square's stresses can be used on the circle. Each ellipse also fits neatly into a specific rectangle, and, likewise, that rectangle's armature will be useful in discovering the ellipse. Many of the rectangular structures we've discovered in the rectangle can be turned into curvilinear structures to rhyme with the outer edges of the circle or ellipse, and these curving lines can even be used in a rectangle.

If you're interested in other shaped drawings, regular or irregular, the same idea holds: Understand the internal structure of the format shape, and relate the divisions and shapes in the interior to the whole.

Earlier I'd said that a good way to develop a feeling for composing is to draw basic geometric divisions into a range of different rectangles. This will acquaint you with their underlying structures. I also mentioned that it's very useful to pay close attention to what emerges as you add each new line. Let's return to where we started today—to that single diagonal crossing the page. Even something this simple will reward our attention.

By making that one line, I've actually accomplished quite a lot: I've divided my rectangle in half; I've created two shapes—two triangles; I've created contrast; I've created a new direction—diagonal—that contrasts with the format itself, which is made up of two vertical and two horizontal lines; I've created asymmetry where, earlier, there'd only been symmetry; and while you may read it as flat, as two right triangles, there's a lot more to it. I've actually begun to create an object/ground relationship and the illusion of three-dimensional space.

Add a tree and a stump, and it's a sloping hill. Add a couple more humble marks, and we see the ocean, and the sun, and the clouds above. In this case, the lower triangle is forward in space, and the upper triangle represents the space behind it. This is an object/ground relationship with the lower triangle as object and the upper as ground.

But I could flip that space. If I double the diagonal and add a couple objects, I have a still life on a table with the floor below it. Now the upper triangle is object—the lower one, ground. We could also interpret this single line as a drawing of a cardboard box seen at an angle, or a pitched roof seen from above, or a wall meeting a floor.

Coming back to the diagonal itself, if it were a hill, it's one with a relatively gently sloping rise—about 37 degrees. We could hike up to the top without too much trouble. And if we chose to ski down? Well, it wouldn't test our skill; it's a beginner's slope. But turn your piece of paper to the portrait position, and now that slope's over 50 degrees. Walking up would be a real hike. And skiing down? Well, you'd want to be sure you knew what you were doing. And that translates to drawing: The greater the slope, the greater the sense of activity and instability.

Let's add that second diagonal. We've now created four shapes—triangles. We've restored balance and symmetry, and we have a new illusion of three-dimensional space. We could be looking down at a four-sided pyramid, or we could be lying on our backs inside the pyramid, staring up at the ceiling. Equally, we could be looking into a deep room or tunnel.

And this relates directly to Frank Stella's *Mitered Squares*, which we looked at briefly in an earlier lecture. Try looking at the left rectangle and seeing it as a deep room. Simultaneously, try to see the right panel as a pyramid viewed from above; then switch. Then try and see them as two rooms. Then two pyramids from above. Mazelike, no?

Coming back to lines, one way to think about drawing—line drawing—is that what we're really trying to do with every line we make is to transform the white of the page from something inert and flat to something that creates some illusion of three-dimensional space. So it's a good idea to stare at the lines you draw and ask yourself how they're changing the white of the paper or a portion of it, making it bulge, or dip, or shift into an oblique plane orientation.

You'll note that all the lines we've drawn in this lecture fall into one of three categories: horizontal, vertical, or diagonal. Our feelings about these directions in drawings parallel our experience of them in everyday life, and this likely goes back to our very first ancestors.

Imagine a young *Homo sapiens*. He's walking along and comes upon a sleeping Neanderthal. The Neanderthal's got his club lying beside him—all horizontal. That's not a big deal. But if the Neanderthal were standing, vertical, with his club held up vertically, well, you can imagine the youth would pay a lot more attention to that. And if that Neanderthal were lunging with his club, everything all diagonal? The early *H. sapiens* who didn't pay a lot of attention had a very low probability of passing on his genes—probably not one of our ancestors.

Horizontals are like a calm sea; verticals less so, but nothing like diagonals, which are active, unstable, and grab our attention. And the greater the pitch, the greater the feeling of action and instability.

Composition: How Artists Compose
Lecture 8

Choosing the right kind of rectangle for a given drawing is crucial. The drawing's basic character will be flavored by that choice. Artists often choose to orient the format in sympathy with the subject. Although there's no rule about this, you'll find that most landscapes and still lifes are horizontal, and most full-length portraits are vertical, except, of course, when the subject's lying down. Most people make the same choice instinctively when they take snapshots. Generally, artists want the various parts of a drawing to relate to one another, and they want to construct a unified whole out of the parts. Thus, we'll often find that the largest shapes, the object and ground and the aggregate shapes, relate to the drawing's armature. In this lecture, we'll look at some of the ways in which artists apply an understanding of the underlying structure of the rectangle to their drawings.

Low, Mid, and High Horizons
One of the most common compositional strategies we see is a division of the format rectangle into two horizontal sub-rectangles. In the Eakins watercolor, this division occurs near the midpoint. Other works may use a thinner rectangle below and a wider one above (*low horizon*) or a large rectangle below and a smaller one above (*high horizon*).

Other Divisions

Of course, the primary divisions in a drawing don't need to be horizontal. Artists also make use of vertical divisions. And in some cases, you might want to think in terms of dividing the rectangle into thirds, diagonals, and quarters. Yet another compositional strategy is to slightly skew the main division in the ground. In other words, the division sits along a diagonal that divides the rectangle into two wedge shapes, something like the blade of a guillotine.

Focal Point, Focal Area, and Compositional Shapes

This discussion of large compositional shapes leads naturally to the subject of focal area and focal point.

There's a reason that most people aren't aware of the ground when they look at a drawing: Artists purposely construct their drawings so that we focus on the objects. But the artist must pay a great deal of attention to both the focal point and the ground so that the viewer experiences the hierarchy of visual events in a specific way.

In Eakins's watercolor, the focal point is clearly Biglin's head and upper torso. The focal area is Biglin in his scull. Why? First, Biglin and his scull represent the largest figure and boat in the watercolor. They dwarf all similar events. All else being equal, we'll look at the large thing first. Next, Biglin is in the center. All else being equal, we'll look to the center first.

Direction also plays a role here. Not all directions attract the same attention. All else being equal, horizontals are sleepiest; verticals, a bit more energetic; and diagonals, the most dynamic. If we eliminate Biglin and his boat, what remains is very horizontal, with a couple of minor verticals and tiny diagonals. The result is sleepy. Biglin supplies the directional fireworks. He and his oar create the zig-zagging lightning bolt in the composition's center.

Many drawings and paintings—even stylistically different ones—use these and similar abstract strategies to create focal points and focal areas in a composition.

Balance and Visual Weight

We've seen that the center of the format is an important place. Of course, artists don't always locate their focal point in the center, though drawings often find their balance in relationship to it. And balance is a key compositional concept.

We can imagine the bottom horizontal of the format as a plank sitting on a fulcrum. Every line or mark we make has what we refer to as *visual weight*, and just about all the artworks you know are structured to balance in one way or another. You won't see the plank tipping too much in one direction or another.

There are many options in structuring balance. In the Biglin watercolor, Eakins's strategy is based on centering, complemented with counterweights to the left and right. Biglin occupies the center; he's balanced. The thrust of his arm on the left is counterbalanced by the oar on the right. In the foreground, we get the major weight in the center—Biglin's reflection—and there are equal counterweight reflections to the left and right. On the water behind him, we get a portion of a cropped scull and the long scull on the left. That's countered by the two sailboats on the right. The events in the landscape and sky balance out, as well.

Arranging Furniture

Everything we've discussed so far has to do with ordering and balancing things in relation to a given rectangle. In that sense, composing a drawing is similar to arranging furniture, which we do in relation to the proportions of a given room. How we arrange the furniture depends on the room itself. What kind of rectangle it is? How long? How wide? We also create aggregate groupings and relationships when we arrange furniture. In your living room, for instance, you position the area rug, sofa, coffee table, and armchair so that the individual objects form a grouping.

Most drawings, prints, and paintings are rectangles, and most artists structure their compositions in relation to the specific rectangle they've chosen, though in most cases, as with the works we've seen, they don't end up looking geometric. But the act of composition seeks to tie the specific subject matter to the underlying structure of the given rectangle. The structure generally remains hidden—unless you look for it.

Self-Critique Questions

There are several key points to consider when working on compositional problems like the ones we've covered in this lecture:

- Choose what you draw carefully.

- Take time to select a point of view and framing.

- Think about the large planes and planar divisions, such as the tabletop and wall in a still life, floor and wall in an interior, and land and sky in a landscape.

- Relate observed reality to large geometric shapes and draw through the format in sympathy with this.

Here are some questions you can ask yourself as a guide in critiquing your own work:

- Is the whole format activated?

- Are there dead areas?

- Does the composition balance?

- Does the drawing feel alive and fresh?

- Is there a unique perception or point of view?

- Does this perception come to life on the page?

- Does the drawing have a focal point and a focal area?

- Is there a strong sense of design in the composition that directs the viewer to move through the drawing in a particular order?

- Have you looked at what you're drawing closely and with an intelligent and analytic eye?

- Do your objects sit convincingly in relation to the large planes?

- Are you creating space and volume convincingly?

- Have you been attentive to clarifying overlap situations?

Suggested Reading

Loomis, *Creative Illustration*, pp. 29–34 and 47–53.

Mendelowitz, Faber, and Wakeman, *A Guide to Drawing*, chapter 8, "Composition," pp.138–160.

Pumphrey, *The Elements of Art*, chapter 5, "The Organizational Components of Art," pp. 62– 89.

Rockman, *Drawing Essentials*, "The Principles of Composition," pp. 22–38.

Composition: How Artists Compose
Lecture 8—Transcript

Let's take a look at some of the ways artists apply an understanding of the underlying structure of the rectangle to their drawings. As we analyze their work, you'll have the opportunity to put these concepts into practice. For your drawings, you'll need: pencils, sharpening tools, erasers, a drawing board. You'll also need: your viewfinder, some printer paper or a sketchbook of a similar size, some very simple still life objects. For this project, the simpler the better.

Choosing the right kind of rectangle for a given drawing is crucial. The drawing's basic character will be flavored by that choice. Generally, artists choose to orient the format in sympathy with the subject. While there's no rule about this, you'll find that most landscapes and still lifes are horizontal. Most full-length portraits are vertical, except when the subject's lying down. Most people do this instinctively, even when they're taking a snapshot. Unlike a snapshot, we can decide exactly how vertical or horizontal to make a drawing.

In the examples, you'll note that each drawing uses a unique rectangle, some more vertical, some more horizontal, some more square. Each makes use of specific shapes and divisions to structure the drawing. Generally, artists want the various parts of the drawing to relate to one another, and they want to construct a unified whole out of the parts. So we'll often find that the largest shapes, the object and ground, and the aggregate shapes, relate to the drawing's armature.

Here's a drawing by Rembrandt. You'll note the uniquely shaped rectangle. Just about every one of his works has a unique format shape. While the subject is a landscape, the underlying compositional strategy is to divide the rectangle into two horizontal sub-rectangles, and this is among the most common compositional strategies you'll find. Here, we get a thinner rectangle below and a much taller one above. We could refer to this as a low horizon.

This is a 12th-century Song Dynasty drawing by Xià Guī. We looked at it in an earlier lecture. The format shape's vertical to the Rembrandt's horizontal, but we find the same compositional idea. Divide the rectangle into two constituent rectangles. In this example, it occurs at the format's horizontal half.

And what about the Eakins watercolor we looked at earlier? We find a similar division, near the mid-point. And note that the boat sits conveniently on the quarter. It sub-divides the lower half into two more-or-less equal rectangles.

And here's a Goya. We're in the bullring. What do we find? The same abstract compositional structure, division at the horizontal half. This isn't just about landscape and bullfights.

And, here's a figure painting by Lucian Freud. What do we find? A strong division at the half. Just like Xià Guī about 800 years earlier though unlike Xià Guī, Eakins, and Goya, Freud locates his main subject in the upper half.

Here's Vincent Van Gogh employing the same idea as his countryman, Rembrandt, but inversely. Here we have a large rectangle below, about three-quarters of the whole, and a slight one above, about one quarter, a high horizon. And note the gentle way the topography is divided or stressed, at about the half and the quarter, both slightly diagonal.

I've seen many students try to imitate Van Gogh's drawings. They're generally attracted to the mark making. It's very beautiful and it's a real hallmark of Van Gogh's work. But they miss the underlying structure. This grid of horizontals and diagonals related to the format shape, which hold all those marks together.

Now, I don't think anyone looking at these six drawings would say that they look particularly geometric, but in each case, the ostensible content—a landscape or figure—has, at an abstract level, been married to the geometric underpinnings of a given rectangle, a format shape.

So here's a useful exercise to do at this point. It's all about using a range of different rectangles and horizontal ground divisions related to the armature of the rectangle. Doing this helps you begin to develop an intuitive sense about composition. You'll be making a number of small compositional studies.

So keep the objects simple, a bottle, a coffee mug, a saltshaker, or the like. We want to concentrate on the large compositional shapes. We don't want to spend a lot of time drawing intricate objects. In fact, many of the drawings you'll be making will work fine with a single object, and using some of the same objects repeatedly will heighten your awareness of how much the compositional decisions contribute to the drawing, that as opposed to the objects.

For the first drawing, use one object. Make sure your table is pushed back against the wall, then pose the object. The goal is to find a point of view and frame with the viewfinder to capture specific compositional structures.

One word of caution. Some of my students will, at first, try to create the compositional divisions with the object. That can work, but it's generally much stronger if you can do this with the large planes, the ground shapes. The tabletop and wall in a still life, the floor and wall in an interior, or the land and sky in a landscape.

Let's start with a low horizon, someplace around the horizontal quarter or third, like the Rembrandt. You want to get in a position so that the division of the table and wall will be a true horizontal, not a diagonal, so you see a smaller rectangle below and a larger one above.

Once you're satisfied with your point of view and framing, trace the shape of your viewfinder on your page with a 2H or 4H pencil. Then make your drawing with a somewhat softer pencil, a B or a 2B.

Start with the two ground shapes, your tabletop and wall, and then give yourself a centerline, relating the placement of the object to the large divisions. Then build your object using shape. Check your proportions using your centerline and your negative shapes. Don't worry about shading or shadows, we just want to concentrate on moving through compositional strategies so this sense of ordering shape is embedded in the way we see the world. Now try reframing to get a mid-horizon. After completing that drawing, do a high horizon.

Each time you'll have to think about: How you pose the object or objects, how you position yourself, how you change the viewfinder window's shape. The viewfinder window's shape will be the shape of your drawing. So far, it's likely that your object or objects have been in the lower rectangle or straddling the two rectangles.

Here's a challenge. How could you get the object in the upper rectangle? We have Freud's example to contemplate. You may have to move around a bit, but if you look up at your table from below, so that the front edge of the table forms the horizontal division, you've found one solution to the problem. Or we could look down at an object on a bed, or on a low table. So try another three drawings—low, mid, and high horizons—but this time, with the object or objects occupying the upper rectangle.

Of course, our primary divisions don't need to be horizontal. Here's a drawing by the American artist Norman Lundin. It's from 1974 and it's titled *Model Standing Before a Blackboard*. Note the division along the vertical half. It's accompanied by stresses at the vertical quarters. Also, note the projection of light on the blackboard, pretty much parallel to the rectangle's diagonal.

Most of the artists we've talked about here are long gone, but Norman Lundin's someone that I've had the great good fortune to know and call a friend for close to two decades. He was my colleague at the University of Washington before retiring a couple years ago. I interviewed him in 2006 for a piece that was published in a catalog on his work

This is what he had to say about composition in painting, of course, it applies to drawing, too:

> Paintings are, by and large, rectangles. In both figurative and non-figurative art, being conscious that the interior rectangles and diagonals relate to the overall rectangle is an important concept.

When I compose, I consciously relate the rectilinear aspects of the imagery to the edges of the painting.

So let's try this, too. How could you get a vertical half? I'll give you three examples. I'm sure you'll be able to find many more. You could place a tall bottle, a big bottle, in the foreground, and then put a shorter bottle in the mid-ground. Then frame so that the edge of the tall bottle occurs at the half. We could also look down at a table and frame so that its edge creates the half. Moving from still life into an interior, we could frame so that a door opening onto an adjacent room acts as the vertical half.

Another motif involves thinking of the page in terms of quadrants. Here, Leonardo locates the woods in the upper right. This kind of decision impacts the way we read the illusionistic space in the drawing. Locating the woods, as he did, pushes it far back in space. The blank page functions like a field we traverse to reach the trees. Had he drawn the woods in the lower left, the woods would appear right in front of us.

So try this, too. Set up an object or objects and locate the drawing in the lower left quadrant. Repeat in the upper right quadrant, then note the difference in the way the spatial illusion appears.

In the Freud, we not only get the horizontal half. The center floorboard and the white drape stress the vertical half and the edge of the figure overlapping the white drape rides the horizontal quarter.

Here's a drawing attributed to someone in Rembrandt's circle. Here we have horizontal thirds, stresses at the vertical quarters, and the figure's upper torso falls into the diagonal of format.

And here's a drawing by Rembrandt himself. The drawing's divided into vertical thirds. The figure sits in the diagonal. It's also pinned to the horizontal and vertical halves.

And Picasso not only gives us vertical thirds but sixths as well, not to mention the stress at the vertical half, the horizontal thirds, the diagonal of the format in both directions, and the diagonals of the vertical halves.

I want to be clear here. This isn't about style, period, or country. Here is from the 15th-century Japanese artist Sesshu Toyo, middle Muromachi period. Like Picasso, he ties his composition to the rectangle's armature. There's a division along the horizontal half, stresses at the horizontal quarters, another along the diagonal of the format, along the diagonal of the horizontal half, along the bottom two horizontal quarters, and subtle stresses along the vertical half and quarters.

A couple 100 years earlier in China, Mǎ Yuǎn composed this piece, and we find very similar divisions. Horizontal half, a stress along the diagonal of the format, others along the diagonal of the bottom horizontal halves, and a light accent at the vertical half, too.

So let's try all this. Your goal is to set-up or find visual situations that can be framed from a specific point of view so that your drawings use: horizontal thirds, vertical thirds, the diagonal of the rectangle, quarters. Try this out when you finish this lecture. For now, let's take a look at some examples to stimulate your imagination. So here are a couple examples.

We can get horizontal thirds by framing so that the top of the table is the center third, the area below it the lower third, and the wall the upper third. We can get vertical thirds by framing a door with equal amounts of wall on either side. You can get a diagonal by viewing your still life table from an angle and making sure the viewfinder is adjusted so that the diagonal is the diagonal of the rectangle itself.

It really helps to pay attention to the large planes, like tabletops, walls, and floors and understand them as flat shapes. To bring this home, here's the drawing by Richard Diebenkorn we looked at earlier. This isn't just a drawing of a couple of nude models. It involved a very careful consideration of three interrelated things: the position of the models and the furniture, choosing the point of view, choosing the framing and format shape. The result? A tightly-knit drawing that's melded to the rectangle's armature. We have stresses, things lining up, at both the vertical and horizontal halves, at the vertical and horizontal quarters and eighths, along the format's diagonals and along several of the diagonals of the horizontal halves, and diagonals of the vertical halves.

This composition also evinces a strategy of the main division in the ground being slightly skewed. It sits along a diagonal that divides the rectangle into two wedge shapes, kind of like a guillotine blade.

We find the same strategy employed in Picasso's *Portrait of Apollinaire*. The drawing's hinged on the vertical center, dividing the nose and lips in half, with one eye to the right, the other to the left. The figure and chair are pegged to the vertical quarters. One arm rides the center of the right quarter, while the other chair leg echoes it on the other side, riding the center of the left quarter, one side balancing out the other.

Norman Lundin uses a similar wedge-shaped division in his drawing *White Doe at Home*. We also get stresses along the horizontal half, the vertical half, and along several of the vertical and horizontal quarters.

None of the drawings we've looked at would be considered geometric drawings, but they all have a strong geometric underpinning. They all rely on large shapes, usually in the ground, that are related to and construct the format shape of the drawing.

So, try composing using two wedge shapes. Try a vertical version, like the Picasso, and another horizontal version, like the Lundin. You could also try varying the relative amounts of the wedges. Start with both about equal. Then try one small on top, big on the bottom, then the inverse. Like the artists we've been looking at, you could compliment the primary wedge division with a vertical half or diagonal half, or some other measure. Mix it up, and remember to consistently vary that rectangle.

You can draw just about anything with this approach, still lifes, interiors, landscapes, cityscapes, all of it. If you have someone who can pose for you, try the figure, too. If not, use a mirror and compose some self-portraits. The mirror itself can be used structurally in the composition.

Another good way to develop a feel for this aspect of composition is to get reproductions of some of your favorite drawings and paintings. Put a piece of tracing paper over the reproduction. Trace the shape of the rectangle. Measure the rectangle and note the ratio of height to width. Then remove the acetate or tracing paper and draw an armature into the rectangle. You don't need every line we drew in the last lesson, but give yourself the most important ones. Then put the tracing paper back on top of the reproduction. Note what lines up with or echoes the important divisions and directions.

Most drawings are constructed with some kind of hierarchy in mind, and our discussion of the armature and large compositional shapes leads quite naturally to a discussion of focal area and focal point. There's a reason why most people looking at a drawing aren't even aware of the ground. It's because artists purposely construct their drawings so that we focus on the object. But the artist has to pay a lot of attention to both so that the viewer experiences the hierarchy of the visual events in a specific way.

In Eakins' watercolor, the focal point is Biglin's head and upper torso. The focal area is Biglin in his scull. We've noted that the two large rectangular ground shapes hinge near the horizontal half. The drawing's also clearly hinged to the vertical half. The figure grouping, Biglin, and his boat, sit into a rectangle. Our main character sits into a central triangle within this. Eakins has positioned Biglin's shoulder and arm directly below the format's center so that they echo the page's diagonal. He's also placed the oar parallel to the diagonal of the figure's rectangle. All in all, lots of triangles. This means lots of diagonals in this part of the image.

The reason's clear. Biglin's a focal point. Eakins also wants to express energy and movement. The guy's an athlete. He's rowing. So the choice is not only rational but expressive of the content.

We have a second figure group in the distance made up of three boats and landscape events. This sits into a rectangle as well, a smaller one, more horizontal one. The major stresses are more horizontal and vertical, very stable, less eye-grabbing. There are a couple minor diagonals in the distant boats. This helps to make them more compelling than the even quieter landscape beyond.

In the Indian drawing, the man and woman are the focal point. They form a central triangle with attention-grabbing diagonals. This drawing, too, is hinged at the center. The place where the two lovers touch hands is dead center, with their arms paralleling the vertical and diagonal centers respectively. Adding the still life objects, we get a larger focal area that fits into a square centered in the large rectangle. The still life objects form a rectangular sub-compartment.

The Rembrandt follows a similar strategy. The focal point is Saskia's head and upper torso. Where do we find it? In the center. What kind of shape is it related to? A triangle. Picasso follows suit. The model's the focal point. She's placed in the center. She's constructed using sets of triangles.

The Rembrandt, the Punjab Hills drawing, the Eakins, and the Picasso are all stylistically different, but they follow similar underlying compositional strategies, similar abstract strategies. In these cases, that means locating the focal point and focal areas in the center, and hinging these to diagonals associated with the rectangle.

That brings us to the next set of drawing projects. The idea is to extend on what we did in the last set of compositional exercises. You'll introduce more complexity in terms of the objects and their relationships. The goal is to: select objects, pose them, select a point of view. Frame them so that there's a natural hierarchy to the organization.

This means that, relative to the large ground shapes, you'll have a focal point and focal area. Start with still life, three to five objects will work well. Once you've done this observationally, try it again from your imagination. You can invent objects of differing shapes and sizes so that they create a natural hierarchy relative to the ground in the drawing. You can also go back and consult your earlier drawings, both from life and from your imagination, and begin to composing, using them as source material.

We've seen that the center of the format is a very important place. That's not to say that artists always locate their focal point in the center, though often drawings find their balance in relationship to it, and balance is a key compositional concept. We can imagine the bottom horizontal of the format as a plank sitting on a fulcrum. Every line or mark that we make has what we refer to as visual weight. That's another important compositional concept, and just about all the artworks you know are structured to balance in one way or another. You won't see that plank tipping too much this way or too much that way.

There are many options in structuring balance. In the Biglin watercolor, Eakins' strategy is based on centering, complimented by the use of counterweights, left and right. Biglin occupies the center. Balanced. The thrust of his arm on the left is counter-balanced by the oar on the right. In the foreground, we get the major weight in the center, Biglin's reflection. There are equal counterweight reflections left and right, balanced. On the water behind him we get the portion of the cropped scull and the long scull on the left. That's countered by the two sailboats on the right. The events in the landscape and sky balance out as well.

In this drawing by Norman Lundin, we get a balance which is symmetrical in nature. The two figures balance each other out. Now, too much symmetricality can be monotonous, but managed artfully it can serve as a strong basis for a composition. The obvious symmetricality is offset by the way the figures twist in opposing directions in space, one forward, and one away. That's complimented by the differences in the position of the arms and the feet.

While not as symmetrical as the Lundin, this Rembrandt is by no means asymmetrical. It's still a drawing where the visual weights are balanced out, right and left. The big division in the ground occurs at about the horizontal third. That gives us a small rectangle below and a larger one above, about twice as big. The large tree sits just off center with the limb on the right tied to the format's diagonal. The right side of the tree balances with the left. The bifurcated buildings, divided by the tree's trunk, balances out left and right, as do the buildings on the left with the horse and the cart on the right.

In this brush painting by Zhào Mèngfǔ the large division in the ground occurs at about the three-quarter mark. This divides land from sky. Here, too, we get balance from the center, but the hierarchy is inverted. The focal points are on the right and left. The foreground landscape grouping on the right is counterbalanced by the colophon and the distant mountains on the left.

Lundin's Model *Standing Before a Blackboard* embraces a greater degree of asymmetry. The drawing hinges along that vertical half. The full weight of the figure is on the right, but it's counterbalanced by the visual weight of the notations and play of light on the chalkboard.

In this drawing, the figure splays right and left of center, balancing out around it. The triangular shape of the floor and the wall molding provide an added counterweight to the portion of the figure on the right.

This other drawing by Eakins is more asymmetrical, but not without balance. The two rowers and most of their scull weigh down on the left, as does the small boat in the upper left. To balance this out, Eakins adds a second long scull, horizontal and straddling the center, and a tugboat and large paddleboat anchored on the right. It's worth noting here that the large division is a variation of the high horizon, dividing the rectangle into two primary rectangles, a larger lower one, about two thirds, and a smaller higher one, about one third.

Everything we've discussed so far has to do with ordering and balancing things in relationship to a given rectangle. In that sense, composing a drawing is a lot like arranging furniture, which we do in relation to the proportions of a given room. How we arrange the furniture depends on the room itself. What kind of rectangle it is. How long. How wide.

We also create aggregate groupings and relationships when we arrange furniture. In your living room, for instance, you position the area rug, sofa, coffee table, and armchair so that the individual objects form a grouping. Similarly, in your office you relate the chair to the desk, to the computer table, to the file cabinet. It's all about establishing relationships. There's generally a hierarchy here, too.

Most drawings, prints, and paintings are rectangles, and most artists structure their compositions in relation to the specific rectangle that are chosen. Though in most cases, as with the works we've been looking at, they don't end up looking geometric. But the act of composition seeks to tie the specific subject matter to the underlying structure of the given rectangle. The structure generally remains hidden, that is unless you look for it. Kind of like the two-by-fours and joists in the walls and floors of your homes. Most of us don't tend to think about them much, but they're really holding all the stuff we see on the surface—the wallpaper, moldings, paneling, mirrors—it's holding all of that together.

Learning to draw is a bit like learning to juggle. You have to keep a number of balls in the air at the same time. There's the choice of a particular rectangle, the format shape. Then, there are the large ground divisions. Next, we have to think about the internal aggregate shape or shapes and how these relate to the armature. All of the above is often related to a consideration of focal point and focal area, and now we have to start to think about structural balance.

This leads us to our next drawing exercise. The goal is to pose your still life objects, find a point of view, and frame to make three new studies. For the first, try symmetry. Next, try one that's balanced. It could have elements of symmetry, but it shouldn't be truly symmetrical. Last, structure a composition that's clearly asymmetrical, but also balanced. Once you've done this from observation, try it from your imagination using the constructive methods we've covered earlier.

There are a couple key points to consider when working on compositional problems like the ones we've covered in this lecture. You want to choose what you draw very carefully. Take time to select a point of view and framing. Think about those large planes and planar divisions—the tabletop and wall in a still life, the floor, and the wall or walls in an interior, and the large divisions of land and sky in a landscape.

Relate observed reality to large geometric shapes and draw through the format in sympathy with this. And here are some questions you can ask yourself as a guide in critiquing your own work: First, is the whole format activated? Are there dead areas? Does the composition balance? Does the drawing feel alive and fresh? Is there a unique perception or point of view? Have you taken care to bring this perception to life on the page? Is there a focal point and focal area? Is there a strong sense of design in the composition that directs the viewer to move through the drawing in a particular order? Have you looked at what you're drawing closely with an intelligent and an analytic eye? Do your objects sit convincingly in relationship to the large planes? Are you creating space and volume convincingly? And, have you been attentive to clarifying overlap situations?

All these questions will help you identify problems in your work and improve the results.

Line and Shape: Line Attributes and Gesture
Lecture 9

At first glance, line might seem a simple matter, but as you begin to look more closely, it reveals a surprising degree of complexity. There are quite a number of choices to make when using line and a great deal of "art" involved in making those choices. So far, we've discussed three kinds of line: contour, cross-contour, and construction line. In this lecture, we'll dig deeper. We'll learn about the attributes of line that directly bear on its function and expressive potential, and we'll learn about a new kind of line, gestural line.

Types of Line and Their Attributes
The visual attributes of various lines account for the way a drawing "feels"—its expressive quality. Major attributes of line include the following:

- Value: light versus dark

- Width: thick versus thin

- Continuity: continuous versus discontinuous

- Length: long versus short

- Direction: horizontal, vertical, or diagonal

- Shape: straight, angular, or curvilinear

- Degree of closure: a range running from straight with no closure to curving and fully closing in on itself, making a shape

- Speed: drawn quickly, slowly, or at any speed in between

- Texture: smooth versus rough.

Value and Width

Line value can be controlled by pencil choice—a soft pencil produces a darker line than a hard one—and pressure applied when drawing.

Line width is controlled by pressure (increased pressure results in increased width), the way in which the pencil comes into contact with the page (point versus side), and the way in which the pencil is sharpened (sharp edge versus flat wedge).

These first two factors, line value and width, are often taken together and referred to as *line weight*. The greater the line weight, the greater the contrast to the page. And, all else being equal, the part of the drawing with the greatest line weight will function as a focal point and draw the viewer's eye to that section. This is a primary means for creating a hierarchy in a line drawing.

Continuity

Some lines are discontinuous or fragmented (sometimes referred to as *implied lines*), while others are continuous. Highly continuous lines present things in sharp focus, while discontinuous lines may create the appearance of broken edges and things seen peripherally. Greater line weight and continuous line create focal zones and, all else being equal, tend to pull forward in space. Lighter, thinner, and discontinuous lines receive less of the eye's attention and, all else being equal, recede in space.

Length

Related to continuity and discontinuity is line length. Varying line lengths can be used to create rhythm in a drawing, just as in music, where varied durations or lengths of notes create audible rhythm.

Direction

Another factor affecting line is direction and stability. As we've noted, horizontals are stable, at rest; verticals are less so; and diagonals are the most dramatic lines.

Shape, Degree of Closure, and Speed

Lines can be relatively straight, angular, or curvilinear and flowing. Related to a line's shape is its degree of closure. Some lines in a drawing may be very open; they make no move toward closure. Others, however, close to make clearly delineated shapes. In some cases, lines may exhibit degrees of closure. They begin to suggest shape but don't fully close in on themselves. Lines are also imbued with character by how quickly or slowly they seem to be drawn.

Texture

Line texture is often the product of the way the line interacts with the paper's surface. Not surprisingly, a smooth surface yields smooth lines—lines that are consistent in value, both internally and along the edges. But a textured paper—one with a noticeable tooth, such as many charcoal or watercolor papers—results in rougher lines. Such lines have irregularities both internally and along their edges.

Combining Attributes

Overall, you can think about each of these attributes as existing on a sliding scale. You can increase or decrease any of the factors and make a fairly unlimited number of line types by combining diverse attributes. For instance, you could make a thick, light, short, straight line, drawn slowly, with a lot of texture. Or you could make a dark, thin, long, curved line, drawn quickly and smoothly. In the end, these types of choices contribute to the way we experience a drawing emotionally.

Line attributes are also affected by the artist's choice of materials. Different tools and papers or surfaces have different intrinsic qualities and personalities that will create different opportunities and limitations. In addition, line attributes are affected by how you physically draw. To test this out, try drawing by moving only your fingers; then, move only your wrist, arm, or shoulder. You'll see that each of these choices can affect the lines you draw.

Gestural Line

Rather than trying to find the specific boundaries and edges of objects or planes, *gestural lines* describe the approximate location and character of things. Gestural line generally has the attribute of speed and some quality of wildness. It's much less sober and orderly than the kind of contour or cross-contour lines we've seen in Eakins.

In the example below, although it's clear what's being depicted—an older man holding a small child—the lines are abstract and scribbled. If we zoom in on the man's head, we see that a line whips from the back of the skull over the ear to a point and back into the ear itself. The lines don't necessarily hew to the edges of objects or parts of objects, and they're certainly removed from the idea of outlining. With the gestural approach, we often note the wildness and speed of the lines and multiple lines that result in the approximate definition of edges and changes of plane.

A useful way to think about gestural line is that it combines the work that contour, cross-contour, and even construction line each do separately. And it does all that much more rapidly than you could do with contour, cross-contour, and construction line separately. But the emphasis is on approximation, not certainty.

In using gestural line, you want to skip over the surface in a discontinuous manner, quickly flitting back and forth across the page, not moving sequentially along a line. Your goal is to find approximate positions, directions, and amounts through a series of repeated tests and probes.

As you probe for visual data, ask yourself these questions:

- Where will the drawing begin and end?

- What will be the format shape?

- Where are the large divisions?

- What are the farthest points to the right and left of the aggregate shape?

- What are the farthest points up and down?

- How would you describe the negative shapes between the objects?

- How far does your eye travel from one side of the arrangement to the other?

- What are the widths and heights of the objects?

Suggested Reading

Brown and McLean, *Drawing from Life*, chapter 4, "Line."

Curtis, *Drawing from Observation*, chapter 4, "Intuitive Gesture."

Sale and Betti, *Drawing*, chapter 2, "Learning to See," pp. 33–71.

Smagula, *Creative Drawing*, chapter 4, "Line."

Line and Shape: Line Attributes and Gesture
Lecture 9—Transcript

At first glance, line might seem a simple matter, but as you begin to look more closely, it reveals a surprising degree of complexity. There are quite a number of choices to make when using line, and there's a great deal of art involved in making those choices.

So far, we've talked about three kinds of line: contour, cross contour, and construction line. Now, we'll dig deeper. We'll learn about the attributes of line that directly bear on its functions and expressive potential, and we'll also learn about a new kind of line, gestural line.

Here are three drawings we've looked at before: The Holbein, the Schiele, this Rembrandt. Each one's primarily a line drawing of multiple figures, but in each case, line is used in a somewhat different way.

We'll take a close look at these drawings as well as several others, to help us understand how and why artists use different kinds of line. You'll need: pencils, erasers, sharpening tools, brush, and ink. You'll also need some 8½ × 11-inch paper or a medium-size sketchbook.

Edgar Degas not only drew, painted, and made sculpture, but also wrote poetry. He was once speaking to the poet Stéphane Mallarmé and said, "Your métier, your field, is hellishly difficult. I'm never able to really get at what I'm going for and yet I'm so full of ideas." Mallarmé responded, "My dear Degas, one doesn't make poetry out of ideas. You make poems out of words."

This applies to drawing, too. As we've noted, we can't really draw a person sitting in a room. We can only draw lines that create the illusion of a person sitting in a room, and we can accomplish this with many different types of lines.

Many people beginning to draw, though, often have trouble even seeing the lines. That's because they're so intent on what the lines construct, fruit in a still life, trees in a landscape, or a model on a model stand. To bring the point home, here's a detail of a drawing.

Unlikely, you'd be able to tell me what it is, but clearly, these are marks on a surface. They're medium gray lines on a neutral orange paper. Neutral orange means it's like an orange, but the saturation or orangeness is turned down a bit.

Here's the drawing in its entirety. It's the Schiele. The personality of the figures is so present that it can be difficult to even see beyond that illusion. Many people wouldn't even pay attention to the lines themselves.

But if we do, it becomes evident that the drawing's constructed of some very particular lines, and these lines actually account for the way the drawing feels. The kinds of lines used have everything to do with the drawing's expressive quality.

Going back to Degas and Mallarmé, we can't really make a neck, shoulder, or arm; we can only make lines, which in the aggregate, suggest specific physical form. And the way those lines are inflected, the visual attributes of the various lines has a lot to do with the feel of the drawing.

Schiele's drawing exemplifies many major attributes of line, and we're going to talk about nine: value—that refers to how light or dark a line is; width—that refers to how thin or thick; continuity—that'll refer to how continuous or discontinuous a line is; length—how long or short; direction—that'll refer to how horizontal, vertical, or diagonal; shape—that refers to qualities like straight, angular, and curvilinear; degree of closure—lines run the range from straight with no closure to those that curve and fully close in on themselves, making a shape; speed—you can draw a line quickly, slowly, or any place in between, and this will really affect the way they look; texture—lines can have textural qualities from smooth to rough.

Let's start with value. When we speak about value, we're referring to the lightness or darkness of a line. Here, some lines are light and some are much darker. In fact, there's a range of line value throughout the drawing. In addition, some line segments shift from light to dark or vice versa.

There are two major ways to control line value. The first involves pencil choice. Take out your softest pencil, the highest B number, and also your hardest pencil, the highest H number. Make a line with each. As we noted in an earlier lecture, the B produces a darker line than the H.

The other factor affecting line value is pressure. Again, using both your softest and the hardest pencil, exert the least amount of pressure possible and produce a line, then up the pressure. The line's going to get dependably darker. The softer the pencil, the greater the range of value; the harder, the less range you have.

So experiment with that full range of pencils. Following Schiele's example, try drawing a range of lines from light to dark. And then try moving from light to dark and dark to light in a single line.

Next, there's line width. Some lines in the drawing are comparatively thin while others are thicker, and we see some segments shift from thin to thick. There are three main ways to control this. The first is, once again, pressure, more pressure, thicker; less pressure, thinner. In fact, as you upped the pressure earlier, you likely noticed an increase in width as well as darkness. As with line value, as far as pressure's concerned, the softer the pencil the greater the range of widths. So try this with a couple of your pencils to get a feel for how they behave.

The second factor is how the pencil comes into contact with the page. We can control this by how we hold the pencil. With a pointed pencil, holding it like a writing implement, we get a fine line. By twisting it so that the side comes into contact with the page, we get a thicker line.

As we saw in an earlier lecture, another factor is how we sharpen our pencils. We can expose more of the graphite with a utility knife, and then shape the pencil into a wedge shape on our sanding block, and this will give us a sharp edge for thin lines and a flat wedge for thicker ones. This makes it much easier to flow from thin too thick by simply rotating the pencil between the thumb and first finger. And we could equally blunt our pencil on our sanding block to get a dependably thicker line without increasing pressure.

Now you're ready to draw lines of varying width and value. Try thin lines that are light, medium, and dark. Now try the same on the thick side, light, medium, and dark. Now try to get a thickness between your thin and thick line and repeat with three different values, light, medium, and dark. Next, move gradually from thin to thick and back again. Now try to do this while also moving light to dark, and then, dark to light.

Let's take another look at this detail. Notice the line that moves from the upper right, down at a diagonal and then turns 90 degrees and cuts down at a diagonal in the opposite direction. You'll likely have a sense how Schiele went about this. Start more on the point or sharp edge for the thin segment, then rotate to the side or wedge for the thicker one. You can also see how he's changed pressure. Note the slight dig right after the change of direction.

These first two factors, line value and width, are often taken together and referred to as line weight. The greater the line weight, the greater the contrast to the page. And all else being equal, the part of the drawing with the greatest line weight will function as a focal point and draw the viewer's eye to that section. This is a primary means for creating a hierarchy in a line drawing.

So in this sense, line weight functions compositionally, and this is an abstract visual phenomenon. It has nothing to do with what you're drawing. It applies to everything.

Here's a thin, light diagonal line. It attracts your eye and becomes a focal point because it's the only thing on an otherwise blank page. Now, let's add another diagonal line but a bit darker and thicker. You'll note that your eye goes to the new line first. Now I'll make another line and increase the weight. The focal point predictably shifts. We'll add one more line, darker and thicker yet. We have four distinct line weights, and they direct you to move through the drawing in a particular order.

Artists apply this principle routinely. Let's say I want you to go to the apple in the still life first, the bowl second, the patterned drape third, and the table and wall fourth. One way to achieve this is to stack my line weights. This functions the way relative volume does in music. We'll generally pay more attention to the wailing guitar above the accompanying keyboards and drums, or the trumpets in the high range above the accompanying violins. You can think about line weight as visual volume.

The reason that this works is that it's precisely the way we see. We've already noted that when we focus on something we see more of its detail. Additionally, when we focus on something, say me, as the camera's doing now, my value contrast is high relative to Jamie, my producer behind me. But if the camera's focus is Jamie behind me, my contrasts go down. When we focus our eyes on something, its value contrast and edge definition increases. We can create just this visual sensation by manipulating our line weights on the page.

In Schiele's drawing, some of the highest value contrasts are located in both the model's and Schiele's eyes, and that's a good choice because the drawing's all about looking. She's posing in the mirror, checking herself out, appears to be quite pleased with what she sees. And he's deeply involved in studying her. He's knitting his brows, pursing his lips, and trying to make drawing sense out of what he's seeing. Through the use of value, we're made to look at them looking. Abstraction orchestrates the narrative.

Our next factor is continuity. Some lines are discontinuous or fragmented, and some artists refer to these as implied lines, while other lines are continuous. We can relate continuity and discontinuity to focus, too. Highly continuous lines present things in sharp focus. That's because when we focus in on something, its edges appear clear. When we see something out of focus, say in our peripheral vision, its edges appear somewhat broken.

Discontinuous line can create just this sensation. Take a look at the long continuous line moving down the model's rib cage, and also down her pelvis and thigh. Compare Schiele's arm and elbow. The long continuous line creates a sensation of focus. In contrast, Schiele's arm and elbow are drawn as if we're seeing them in our peripheral vision.

In fact, the way the model's right arm fades out and the line breaks up a bit below her right hip echoes the breaking-up in Schiele's elbow. It's as if his vision's focused into the center of the drawing where we get our greatest accumulation of long continuous lines.

Picasso's portrait of Apollinaire represents another great example of contrasting line weights and continuous versus discontinuous line. Apollinaire is mostly drawn in robust weights and continuous line, but when we get to the shelf and objects behind him, the line becomes lighter, thinner, and discontinuous. This cements our focus on Apollinaire and also fosters the illusion of spatial depth.

Greater line weight and continuous line will create focal zones, and all else being equal, tend to pull forward in space. Lighter, thinner, and discontinuous lines will receive less of the eye's attention and will, all else being equal, recede into space.

Related to continuity and discontinuity is line length. In the Schiele, we find line segments that are relatively short and others that are relatively long. Varying line lengths can be used to create rhythm in a drawing. Just as in music, where varied durations or lengths of notes create audible rhythm, here we can create visual rhythm.

Here are some lines of different lengths. Can you feel the rhythm? It's almost audible. I based the example on the William Bailey still life. So this not only applies to line length but measure in general. Can you feel the rhythm in the objects?

Another factor effecting line is direction and stability. As we noted earlier, horizontals are stable, at rest, verticals less so, and diagonals the most dramatic.

In the Schiele, a dramatic drawing to be sure, there are few horizontals to speak of. We find the greatest degree of horizontality in the woman's reflected head, and indeed this is the place of rest in the drawing. The remainder of the drawing's all verticals and diagonals makes things feel dynamic.

Contrast that with the Bailey. It's peaceful, at rest. The format shape's a stable horizontal to Schiele's gangly vertical. And not surprisingly, it's full of repeated horizontals, no dramatic diagonals to speak of.

Another factor affecting line is the shape quality of the line. Here, we have lines that are relatively straight, others are angular, and others curvilinear and flowing. Overall, there's a much greater reliance on straight and angular lines in the Schiele's self-portrait and a much greater use of curvilinear line in the female figure. This functions to create contrast between them and express their different characters, male versus female, artist versus model.

Related to a line's shape is its degree of closure. Some lines here are very open. They make no move toward closure. Other lines or sets of lines close and make clearly delineated shapes. Others yet, exhibit some degree of closure. They begin to suggest shape but don't fully close in on themselves.

Next, there's the attribute of speed. Lines are imbued with character by how they're actually made. Here, some were clearly drawn very quickly, while others were drawn much more slowly. Though it's not functioning prominently in this drawing, we can also speak about line texture.

This is often the product of the way the line interacts with a paper's surface. A smooth surface will give us smooth lines, lines that are consistent in value, both internally and along the lines edges, like the lines in the Schiele. But a textured paper, one with a noticeable tooth, like many charcoal or watercolor papers, will give us rougher lines, lines with irregularities both internally and along their edges. That is unless we apply significant pressure to get the drawing material into the recessed parts of the surface. And we're going to speak more about this factor more fully when we talk about texture later on.

Overall, you can think about these nine attributes like sliding scales. We can increase or decrease any of these factors and make a pretty unlimited number of line types by combining diverse attributes. For instance, we could make a thick, light, short, straight line, drawn slowly with a lot of texture. Or we could make a dark, thin, long, curved line, drawn quickly and smoothly. Or we could do this last line again, but shift gradually from very light to very dark along the line's length, applying greater pressure as we went. Like I said, it gets complicated pretty quickly, and we're not even talking about drawing objects, just lines in the abstract.

It's a lot like the range of choices you have when you play a note. For each note, there's the duration, attack, and dynamics, among other variables. For instance, you could play a given pitch as a 16th note or a whole note, and you could also play it legato or staccato, and pianissimo or fortissimo. And these, among many other choices, affect the way we hear the pitches being played. In the end, all of this contributes an enormous amount to the way we experience the music emotionally.

We also affect line attributes by our choice of materials. Different tools and papers or surfaces have different intrinsic qualities and personalities that will create different opportunities and limitations and we're going to learn more about this later.

We can also affect the attributes of line by how we physically draw. To test this out, try drawing by only moving your fingers, then only your wrist, then arm, then your shoulder. You'll see that each of these choices can affect the lines you draw, and that can be compounded by how you hold the drawing implement and by the decision to sit or stand.

These discussions lead us to our final topic, gestural line. If we go back to Schiele's drawing and look at the wiggly line describing the sloping part of the model's hat or the lines describing Schiele's arm, we would classify these lines as gestural.

Rather than trying to find the specific boundaries and edges of objects or planes, gestural line describes the approximate location and character of things. It generally has the attribute of speed and some quality of wildness, much less sober and orderly than the kind of contour or cross contour we've seen in Eakins or Holbein.

To get a better sense of this, let's take a look at the Holbein in relationship to the Rembrandt. Both drawings are largely line drawings, both depict a group of people, but Holbein and Rembrandt are using line very differently.

How long do you think it took to make the Holbein? Got to be hours. And the Rembrandt? I'd say minutes. In the Holbein, the figures are clearly countable, 10 in the front room, two in the back. In the Rembrandt, it's not so clear. As we move from that central grouping to the far right and left, well, just hard to say.

If I zoom in on just about any detail in the Holbein, it's pretty clear what's being depicted. If I do the same in the Rembrandt, it's much less clear. The lines are more abstract. They're more scribbled. They don't necessarily hew to objects or parts of objects. They're certainly removed from the idea of outlining.

Different kinds of drawings have different utilities, different goals, or purposes, and different approaches solve different kinds of drawing problems. Artists choose to draw one way or another depending on the type of problem they're trying to solve.

In this drawing of Jesus among the doctors, Rembrandt's trying to figure out a composition, his format shape, and his object-ground relationships. He wants to identify where things are and about how large they are, one relative to the other. But for this, he doesn't need a lot of detail in the figures, or drapery, or environment. He wants a quick and ready, all-encompassing drawing language, one that'll allow him to move through multiple compositional permutations, multiple drawings, in rapid succession.

Our first compositional ideas are not always our best. Let's say I want to move through 5, 10, or 15 different compositional ideas for a given drawing. Adopting Holbein's language would consume all my time. But if I could work through my ideas using Rembrandt's language, well, it'd be a real time saver. Once having found a strong compositional structure, I might then study all the specifics in a drawing like Holbein's.

While many people grasp that drawing is about expression, to get to that expression, we may use drawing as a problem-solving tool, and a primary problem is to identify a winning composition.

There are other reasons why artists choose a gestural approach. Not everything stays still. Clouds in the sky, passengers on a train, boxers in the ring, they're all in motion. Many things you may want to draw will be, too. Working from observation, we don't always have the luxury of drawing slowly, so we need to develop an approach that allows us to note things quickly.

Let's take a look at a couple more examples of gestural drawing. You've likely seen Sargent's painting *Madame X*. This is a drawing of the same woman. And here's a Delacroix. And this by Daumier, one of the greats associated with gestural line.

In each case, you'll note the wildness and speed of the lines, the small marks, and bits of line associated with longer line segments, and often, the multiple lines that result in the approximate definition of edges and changes of plane.

What Holbein does involves a great deal of skill and artistry, but the approach, using contour and cross contour, comes pretty naturally to most people. On the other hand, what these artists are doing, gesture, that can be hard to get at first. Students often struggle with it because it's just so different than following the edges and plane changes in objects in a linear way. But give it a shot. There's nothing to lose, just pencil and paper.

To get started, let's return to basic shapes. Pull out your first contour drawings, the ones of the circle, square, and triangle. These are more or less in Holbein language. We'll use them as models with the goal of translating Holbein into Rembrandt, to the language of gesture.

Let's start with that circle. First, in preparation, without drawing anything, let your eyes flit around all over the drawing from the circle's perimeter, across its width, quickly moving back and forth and up and down, as if your eyes were like a fly darting back and forth over a pie at a picnic. Now, while your eyes continue to move rapidly over your prior drawing, let your pencil begin to flit above the surface of your new sheet of paper, tracking your eyes.

The pencil should move across the intended circle shape like an electron around the nucleus of an atom. We're at the top, we're at the bottom, we're at the side, skipping across its diameter. At this point, begin to touch down on the paper, first on the right, then the left, then towards the top or bottom. We might even leave some bits of line in the middle of our circle as we feel the distance from one side to other. We're getting in touch with its measure.

Each time we touch down on the page, we leave a bit of line. In the aggregate, it defines a set of approximations of where we think the edge of our circle might be. Let's take this one more step, and it's already suggested by some of the internal marks, bits of cross contour. Let's use more of these internal lines so that we can transform the flat circle into a three-dimensional sphere.

A useful way to think about gesture is that it combines the work that contour, cross contour, and even construction line each do separately. And it's doing all of this efficiently, much more rapidly than you could do it with contour, cross contour, and construction line separately. But the emphasis is on approximation, not certainty.

We're finding the shape of what we're drawing. That matches-up with contour's function. We're diagramming its measure, pulling our pencil across its height and width. That's a construction line function. And we're creating the illusion of its three-dimensionality with interior markings. We can even suggest further three-dimensionality by drawing the interior, drawing through as it's called as if our object were transparent. That's the cross contour function.

One of the common hallmarks of gesture drawing are small marks or bits of line that don't really appear to be attached to anything. I understand these as probing marks, as initial attempts at locating the edge of a form, but as the drawing progresses the artist gains greater confidence about the location of visual events. And longer line segments appear above or below, or to the right or left of those initial marks.

Now that you've drawn a sphere with gesture, try it with your rectangle and triangle. Follow the same steps, then add adjacent planes and turn the rectangle into a block, the triangle into a pyramid.

It's going to take some practice to get this going, so take out a dozen of your earlier contour and cross contour still life drawings, the figure-ground or compositional drawings you did. Using the same method we just used, translate these drawings into gesture drawings.

And try this with brush and ink. It'll feel a little less comfortable at first, but because it's a less-familiar tool, one you can't control like a pencil, you'll be less likely to use it in a contour-like way. It will help you get a grasp of drawing with gestural line.

Start with a fairly dry brush. Dip the brush's tip into the ink and dry some off. You should get a light gray mark. Knowing you can't erase will push you to search out the approximate position of things with bits of line rather than continuous line. You want to be skipping over the surface, quickly flitting back and forth across the page, not moving sequentially along a line. Your goal is to find approximate positions, directions, and amounts through a series of repeated tests and probes.

Think about gesture as an all-encompassing type of line. You want your bits of line and mark to note what your construction lines, armature lines, and the lines defining your large ground shapes would have done in past drawings. You want to note the large aggregate shape of your objects. And this is very important, you want to measure the negative shapes between your objects with your probing gestural marks and lines. Gesture can do all of this at once.

It will help you out to do these drawings with a timer, two minutes each. Once you've done some gestural drawings based on your earlier drawings, try this directly from life, too. Set up three simple objects on your still life table. Think about their aggregate shape as you set them up. Next, frame them in your viewfinder. With a light H pencil, draw the format shape on your page. Then put aside the pencil and the viewfinder, and with brush and ink, do a two-minute drawing.

Here's a helpful technique. Some refer to it as rehearsal drawing or phantom drawing. The idea is this, before actually drawing, close one eye and hold your finger or brush out over the subject, then do a gesture drawing in the air to familiarize yourself with where things are and with the relationship among the objects, the ground, and the negative shapes, and also the space they will sit in.

You're probing and searching for visual data. Where does the drawing begin and end? What would be the format shape be like? Where's the large division? Where does the back of the table meet the wall? What's the farthest point to the right? What is the farthest point to the left of the aggregate shape? What's the farthest point up? What's the farthest point down? What are the negative shapes like between the objects? How far do we have to travel from one side to the other? What are the widths of the objects? Their heights?

Once you've done your phantom drawing, set the timer. This time, give yourself one minute to do each drawing. Use little bits of line at first, small light marks, mere approximations. You're giving yourself positioning marks in answer to the questions we're asking about where things occur and where they don't. Absence and presence are equally important. As you begin to be more certain of the locations, use a bit more pressure, a darker and somewhat more continuous line.

When you're ready, try gesture drawing with more challenging subjects. Try the interior of your home or other building. Try a landscape or cityscape. Draw while watching TV and this is really great practice because the scene is constantly shifting. It pushes you toward speed. It's the same with drawing at a playground, or at a sporting event, or on the subway, any situations where the world is not standing still for you. All these experiences will help you expand your abilities with gesture.

As you do this more and more, you'll find your own natural handwriting and calligraphy. I see it with my students all the time, it just takes some persistence.

Next, we'll expand our understanding of how artists think compositionally. And very soon, we're going to be putting all these pieces together to make a very complex drawing.

Composition: Shape and Advanced Strategies
Lecture 10

In this lecture, we'll conclude our investigation of composition. We'll start by looking at some of the major attributes of shape. Then, we'll dig deeper into the compositional strategies that artists use in their work. Now that we've studied gestural line, we can also apply it to test out these new compositional structures.

Types and Attributes of Shape

Different kinds of shapes, like different kinds of line, have different attributes or qualities. And most of us associate different feelings or sensations with shapes because of these differences. Attributes of shape include the following:

- Geometric (including rectilinear and curvilinear) versus organic.

- Degree of symmetry.

- Degree of complexity. All else being equal, we generally reward complexity—a source of visual excitement—with our attention.

- Personality. Rectilinear and symmetrical shapes generally appear serious and sober; curvilinear shapes can appear elegant and flowing; and asymmetrical, loopy shapes can seem humorous.

- Degree of closure. Open shape equals gentle overlap and continuity; closed shape indicates emphatic overlap and discontinuity.

- Degree of stability.

All these are important compositional factors and, ultimately, affect the expressive quality of a drawing.

Compositional Strategy: The Target or Bull's Eye

With all this in mind, let's return to some examples of compositional strategies used by artists. A balanced strategy related to the use of symmetrical shape is what we might call the *target* or *bull's eye*. It uses centered rings or successive units of framing to bring the viewer into the center of the drawing.

Several compositional factors can be used to bring the viewer into the target's center, including contrasts of shape, contrasts in degree of density and complexity of line or mark, and contrast of direction. All these factors are used to induce a viewer to look to the target's center first and the outer rings later. We prompt the viewer to attend to the parts of the drawing in a certain order, which is one of the goals of composition.

Compositional Strategy: Repetition, Variation, Pattern, and Visual Rhymes

Repetition and variation are key compositional concepts in their own right. Musical composition can revolve around this structural idea, as well. A Bach two-part invention is all about repetition and variation, as are popular songs. Choruses repeat, and verses vary, generally, with the same melody but new lyrics. This would indicate that we like a certain amount of repetition, but too much is monotonous.

We can see this idea of repetition with variation in the Eakins watercolor. Note the many horizontal events: Biglin's scull, the scull's reflection in the water, other sculls, wavelets in the water, the landscape in the distance, and striations in the sky. This is often referred to as *visual rhyming*. Shapes and directions are repeated rhythmically to create relationships among the parts.

© Yale University Art Gallery.

Spatial Considerations: Bas-Relief and Three Depths of Space

So far, we've looked at relationships that occur on the surface of the drawing, basically, in the realm of the flat. We've seen how artists organize what they want to draw in relation to the geometry of the specific rectangle they've chosen. We've also seen that there's a relationship between the main things being depicted—the ostensible subject—and the environment in which they sit.

In addition, we've noted that we must think in two ways simultaneously. First, we have to think about how things relate flatly—to the rectangle's edges and armature. Second, we have to think about how they relate to any illusion of depth. Inextricably related to both of these considerations is the specific spatial organization of the drawing.

Shallow spatial depth is referred to as *bas-relief* ("low relief"). Think here about the slightly raised profile of Lincoln on a penny.

Deeper spatial organization may be achieved through the use of three depths. Again, in the Eakins watercolor, water and the reflection of Biglin are located in the foreground, the main subject is located in the mid-ground, and there's a depth of space with a number of supporting events occurring in and around the horizon. This approach to composition is often accompanied by placing the main subject in the topographical center of the page.

Composition and Narrative

The way we pose things and organize them on the page in a drawing can also have narrative import. In an old-fashioned family portrait, for example, the father might be elevated over the other family members to highlight his position as head of the family. In a modern advertisement, a political leader might be posed in the center of his advisors.

Uncomposed Drawings

Not all drawings are composed in the ways we've discussed in this lecture, primarily because not all drawings are intended as complete or finished artworks in their own right. Some drawings concern themselves with problem solving; others function as exercises to explore perspective, pattern, or color relationships; and others are done as studies in preparation for more involved works. The choices we make regarding how we draw are often based on the goal we have for the drawing in question.

Suggested Reading

Curtis, *Drawing from Observation*, chapter 9, "Composition," p. 279.

Guptill, *Rendering in Pencil*, chapter 10, "Composing Your Drawings," p. 110.

Smagula, *Creative Drawing*, chapter 7, "Composition and Space," pp. 150–167.

Composition: Shape and Advanced Strategies
Lecture 10—Transcript

In this lecture, we'll conclude our investigation of composition. We'll start by looking at some of the major attributes of shape, and then we'll dig deeper into the compositional strategies that artists use in their work. And now that we've studied gestural line, we can apply it to test out these new compositional structures.

Different kinds of shape, like different kinds of line, have different attributes or qualities, and most of us associate different feelings or sensation with them because of those differences. Let's look at both the Holbein and the Indian Punjab Hills drawing in this regard.

In both, we can see a range of shapes deployed. Some are geometric. Among those, some are rectilinear while others are curvilinear. And some are not geometric but organic. Some geometric and some organic shapes are symmetrical while others are asymmetrical. And related to symmetry, some shapes are simple, while others are complex.

All else being equal, we'll generally reward greater complexity, a source of visual excitement, with our attention. That explains why, in both drawings, the figures and their drapery are drawn in elaborate line and shape, very organic, complex, and asymmetrical. It also explains why the drapes hanging behind the figures are simplified. They're geometric and symmetrical. Both artists want us to look at the figures first and use complexity of shape compositionally to focus our attention on the figures.

These same factors, geometric versus organic, and the level of symmetry, also communicate personality. Some shapes appear serious and sober. Rectilinear and symmetrical shapes generally have this quality. Curvilinear shapes can appear elegant and flowing. And very asymmetrical, loopy, organic shapes can seem humorous. Superheroes like Superman, Batman, and the like are constructed using symmetrical and relatively angular shapes. Homer Simpson, in contrast, is much less symmetrical. He's curvilinear to the point of being bulbous.

Forgetting about a given plot, the dialogue, or the expressions on an animated character's face, their silhouettes alone, their very shapes, will conjure a specific emotional response. And, of course, this plays out in real life as well. Network executives tend to hire sober-shaped people to serve as news anchors. These jobs generally require symmetrical features, strong angular jaws, and an upright posture. Think Charlie Rose.

Men like Danny DeVito or Louis C.K., however brilliant, are unlikely to be given these kinds of opportunities. You could say that many of us, in terms of shape, are biased. We're predisposed to certain conclusions about an individual based on their shape. Put another way, shape, at an abstract level, can foster an emotional response in us. All of these considerations relate to composition and expression.

Earlier, we noted that lines can have different degrees of openness or closure. The greater the degree of closure the more the line appears to be a shape. Let's take a look at a rectangle. We'll draw one side, clearly not a shape. Draw another side, again, not yet a shape. But as we begin to draw the third side, it begins to suggest its own completion. Halfway through the final side, it's looking pretty much like a shape. We can try this with a circle too. As we begin to move past the halfway point, it begins to feel more and more shape-like. Even with very unpredictable and irregular shapes, once we get close enough to the point of origin, we begin to read shape, even though it's not completed.

In the Holbein, we see these implied shapes in many places. For instance, in the central figure, in Sir Thomas More's cloak, the pleats aren't fully closed yet they feel very much like shape. These two feel like triangles though the shapes haven't been closed. And in the drape hanging behind the figures we see rectilinear and triangular shape-like entities. But these are also open though they clearly imply shapes. The Punjab Hills drawing yields similar results in both the man's and the woman's drapery and in the drapery hanging behind them.

The reason why shapes are left somewhat open is often for practical reasons. It's done to create the sensation of continuity. The overlaps of the pleats in More's robe are gentle. We're meant to move from one pleat to another and feel that they're all part of the same piece of continuous fabric. We can contrast this approach with the one taken in More's fur collar, or the wide sleeve on his left arm. Both are closed and read as strongly overlapping the rest of the robe. They're discontinuous.

Open shape equals gentler overlap and continuity. Closed shape indicates emphatic overlap and discontinuity. When drawing, ask yourself, how discretely or emphatically do you want a planar junction to read? If we look at the footstool in this regard, we see that the shapes are about 90 percent closed and the planes read emphatically.

Shape stability is directly related to what we've already noted about line direction and line stability. A shape, like this rectangle resting on its horizontal base, projects stability. A triangle resting on the same size base appears a bit less stable, it's those active diagonals; a triangle with a smaller base, well, less so. Now rotate the triangle 180 onto its tip, and we're much less stable. And tilt the triangle so it sits on a diagonal and there's very little sense of stability at all.

Tilting things is a visual trope we often see on television and in film. The director changes a camera's angle relative to what we know should be horizontal and vertical in the shot. Floors and walls and the things that sit on them, or trees and houses in a landscape, go all diagonal. Without anyone saying a word we know something's amiss.

Let's try it here. As the camera tilts, I look less in control and authoritative, more like a passenger on the Titanic. All the shapes have shifted from stable horizontals and verticals to less stable ones. Everything's pitching diagonal.

The factors we've just discussed—how geometric or organic our shapes are; how open or closed; their degree of symmetry, complexity, and stability—are all-important, compositional factors and will, ultimately, affect the expressive quality in a drawing. With all this in mind, let's return to some examples of compositional strategies used by artists in their drawings.

A very balanced strategy related to the use of symmetrical shapes is what I call the target. It uses centered rings or successive units of framing to bring you into the center, or bull's eye. It's what Rembrandt uses here.

The positive shape of the doghouse turns the aggregate negative shape bounded by the drawing's border into a framing outer ring. The doghouse itself becomes the next ring. The dark interior around the dog's body the next, then we get the dog's body, and finally the bull's eye, the dog's head. It's clear that the focal area is the sleeping dog; the focal point, the dog's head.

There are several compositional factors, which lead us to read the drawing in this way. The first has to do with contrasting shape types. A rectangle is, well, just a rectangle, and an ellipse is an ellipse. But put a rectangle next to an ellipse and we tend to feel their rectilinear and curvilinear qualities in a heightened way.

The second type of contrast has to do with sameness, or repetition and difference, or uniqueness. If we have one rectangle and one ellipse, we'll pay about equal attention to both. But if we have five rectangles and one ellipse, we'll pay more attention to the ellipse. We'll generally pay more attention to whatever's different in our field of vision. Our eye will go to the guy in the Speedo walking down Madison Avenue, and to the guy in the suit and tie playing volleyball at the beach.

The way this plays out here is that the drawing's shape is rectilinear. The internal frames representing the doghouse are rectilinear, too. Only the dog is curvilinear, so it'll get more attention.

A third and related type of contrast has to do with geometric versus organic. The rectilinear elements are relatively geometric, the curvilinear ones relatively organic.

A fourth type of contrast has to do with the degree of density and complexity of line or mark. This is often related to detail.

Here's the principle. The more dense and complex the marks in a given part of a drawing, relative to the drawing as whole, the more we'll often pay attention to that part. Here, the dog's head gets the densest and most complex marks, and that translates as detail. And that, once again, mimics the way we see. When we focus on something, we literally bring out the detail in what we're looking at.

As we've seen already, when the camera focuses on me, my detail emerges and the details of my producer, Jamie, behind me, become obscured. If we invert this and have the camera focus on Jamie, I lose my detail.

Let's note Rembrandt's choice of rectangle and its divisions. The rectangle itself is more horizontal than vertical, expressive of sleeping. And let's look at the divisions. We get a stress along the horizontal half and quarters. We also get a stress along the vertical quarters. In addition, a number of things, including the dog's head, line up along one of the rectangle's diagonal. Similarly, we get the ears and a number of other things lining up with the contrasting diagonal. And remember, diagonals are our most powerful, attention-grabbing direction.

This brings us to our final type of contrast, contrast of direction, diagonal versus horizontal and vertical. The dog gets the most powerful diagonals. Most of the rest of the drawing is constructed using horizontals and verticals. And the most prominent diagonals not related to the dog, those on the top of the doghouse, are mitigated by being close to vertical.

So there are multiple compounding abstract factors, compositional factors, that make us read the drawing the way we do. We see it's a drawing of a dog in a doghouse, but without anyone telling us anything, we know the sleeping dog's the star of the drawing, and we zoom in on the dog's head. We're brought to do this in a totally non-verbal way, it's automatic. We've been visually manipulated, and that's a very good thing. That's just what composition does.

Rembrandt's made us read the drawing this way because he chose a horizontal rectangle communicating stasis, rest, and sleep. He constructed the drawing like a target, putting the dog's head in the center, in the bull's eye position. He not only puts the dog in the topographical central position, but also in the middle depth of space. In other words, there's a foreground, a mid-ground, and a background, the dog goes in the middle. He links the dog's head to the central diagonals, among the most attention-grabbing directions. The dog's association with the diagonals is in marked contrast with the rest of the drawing, which Rembrandt constructs primarily out of horizontals and verticals. He also makes the dog different from most of the rest of the drawing. The dog's curvilinear in contrast to the rectilinear; the dog's organic in contrast to all the geometric elements. The treatment of the dog's head exhibits more dense and complex marks, more detail. That draws us in and causes us to focus. It seems like a simple little drawing of a dog sleeping, but as you see, there's really quite a bit of abstract visual thinking involved.

So I'd like you to try a drawing using the target strategy. Walk around your home or office and look for things that could lend themselves to this treatment. Here are a couple of ideas to stimulate your imagination. You could pose a log or two on a grate in a fireplace framed by the surrounding fireplace walls. You could look down at an object, for example, a folded scarf in a rectangular drawer. Again looking down, you could pose an apple or flower on a plate on a placemat on a small low table with the floor seen around it on all sides. There are many other possibilities. It's a matter of engaging your curiosity and imagination to uncover some possibilities.

Try to follow Rembrandt's model. Choose a format shape, objects, and a point of view so that you get a variety of contrasts. Think about: contrast of direction, contrast of the curvilinear with the rectilinear, contrast of the organic with the geometric, and contrast of complexity and density of line with simplicity and paucity of line.

Do the drawings that accompany this lecture with gestural line. You'll move through the drawing problems much more quickly than with contour or cross contour. And as you work through each drawing, use a range of line weights and qualities: from thin to thick, light to dark, slow to fast, from angular to curved, from short to long, and from open to closed.

In our analysis of Rembrandt's sleeping dog, we noted a number of instances of repetition and variation, and these are key compositional concepts in their own right. Most of the drawing is built on a repetition of vertical and horizontal stresses, all geometric. The dog introduces variation through the use of diagonals, curvilinear directions, and organic shape. A lot of composing deals with repetitions and variations on those repetitions.

Musical composition can revolve around this structural idea as well. A Bach two-part invention is all about repetition and variation. So are popular songs, choruses repeat; verses vary; generally same melody but new lyrics. This would indicate that we like an amount of repetition, but too much is monotonous. A simple grid would likely be too simple for most. An intricate pattern based on that grid would probably be more interesting to look at. What pattern proposes is similarity, we get the same grid unit, but different units get different structures or visual event, repetition with variation.

We see this in the Eakins watercolor. We have lots of horizontal events. Start with Biglin's scull. It's echoed by his reflection in the water, by the other sculls, by the wavelets in the water, by the landscape in the distance, and by the striations in the sky, repetition with variation.

This is often referred to as visual rhyming, shapes and directions that get repeated rhythmically to create relationships among the parts. The triangles in the Picasso are not limited to the figure but occur in the negative shapes around the figure and in events in the room itself. There are many rhyming rectangles as well. We find something similar in the Diebenkorn. Triangles and spheroid shapes, completed and implied, in both the positives and the negatives.

And the Morandi rhymes the bottle shapes with the negatives that occur between them. The negative between the two bottles on the right is an inverted and contracted version of the bottles themselves. The large, aggregate negative between the bottle on the left and the bottle to its right is an inverted and contracted version.

As a first go, you might want to try this with a couple of bottles. The trick is to find shapes that, when combined, produce negatives that rhyme with the positives. Another dependable way to get rhymes is to pose something in front of a mirror. Or look for objects that have similar structures, rounded objects, triangular objects, or rectangular objects. Or find objects that rhyme with the ground they sit in. And, like Morandi, pay a lot of attention to those negatives.

So far, we've looked at relationships that occur on the surface of the drawing, basically in the realm of the flat. We've seen how artists organize what they want to draw in relationship to the geometry of the specific rectangle they've chosen. We've also seen how there's a relationship between the main things being depicted, the ostensible subject, and the environment in which they sit. I'm alluding to object-ground or figure-ground relationships.

We've already noted that we have to think two ways simultaneously. First, we have to think about how things relate flatly to the rectangle's edges and armature. Second, how they relate to any illusion of depth. Inextricably related to both of these considerations is the specific spatial organization of the drawing. Now, I want to think if you can imagine seeing the space in a drawing from the side. Try to imagine the space as accordion-like. It could be pushed in and condensed toward flatness or pulled out to create a very great depth indeed. And using the same subject and the same rectangle, we'll wind up with very different compositions depending on that spatial organization.

Here in the studio, the camera could zoom in, cropping me at the nose and hips. Or zoom out so there's real space in front of me. It might even include something occupying that space to help define it, like the camera here in the foreground. Now, I'm in the mid-ground, we see the furniture, spiral staircase, and windows behind me in the background, three depths of space, just what we saw in the Rembrandt of the sleeping dog. Of course, you do this all the time when you compose a snapshot, you zoom in, and you zoom out. And you'll be missing a lot if you don't consider spatial depth when composing a drawing.

In Norman Lundin's *Model Standing before a Blackboard*, the space is shallow, we're zoomed in right up next to the model. There are only several inches behind her before we get to the blackboard. We refer to this kind of space as *bas-relief*, literally low relief, like Lincoln on a penny.

One way of beginning to open the depth of space is to use an entry space. The white at the bottom of the page below the woman's dress is not inert paper. It's serving to push the woman, Saskia, back in space. Through the entry space, Rembrandt creates a space in which she can exist. She'll appear more volumetric than otherwise, and this without a lot of shading. The key here is that we can make objects feel three-dimensional by thinking compositionally.

Conversely, a ham-fisted cropping can flatten the same figure. In essence, cropping is a form of zooming in. The more severe the crop, the more we diminish the depth of space, and the more we potentially flatten our subject.

Eakins' drawing *Biglin Brothers Turning the Stake* has an expanded depth relative to Rembrandt, it's a much more zoomed out view. And we have three depths of space. As we'll see, that's a very common motif. Here we have water and reflection in the foreground, our main subjects occupy the mid-ground, and there are other events occurring back, deep in space, in the background. We note the same spatial organization in his watercolor, water, reflection in the foreground, our main subjects located in the mid-ground, and there's a depth of space with a number of supporting events occurring in and around the horizon.

And this structure doesn't just apply to landscape or figures in a landscape. Here, the floor is foreground, the figure, mid-ground, and the drapes construct the background, three depths of space.

This School of Rembrandt, *A woman ill in bed*, is set up similarly though here the fore-space is defined by the scribbled line on the right, a gestural line to be sure. We don't know what it is, it could be a bedpost, could be a door opened into the room, could even be a bathrobe hung on the wall. So we don't know what it is, but we do know where it is, it's the out of focus thing in the foreground. We focus on the woman in the mid-ground. The wall in the background is implied by the pillows.

We find the same compositional template in the Picasso. The foreground's defined by the woman at the easel, the floor, and the still life on the right.

The nude, our main subject, is in the mid-ground. The rest of the room is in our third depth of space.

In our Punjab Hills *Two Lovers*, we find the identical structure. The foreground is established by a floor plane and still life objects, our main figures occupy the mid-ground, a wall plane occupies the background. A very common motif—three depths of space with the most important event located in the mid-ground. And, as we see here, and in the Eakins watercolor, the Picasso, and the Rembrandt, it's often accompanied by placing the main subject in the topographical center of the page as well.

The foreground can also be asserted by part of an object or figure. In *White Doe at Home*, Lundin defines the foreground with the model's leg and foot and on the front part of the bed. The arm, chest, head, pillows, back of the bed, and the front portion of the floor establish the mid-ground. And the rear of the floor and the wall establish our third depth of space.

Picasso uses a similar idea in his portrait of Apollinaire. The front leg and hand establish the foreground. The rest of the body, head, and chair establish the mid-ground. The wall and shelf establish the background. We note this same spatial organization in Sesshu Toyo's autumn landscape, foreground, mid-ground, and background disappearing in the fog though here the greatest emphasis is on the foreground. The Mă Yuăn also has three depths of space and it also puts the greater focus on the foreground.

There are other important ideas about composition and space. Many are at the heart of much of the art of the late-19th century to the present, and we'll be discussing them in greater detail in later lectures.

But now you're ready to try a couple of drawings using different spatial approaches. A great first exercise is to place a single object, a bottle, or other similar object, on your table an inch or so from the wall. Frame it very simply, center it, but draw from a distance with your viewfinder opened up wide. Follow this by making a drawing where you're cropping the bottle at the top and the bottom. Then make two more variations at intervals between the wide and close-in view. This will give you a very clear idea about how important a decision this is. There's a very strong correlation between the sensation of space and volume in the subject and the amount of surface we have between the object or aggregate object and the drawing's edges.

A next exercise would be to set up a still life using a shallow *bas-relief* space, and then another with three depths of space. And you can try this with the interior of your home and outdoors, too, in a landscape. The more you look at the world around you for instances of compositional opportunity, the more you'll readily find them. The more you do this, the more thinking compositionally becomes second nature.

Last, once you've done this observationally, try it from your imagination. Draw with shapes and volumes, construct your compositions with reference to these strategies we've discussed.

The way we pose things and organize them on the page can have narrative import as well. Here's a portrait of *The Stamaty Family* drawn in 1818 by the French artist Jean Auguste Dominique Ingres. You'll note he's making use of many of the compositional devices we've already spoken about. There's the division at the vertical and horizontal halves and a strong use of the diagonal half. Though a shallow space, we still have three depths. The foreground is established by the floor and the toy cart, the figures are grouped in the mid-ground, and the piano, wall, and painting sit in the background. The figures fit into an aggregate shape, something like a simple house shape, rectangle with a triangle on top. The weight of the four figures on the right is counterbalanced by the toys, figure on the left, piano, and the painting on the wall. The composition is asymmetrical but balanced.

But there's something new going on here, too. The composition has a narrative aspect. The figures have been posed and framed to tell us something about the family. The father's top dog, elevated. The elder son comes next, he's posed jauntily above his mother. Then we get the two women, mother just a bit above the daughter, and the child last. While the father, son, mother, and child form a solid subgrouping, the daughter is off by herself. Why? Well, she's of marriageable age, she's on the way out. And to make the point that you'd be lucky to grab her, she's posed as the mirror image of her mother, a visual rhyme. She's ready to take on her mother's role, produce children. Even better, she plays piano. You'll have children and the home will be filled with music. It's a piece of high-class advertising.

And, of course, professionals in illustration and advertising, and people choreographing political campaigns use these visual strategies all the time to make their products or candidates look more appealing. Think presidential candidates who argue about podium height before a debate or jockey to be photographed with military hardware.

So, let's try this. We don't necessarily need figures, still life objects will work fine. Pose your objects so that you have distinct groupings, hierarchies, and personalities. As in the Ingres, you could try one against four. You could also try one tall object versus several short ones, or one flamboyant object versus several conservative ones, or a skinny object versus several fat ones. And, of course, we can try the inverse of all of these. Later, you'll be able to try all these same ideas and apply them to the figure.

We've covered a lot of material on composition. Making it your own takes time and practice. All these distinct pieces that we're practicing individually, one by one, will become more and more interconnected. They'll often act in concert. You'll find yourself applying these principles intuitively once you've practiced them for some time. Einstein's quoted as saying, "Intuition is nothing but the outcome of earlier intellectual experience." Like learning to read or learning arithmetic, at first it's painfully slow but with time it becomes automatic.

A note on this, as you look around at drawings, you'll see that not all drawings are composed in the ways we've been discussing here. That's because not all drawings are intended as complete or finished artworks in their own right. Different kinds of drawings have different goals. For instance, some drawings concern themselves with problem solving, or with learning something, or figuring something out.

Leonardo often used drawing as a tool to help himself understand the physical world. In this drawing of a fetus, he wasn't setting out to make a finished art object but was using drawing, along with note-taking, as a means to learn something about a specific subject and record it. Other drawings function as exercises. Dürer made hundreds of diagrammatic drawings investigating human proportions. He used them to gain a greater understanding of proportions in all their variety. And, this Michelangelo is a study, a drawing done in preparation for a specific work.

All three of these drawings are about learning something specific. The goal is gathering information, so there's no need to compose in the way we've been talking about. Other drawings might target studying perspective, pattern, value, relationships of color, or other kinds of relationships.

This drawing by Rembrandt is also not what might be termed a "finished work," and it's also about learning something, but it's about learning something about composition. So, by definition, it's composed. I'd contrast these drawings with this one by Norman Lundin, which is meant as a finished work in its own right.

The compositional choices we make regarding how we draw are often based on the goal we have for the drawing in question.

Next, I'd like to introduce some very effective ways for controlling proportions. Combining these new techniques with what you've already learned about line, shape, volume, and composition will give you the basics to make some pretty sophisticated drawings.

Proportion: Alberti's *Velo*
Lecture 11

We're now ready to turn our attention to proportion and measurement. In this lecture, we'll learn about the discoveries and methods that led to some radical changes in 15th-century European art. These discoveries would spread over the globe and are still very much with us today. As mentioned in the first lecture, human beings have been drawing for more than 80,000 years, but until the European Renaissance, no one had figured out how to convincingly depict a three-dimensional space on a two-dimensional surface. Then, in a relatively short span of time, a little more than 100 years, artists were able to create this illusion. In this lecture, we'll work with some of the tools that enabled this leap forward in naturalistic representation.

Early Explorations in Proportion
One of the first individuals involved in exploring the ideas that led to later artistic discoveries about proportion was an Arab scholar, Ibn al-Haytham, popularly known as Alhazen. In Europe, he was followed by Leon Battista Alberti, Luca Pacioli, Piero della Francesca, Filippo Brunelleschi, Leonardo da Vinci, and Albrecht Dürer. The latter were all interested in the intersection of optics, mathematics, and art, and they enlarged on Alhazen's and one another's discoveries. A number of them published their own seminal works describing newfound systems, tools, and methods.

Around 1490, Leonardo described a method for drawing accurately. It involved placing a pane of glass perpendicular to the artist's line of vision and drawing what was seen directly on the glass. The availability of affordable plate glass may have played a significant role in this type of experimentation. Having seen the three-dimensional world coherently reduced to two-dimensions may well have fueled the great leap forward to naturalistic representation.

In his later book *Instruction in Measurement*, Albrecht Dürer wrote, "There is yet another method of copying an object ... and it is more practical than using a glass pane." Dürer was talking about a device called the *velo*, or "veil." The device had also been discussed about a century earlier by the Renaissance polymath Leon Battista Alberti. Essentially, the *velo* was a grid of threads stretched on a frame that allowed anything seen through it to be transcribed on paper by noting the *xy* coordinates.

Drawing Proportionate Foreshortened Figures

For most of history, people drew things in their iconic positions. In this position, the silhouette of the object would tell us what it is. This also happens to be the position where the long axis of the subject is perpendicular or parallel to the ground. Think of an upright person or a bottle; that position is perpendicular to the ground. A person lying down horizontally would be parallel to the ground. In Egyptian art, the avoidance of other positions accounts for some of the distorted anatomical depictions, with the head in profile; chest facing forward, and legs and feet, once again, in profile. By and large, people avoided other views of objects for about 80,000 years.

All the millennia of avoidance indicate the challenges of drawing objects in certain positions, such as a limb projecting outward from the picture plane. Alberti and Dürer tell us how to tackle this difficult problem: by measuring. Find grid coordinates. Note where and in which grid unit on the vertical picture plane all the important points are located. Then, mark these same points on the second picture plane, the page. Measure carefully and plot enough coordinates, and you get a rather sophisticated connect-the-dots drawing. Artfully connect the dots, and you get a proportionate foreshortened figure. It was this fixation with measurement that fundamentally changed drawing.

The essential idea behind using the *velo* is the same as tracing on glass or studying a reflection in a mirror, for that matter. The three-dimensional world viewed on a vertical plane—here, the gridded picture plane—looks flat. That makes it parse-able. With the *velo*, we have the added aid of *xy* coordinates. We don't even have to worry about drawing a complicated object. We just have to place the coordinates.

Suggested Reading

Alberti, *On Painting*.

Brown and McLean, *Drawing from Life*, "Learning to See," pp. 44–45.

da Vinci, *A Treatise on Painting*.

Dürer, *Underweysung der Messung* (1525).

———, *Underweysung der Messung* (1538).

———, *The Painter's Manual*.

Eakins, *A Drawing Manual*, "Linear Perspective," pp. 47–54.

Hockney, *Secret Knowledge*.

Proportion: Alberti's *Velo*
Lecture 11—Transcript

We're ready to turn our attention to proportion and measurement. In this lecture, we'll learn about the discoveries and methods that led to some of the radical changes in 15th-century European art. These discoveries would spread over the globe and are still very much with us today.

As I'd mentioned in the introductory lecture, human beings have been drawing for over 80,000 years, and there are beautiful examples from just about every place and period. But until the European Renaissance, no one had figured out how to create a convincing depiction of three-dimensional space on a two-dimensional surface.

Then, over a relatively short period of time, artists were able to make the move from works like this, circa 1325, to works like this, by Leonardo, in the early 1490s. All of a sudden plates sat down on tables, tables receded into 3D space of the room, and the rooms themselves had depth. How did this happen? Why, after 80,000 years? After hundreds of thousands of generations of no one being able to figure it out?

Remember, learning to draw is all about learning to see. And there came along a number of people who were fascinated with figuring this out, and certain technologies were evolving, too. And we'll learn how those innovations may have played a part, as well.

One of the first individuals involved was an Arab scholar, Ibn al-Haytham, popularly known as Alhazen. In Europe, he was followed by Leon Battista Alberti, Luca Pacioli, Piero della Francesca, Filippo Brunelleschi, Leonardo da Vinci, and Albrecht Dürer. The latter were all interested in the intersection of optics, mathematics, and art, and they enlarged on Alhazen's, and each other's, discoveries. A number of them published their own seminal works describing newfound systems, tools, and methods.

Around 1490, Leonardo wrote down the following method for getting accurate proportions,

Have a piece of glass as large as half a royal folio paper and set this firmly in front of your eyes, that is, between your eye and the thing you want to draw; then place yourself at about two-thirds of a braccia," that would be about 15 inches, "from the glass, fixing your head with a machine in such a way that you cannot move it at all.

He goes on to tell us to shut one eye and "draw upon the glass what you see beyond it." He suggests transferring the drawing to paper and ends by writing, "paint it if you like, using aerial perspective carefully."

This is a drawing from one of Leonardo's notebooks of an artist using just such a clear-planed device to make a drawing of a sphere. In another entry regarding using flat glass-like surfaces he writes, "You should take the mirror as your master, because on its surface objects have similarities to painting in many respects."

Leonardo was a practical man. How do you get it right? Well, trace or reflect the 3D world onto a 2D surface. That goes a long way toward solving the central problem of understanding the way three dimensions should appear on a flat surface. The glass or mirror translates 3D complexity into a visually understandable 2D version. Then you just copy the tracing or reflection onto your paper or canvas.

Now, I mentioned the role of evolving technologies. It may well have been the availability of affordable plate glass, both in transparent and mirrored form that opened peoples' eyes to what had been going on, well, right in front of their eyes, for so many millennia.

In his book *Daily Life in the Middle Ages*, Paul B. Newman writes, "By the 15th century," and that's what we're talking about here, the 1400s, "while less prosperous people continued to make do with cloth, many could afford glass windowpanes." So this may have been the single technological development that enabled human beings to make the enormous leap into naturalistic representation, seeing things clearly on a transparent or reflective flat surface.

Albrecht Dürer, who many of you may know from his iconic drawing of praying hands, also wrote a remarkable and very technical book on drawing. Part 1 was published in 1525, followed by part 2 in 1538. It was titled *Underweysung der Messung* or *Instruction in Measurement*. Dürer offers the same advice as Leonardo, "Place a clean, flat plane of glass into a quadrangular frame. Now draw whatever you wish." It goes on longer than that, but that's the gist, draw on the glass. And Thomas Eakins suggests the same method in his 1880s drawing manual.

Given Leonardo's, Dürer's, and Eakins' endorsements, try it now. Use a black or other dark, felt-tip pen to draw with, and it's easiest to do this on a window in your home or office. But you want to make a small test first, so you can clean it up after without too much trouble.

Choose a window that has something interesting going on outside, something challenging to draw. For instance, looking out at the backyard you might see a table and chairs. Or out front, a car in the driveway or on the street. Maybe a neighboring home with a complex pitched roof. That would be especially interesting if you're able to look down at it from above.

If you're in an apartment or an office, you may see other buildings, a street and sidewalks, some parked vehicles. All of these situations will contain examples of foreshortened planes, precisely the things people had real difficulty with before the Renaissance.

The procedure's simple enough though it takes a bit of getting used to. You have to close one eye. You also have to stay still. You can't move right or left. Maintain a constant distance from the glass. Start by choosing one thing to draw, a table, a chair, a car, a truck, and work out from that one object. Following Leonardo's suggestions, you'll find that you're able to draw proportionately. So go ahead, try it now.

If you've just done your glass drawing, you're probably seeing the world a bit differently as a result. It's not that after this discovery, everyone drew on glass, but the procedure enabled people to understand how to translate three dimensions into two.

Arthur Guptill offers a nice variation on this in his book *Rendering in Pencil*. He suggests placing a piece of glass on top of a sheet of white paper. Then draw what you're looking at on the glass. When you think you're done, close one eye, and raise the glass up before you. He writes, "When the glass has been shifted to just the right position, the lines of the drawing should coincide with those of the object." If they don't, you know your proportions are off. The glass makes the specifics obvious and you can correct.

There's a key concept behind all this. Drawing on the window is, in drawing parlance, drawing on the picture plane. Here's an illustration by Eakins that he made for his book. It depicts the picture plane.

The early pioneers of optics theorized that when we see an object, what we're actually seeing are reflected light rays converging towards our eye. And we should note that these methods depend on a single eye. Remember, Leonardo instructs us to close one eye. This is monocular seeing and drawing. If we introduce a transparent plane between the object and our eye, we'll note the convergence of the rays on that plane, and we call that plane the picture plane.

You likely noticed, when drawing on the window, that the drawings are much smaller than the objects themselves. You may have also noticed that the closer your eye was to the picture plane, the smaller the object appeared on the glass, the farther, the larger. All of this is evidence of converging rays.

Here's an illustration from Dürer's second volume of his book *Instruction in Measurement*. He writes, "There is yet another method of copying an object, and it is more practical than using a glass plane."

Dürer's talking about a device called the *velo*, or veil. It was described a century earlier by the Renaissance polymath, Leon Battista Alberti, in his 1435 book *De Pictura, On Painting*. Alberti wrote, "attention should be devoted to circumscription," that means outlining, "And to do this well, I believe nothing more convenient can be found than the *velo*. It is a veil, divided up by threads into as many parallel square sections as you like and stretched on a frame. I set this up between the eye and the object to be represented, so that the visual pyramid," that would be those converging light rays we saw in the Eakins' illustration, "so that the visual pyramid passes through the *velo*."

In Dürer's woodcut, we actually have two picture planes, the vertical one, that's the one where we can study what we see, and a second one, the sheet of paper. That's where we transcribe what we see. To this day, artists refer to the piece of paper they draw on, or the canvas they paint on, as the picture plane.

There are a number of important things to note in the woodcut. The grids on the paper and *velo* are identical. Anything seen through the *velo* can be transcribed to the page by noting x and y coordinates. Leonardo's advice for drawing on the glass applies here, too. Keep one eye shut; always the same one. The tall object, like a statuette of the Washington monument, lets the artist know where his eye should be. For accurate and coordinated proportions, the eye must remain in the same fixed position.

Here's Eakins on the negative effects of moving, "If he moved his head upwards, the tracing would go down too low; if downwards, the tracing would go too high. If he stepped back, his tracing would be too small; if he went forwards, his tracing would be too large."

Returning to Dürer's woodcut, a couple other things to note: The artist's eye is coincident with the horizon in the landscape, and that coincidence is no coincidence. That's because the horizon is not a location in nature, it's a function of eye level. Next time you're looking out at a landscape—a flat landscape—or at the ocean, test this out. Take a pencil and place it horizontally level in line with your eyes. You'll note that the horizon is coincident with your pencil. Bend your knees so that you're lower down, and repeat, or climb up on top of something. The horizon's always right there at eye level. And this is a notion we'll come back to when we study linear perspective, which was not coincidentally being codified by many of these same Renaissance individuals we've been discussing.

Let's take a look at the model in Dürer's woodcut. For most of history, people drew things in their iconic positions. That's the position where the silhouette of the object would tell us what it is, men dancing, for instance. This also happens to be the position where the long axis of the subject is perpendicular or parallel to the ground. Think a person or bottle upright, perpendicular to the ground, or laying down horizontally, parallel to the ground. By and large, people avoided other views of objects for about 80,000 years.

This accounts for the mashed-up anatomy in the Greek dancers. Heads in profile, facing left; arms and upper torso, straight on; pelvis and legs, profile right. And earlier Egyptian figures are famous for this. The seated figure's head, that would be Horus, is in profile. Well, that's the iconic view for a bird's head. The shoulders, chest, and abdomen are depicted frontally, iconic view for a human torso. The bent legs, once again, profile, iconic view.

Now, I love both these works, but artists at this point in time had limited options. Why? Well, if I asked you to draw my arm held out like this, laterally, not too hard, but if I put my arm in this position it's a lot trickier. It's the same with the bird head or bent legs, not too hard to draw in profile, but a real challenge if seen frontally. So much so that I know of no good pre-Renaissance example of a limb depicted projecting out towards the picture plane. As some of you have no doubt guessed, we call this type of position a foreshortened one, because the limb appears shorter in this view.

While we're seeing the woman in profile, the artist is seeing her in an extremely foreshortened position, one where her distinctive human silhouette is all but lost.

Alberti and Dürer tell us how to tackle these difficult problems. Measure, find grid coordinates. Note where and in which grid unit on the vertical picture plane all the important points are located, then mark these same points on the second picture plane, the page. Measure carefully and plot enough coordinates, and you get a rather sophisticated connect-the-dots drawing. Artfully connect the dots, and you get a proportionate foreshortened figure. Remember Dürer's book title, *Underweysung der Messung, Instruction in Measurement*. And it was this fixation with measurement that fundamentally changed drawing.

As you'll soon learn, the *velo* is but one of a number of tools we can bring to bear to solve problems of proportion and measure, but it's a really good one to start with. The essential idea behind using the *velo* is the same as tracing on glass or studying a mirror. The 3D world viewed on a vertical plane, here the gridded picture plane, looks flat. That makes it parseable. With the *velo*, we have the added aid of *x-y* coordinates. We don't even have to worry about drawing a complicated object, at least not at first. We just have to place coordinates.

Over the centuries, this tool has been used by many artists and students. Van Gogh went to great expense to make just such a device for himself. Here's his sketch, which he included in an August 1882 letter to his brother, Theo. He wrote, "I've just come back from the blacksmith, who has put iron spikes on the legs and iron corners on the frame. It consists of two long legs. The frame is fixed to them by means of strong wooden pegs. The result is that on the beach or in a meadow or a field you have a view as if through a window."

Note the extra holes in the frame. You see, he could string it up as in his sketch, using the diagonals and cross, a simple armature, like the ones used to practice Chinese characters, or he could string it as a grid, like Dürer.

He goes on to tell his brother that the frame and lines "provide a clear guide, so that one can make a drawing, setting out the broad outlines and proportions. How delightful it is to train this viewfinder on the sea, on the green fields—or, in the winter, on snow-covered land. With considerable and lengthy practice, it enables one to draw at lightning speed. The frame has become an excellent piece of equipment. It has cost me a pretty penny, too. There's no turning back now." He signs off, "Adieu, old chap." So, we're in good company here, following in the footsteps of Alberti, Leonardo, Dürer, Eakins, and Van Gogh.

A great first project using the *velo* is to draw a deep, foreshortened space, something like a hallway. Here are a couple of examples from my students at the University of Washington, and I'd like you to try this, too. We'll be calling on many of the things we've already studied, and adding new procedures. We're really building in complexity now.

You'll use a range of pencils and line weights. Use lighter pencils for construction lines, darker pencils for the drawing itself. You'll use four types of line: gestural line, construction line, contour, and cross contour. You'll use gestural compositional sketches to identify a strong composition. You'll need to think about the drawing's rectangle, its format shape, and its armature, as well as object-ground relations.

You'll scale up from perceived size to a larger dimension and retain proportionate relations, then use grid coordinates to layout accurate proportions, and use negative shapes as a further aid toward this goal. You'll build your drawing moving from large visual events to greater detail.

The first thing to do is to find a hallway or deep room. You want to look down your hallway through your viewfinder and frame it so you see five large planes: a back wall, the two sidewalls, the ceiling, and the floor. As some of you may have guessed, the viewfinder we've been using is a picture plane.

Here's the question. How many points or coordinates do you need to draw these five planes? As you may have guessed, the answer's eight; four coordinates for the corners of the back wall, and another four where the diagonals projecting from the back wall meet the viewfinder. Find eight coordinates, connect the dots, and you'll have drawn the walls, ceiling, and floor, a strong proportionate beginning for your drawing.

A general premise is to find the places where edges intersect in the viewfinder. Place these points on the page. This will create the connect-the-dots underpinning for a proportionate drawing. These intersection points are the places where one direction meets another. This could be in the subject I'm drawing. It could also be where an edge in the subject encounters an edge on the viewfinder.

A second premise is to work from the large to the small, from the general to the specific, and that can be challenging. It's really common for beginners to only see the nameable objects. Some people want to start with a clock on the wall, or a door, or a chair, and they totally ignore the large planes. Draw the large planes first, the walls, ceiling, and floor. They'll be the largest shapes in your drawing. You want to think in architectural order. Before you hang a clock or install a door, you have to build the wall. Before you put a chair in a room, you have to build the floor it sits on.

So find a hallway or, really, any room, the deeper the better. Find one that's not too complicated, you don't want a highly ornamented interior or one that's cluttered with furniture for this project. The drawing's all about determining accurate proportions and measurements. We don't need any value, shading, or hatching, they'll all get in the way. Line alone is fine. We're going to proceed in three distinct steps.

First, make three compositional gesture studies. Next, scale up from the best study to your 18 × 24-inch paper. We'll do this because our *velo*, our viewfinder and grid, is smaller than the drawing we're making. The third step's making the drawing itself. Let's go through each of these steps in detail. You'll need: pencils, erasers, and sharpeners; a pen or brush and ink; viewfinders, clips, masking tape, and the clear acetate grid. You'll also need a ruler, T-square, and drawing board, a couple sheets of smaller paper for gestural compositional sketches, and one sheet of 18 × 24-inch paper for the final drawing.

The first step's to identify a strong composition. Make several quick gestural compositional sketches on smaller paper. Like Rembrandt, draw directly with brush and ink. Using ink means you can't erase and make a finished little drawing. The idea is to quickly give yourself several compositional options. Now, at first, these drawings may not be very proportionate, but they'll help you to begin to see and understand what's before you. As you repeat this process over the coming months, you'll find that you'll consistently improve. Throw yourself into it, there's nothing to fear.

I'm asking you to do three distinctly different studies, each from a different point of view, each using a different format shape. The large drawings are going to take some time, so you want to try to find a promising point of view and framing before committing.

Walk through the room or hallway looking and framing with your viewfinder. Don't worry about the grid yet, we'll get to that later. Make sure you can see the five major planes: back wall, two sidewalls, the ceiling, and the floor. Make sure you have enough of each. If any of your planes are severely cropped, it will make the space feel less three-dimensional. Try different rectangular shapes using your viewfinder, and a heads-up, if you stick to quarter, half, and inch increments in the viewfinder's opening, it will simplify the math when scaling up.

As you try different format shapes, note how the large internal divisions relate. Think about the armature and composition. When you've found a promising point of view and framing, clip the viewfinder together, and you're ready to make your first gesture study. With a harder pencil, with an H of some kind, lightly trace the shape of the viewfinder in the center of the page. If your format shape's horizontal, turn you page horizontally, if vertical, vertically.

Remember, you'll always want to keep that same eye closed, keep your head in the same position, hold the viewfinder at a consistent height, and distance from your eye. Holding it at arm's length is a very good way to go.

Now, with pen or brush, make a quick gestural study. Call on the exercises we did using gestural line. Push yourself to draw quickly and in an all-encompassing way. Establish the major compositional relationships between the format shape and the large planes, walls, floors, and ceilings. Next, attend to the large events on those planes, windows, doors, furniture, et cetera. These objects are figures on grounds.

As your brush darts across the surface, be attentive to the positive and negative shapes. The negatives measure the distances between the positives. Work quickly; you're drawing with gestural line. These drawings really shouldn't take more than a couple of minutes. If you don't like a drawing, try it again. Nothing to worry about, it's a couple minutes, cheap ink, and paper. If you're attentive to what you're looking at, you'll see and understand more with each repetition. The little drawings are going to improve.

Once you've made at least three gestural studies from three different points of view, take a look at them and select the best one. This act of selection, or curation, is an essential part of learning to draw. As you practice doing this and work with the results, this skill's going to improve, too.

The next step is to measure your study then scale it to the 18 × 24-inch paper. For example, this study's 4 × 5¾ inches. The smaller dimension, four, will fit into the smaller dimension of our paper, 18, four times, giving us 16 inches. Next, we'd multiply the larger dimension, five and three-quarters, by the same factor, four, to get to 23. The scaled up rectangle would be 16 × 23. If the larger dimension turns out to be larger than 24 inches, start by dividing 24 by the larger dimension.

Once you've calculated the rectangle's dimensions, lay out the format shape lightly with a well-sharpened H pencil, ruler, and T-square. It's a good idea to get into the habit of centering the format shape in the page. This way you have maximum flexibility to open up the drawing on the right or the left, or the top or the bottom if you need to.

So the first thing we want to do is just take the viewfinder apart and then check the calibration on the viewfinder against the grid to make sure that everything will line up, and you'll do that with the other arm as well. If anything doesn't line up, that means you have to check how you've drawn your inches or how you did your grid.

Next, once we've done that, we can just turn this over and we'll line up our grid with the viewfinder itself, and then we'll just take a piece of tape or two and secure this in place. With that done, we'll just put our other arm of our viewfinder back in place, clip it together, might want to add an extra piece of tape, and we're ready to go.

The next step is to draw a scaled-up grid on your large paper. The acetate grid is one inch by one inch. To draw a corresponding grid on your page, you'll scale that measure by the same factor you used to scale the format's dimensions. In the example, we multiplied the format's measure by a factor of four. So we'd do the same with the grid unit. Since the acetate grid's one by one, the grid on the page will be four by four.

Along the borders of the format shape, on the 18 × 24-inch paper, mark off the grid unit's measure with small marks. Connect the marks with horizontal and vertical lines to create the grid. These are construction lines, best if they're light, thin, and precise. Now, like the artist in the Dürer, you have a gridded *velo* to look through and you have a proportionate gridded horizontal picture plane to draw on.

You're ready to make your drawing. First, put away the small gesture drawing, it's served its purpose. You'll be looking directly at your observational source, the room. Also, put away the rulers and T-square, draw freehand. Take out a well-sharpened F, HB, or B pencil to begin the drawing. As before, keep one eye closed, your head held in a fixed position, and the viewfinder at arm's length.

Find the eight coordinates that will give you the five big planes: back wall, floor, walls, and ceiling. Identify where each coordinate is on the *velo* and transpose that position to the page. Make a very small light dot at each coordinate's location, the larger the dot, the less precise.

When you've placed these eight coordinates, connect each set of points with a single line. Call on those line-connecting exercises you've been doing. We're drawing for proportion and measure, so you don't want to make a lot of sketchy lines, they won't define a measure, instead they'll suggest a range of possibilities, in this drawing the goal's specificity.

Dürer can guide us here. This drawing concerns itself with human proportions. He uses a very specific line, not a sketchy or gestural line. The goal of the drawing is to establish clear and accurate proportions. Gestural lines don't achieve this.

So locate your eight points and draw your lines to create your major planes. Now, take a look at your shapes. Eyeball them. Does the back wall you've drawn resemble the back wall you're looking at? Does it have the same ratio of height to width? Do the other major planes look about right? If not, erase, take another look at the coordinates, and redraw.

Earlier I'd said that the goal is to move from the large to the small, from the general to the specific. In the art building at the University of Washington, once we have our five major planes, we generally move on to the aggregate shape of the light fixtures. All we need are four points or coordinates accurately placed and then we can draw the light fixtures' aggregate shape.

Then, the negative shapes between them. This will define the fixtures themselves. For each negative shape, we need four points. Eyeball your shapes and compare them with what you see. If they're off, erase, and re-measure. Then we go to the aggregate shapes of the corkboards. Then the aggregate shape of the recycling bins. Then I ask my students to eyeball and check. Next, we might locate the moldings and doorways. Last, we move to the smallest visual events, find their coordinates in the *velo*, transpose them to the paper's surface.

Your own drawing will no doubt be somewhat different. The essential thing is to follow this procedure. Remember, you're not drawing things, you're establishing coordinates then connecting those coordinates using clear lines.

As you draw, don't forget to consider line weight. Varying the line will help create the sensation of receding space. It will also create focal areas and focal points. Use a range of line from dark to light, thick to thin, and continuous to discontinuous. Using a range of pencils is really going to help and be attentive to managing your pencil's point.

Next, we'll continue our discussion of proportion. You've already learned about seven tools that help us get things right. We'll add another six. Soon, you'll have a professional repertoire of techniques to bring to bear on complex drawing problems.

Proportion: Accurate Proportion and Measure
Lecture 12

In this lecture, we'll concentrate on the tools we use to arrive at correct proportions. We'll start by reviewing the tools we've already discussed: the centerline, building-block shape, large ground shapes, aggregate shape, eyeballing, negative shape, and Alberti's *velo*. Then, we'll add some new tools: the clock-hand method for determining angles, standard units of measure, level lines and plumb lines, and the method of sighting the half. Although we will study each of these separately, as you use them, you'll find yourself combining them seamlessly in your own way. They'll become part of the way you naturally draw.

Tools for Accurate Proportion and Measurement
The tools for accurate proportion that we've already discussed include the following:

- Centerline, a type of construction line that helps establish an object's placement within the drawing and helps maintain the subject's direction. The centerline also serves as an aid in drawing shapes proportionately in relation to the object's center.

- Constituent or building-block shapes, which help relate both the left and right sides and the width-to-height proportions of an object or part of an object.

- Large ground shapes, which set up proportions for the whole drawing.

- Aggregate shape, or the simple shape that contains the subject and captures the height-to-width proportion. Using ground and aggregate shapes together defines and helps control the overall proportions in a drawing.

- Eyeballing, that is, looking at the shape you've drawn and asking yourself if it corresponds to what you're seeing.

- Negative shape, which we tend to see more accurately than positive shapes because we have no preconceptions about what they look like. This allows us to see them in a purely visual and analytic manner. Taken together, a group of negative shapes will reveal the silhouette of an object in accurate proportion.

The first exercise in this lecture is to make a drawing of a box similar to the one shown below. Follow the steps outlined, concentrating on the large ground shapes and negative shapes, as well as the other tools we've discussed so far. As a second exercise, see how you can apply the grid to the box drawing.

© David Brody.

Determining Angles with the Clock-Hand Method
Our next tool represents a means for quantifying tricky angles. To understand the idea behind the clock-hand method, hold a pencil out in front of you with your left hand, vertically, point up. Closing one eye, rotate the pencil so that it comes into line with the angle of the box. Then, take a second pencil in your right hand and place it pointing straight up from the eraser end of the first pencil.

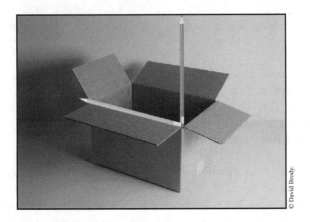

Now, imagine that the pencils are hands on an analog clock face, and tell the time. Here, we have about 13 minutes to noon. This method represents a way to quantify and remember an angle.

We just read this angle as an acute one, but we could equally read it as obtuse. Depending on whether you're right-handed or left handed, one way or the other may be more comfortable.

Once you've practiced this method a couple of times, you can imagine the hour hand, and you'll need only a single hand and pencil to measure the angle. The most important thing to remember here is to hold your pencil parallel to an imaginary picture plane, as if it were held against a glass plane perpendicular to the floor. You don't want to tip your pencil into space.

A Standard Unit of Measure

We've all seen images of an artist, standing in front of an easel, holding out his arm, closing one eye, and looking out over his thumb. This is a version of another tool we can use to create accurate proportions: a standard unit of measure. Here, you identify some part of what you're seeing to be used to measure everything else. In choosing the unit of measure, there are two factors to keep in mind: its orientation and its scale. Regarding orientation, you want something that is parallel to the picture plane, not anything that recedes into space. In fact, it's best if what you choose is a self-contained unit and is vertical or horizontal. Regarding scale, the unit you choose can't be too big or too small.

In the case of the box, the front edge may be a good choice. Although it's a couple degrees off true vertical, it will work for the purposes of this drawing. Hold a well-pointed pencil vertically, with the point up. With one eye closed, outstretch your arm fully, and align the pencil's tip with the top of the standard unit of measure. With your thumb and first finger, hold the pencil at the base of the standard unit. This allows you to capture the unit on your pencil, which you can then use to measure across the picture plane.

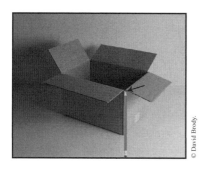

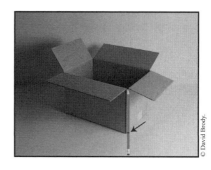

Level Lines and Plumb Lines

Yet another tool is either a horizontal level line or a vertical plumb line. Turn your pencil horizontally and line it up with any point, say, the far left inside corner of the box. Then, look to see if anything to the right lines up with it. In this case, there doesn't seem to be perfect alignment, but we can tell that the far right inside corner is just a bit higher than the left.

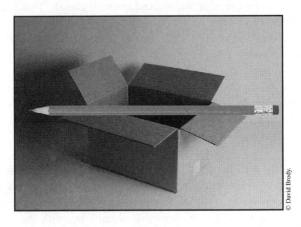

© David Brody.

Of course, you can also use this technique vertically to create a plumb line. Both tools—the level line or the plumb line—can be used to see how things line up and to understand how different points or edges correlate.

With these new tools—clock hands for angles, a standard unit of measure, and level and plumb lines to locate positions—make a second drawing of the box. At first, you should follow the instructions for using these tools as you would a recipe, but once you've worked with them for a period of time, you'll find yourself using them in a much more fluid, organic way. Our method here is to break down the processes into understandable pieces, but as you use them, they'll become natural, embedded in the way you scan everything you see.

Sighting the Half

Related to some of the tools we've studied is an approach called *sighting the half*. This is another method to help you imagine an even grid over your subject and measure through your drawing. You'll then find the key points that help you draw proportionately.

Drawing as an Interrogative Process

As you're beginning to realize, drawing can be an interrogative process. We ask one question after another: How does the picture plane divide? What's the largest shape? What's the angle of that diagonal? How long is it? A drawing can represent the sum of an artist's responses to these questions.

Suggested Reading

Curtis, *Drawing from Observation*, chapter 7, "The Perceptual Grid," pp. 61–74, and chapter 8, "Proportion," pp. 75–92.

Loomis, *Figure Drawing for All It's Worth*, "The Visual Survey Process," pp. 88–89.

Mendelowitz, Faber, and Wakeman, *A Guide to Drawing*, chapter 3, "Learning to See Deeply," pp. 38–56.

Rockman, *Drawing Essentials*, pp. 4–22.

Proportion: Accurate Proportion and Measure
Lecture 12—Transcript

In this lecture, we'll concentrate on the tools we use to arrive at correct proportions. They're not all new to you, you've studied seven of them already. We'll start by reviewing the ones we've already discussed and then add five new ones. While we study each of these separately, as you repeatedly use them you'll find yourself combining them seamlessly in your own way. They'll just become part of the way you draw naturally.

As part of this lecture, we'll be making two drawings, the first with pencil on small paper, and the second with charcoal on 18 s 24-inch paper. You'll also need: your sharpening and erasing tools, viewfinder, and grid.

We'll be drawing a cardboard box. The one I've used in the examples is $14 \times 10 \times 8$ inches. To get a similar view, you'll want to be standing up, looking down at the box. We'll get a lot of interesting angles from this viewpoint, so it's likely best to set up with your drawing board on your easel.

Let's recap our first seven tools. The first is a type of construction line, the centerline. We've seen Dürer use it in his figure studies, as well as Eakins in his drawing of *John Biglin in a Single Scull*, and we've used them to draw still life objects. They help establish an object's placement within the drawing and help maintain the subject's direction, here, vertically. Last, they serve as an aid in drawing shapes proportionately in relation to the object's center.

Our second tool is constituent or building block shape. We often use these kind of shapes with a center line or other construction line. Using these kind of shapes helps us to relate both left and right sides and the width-to-height of proportions of an object or part of an object.

Our third tool is another type of shape, large ground shapes. These set up proportions for the whole drawing. In the drawing we'll be doing here, we'll have a lower rectangle and an equal-sized upper rectangle. Together, they create the overall proportions of our drawing.

Next is aggregate shape. We look at our subject and imagine a simple shape that could contain it, a shape that captures the height-to-width proportion. As we study our aggregate shape, we can even trace over it in the air to get a sense of its proportions, and then draw it on the page. This set of construction lines tells us where our subject should be located and how large it should be. Using ground and aggregate shapes together will define and help us control the overall proportions in our drawing.

Using these concepts helps us avoid running out of space for what we want to include in our drawing. It also helps us to work from the general to the specific. That keeps us from getting bogged down in details prematurely, and that saves us time and exasperation because we're able to avoid drawing time-consuming details that have to be erased because they're not in proportion or they're in the wrong location.

Our fifth tool is used in conjunction with the prior four. We've referred to it as eyeballing. We look at the shape we've drawn and ask ourselves if it corresponds to what we're seeing. This could be applied when evaluating part of a still life object, like the body of a vase or bottle, or it could be eyeballing the height-to-width proportion of a wall in a room as you likely did in the hallway project, or as we'll be doing assessing aggregate shapes in this drawing.

Our sixth tool is negative shape. We tend to see these more accurately than the positives because we have no preconceptions about what they look like. This allows us to see them in a purely visual and analytic manner. In this drawing, we'll have a large upper negative and a large lower negative. Taken together they reveal the silhouette of the object in accurate proportion.

Here's a further refinement on gauging large, complex negatives. By holding your pencil against a negative, arm extended, one eye closed, you can break it up into more memorable pieces. This transforms a complex shape into two simpler shapes, one on the right, and another on the left. Easier to remember like this, and if a shape's easier to remember, it's going to be easier to draw. We can also use our pencil horizontally.

S, let's make a drawing of the box combining these techniques. If you pose your box similarly to the way I've posed mine, it will help you follow the directions. In this example, we're looking down at the box, and it's framed so that there's space on all sides, above, below, left, and right. This guarantees that the box will sit back in space.

The point of view is such that the back edge of the table meets the wall along a horizontal. I've posed the box so that two flaps are pointing up and two are pointing down. This offers a range of angles to deal with.

The format shape in the example is three to four; it's a 3:4 rectangle, specifically four-and-a-half by six inches. You could make yours somewhat different if you like, but make sure to frame your box in your viewfinder using whole or half-inch increments for the format shape.

Once you've framed your drawing in your viewfinder, trace the format shape on our 8½ × 11-inch paper. Look at the two large ground shapes. These are your two largest planes, the table, and the wall. Draw this with a single line at the appropriate height. Eyeball your large division. Then look back out through the viewfinder. If there are discrepancies, correct as necessary.

Next, gauge the aggregate shape of your box. How wide is it? How tall? Lightly draw a rectangle to express this. Now eyeball the rectangle and look back out at your box. Trace a rectangle over it in the air. Then look back at your page. Ask yourself if they're the same. If not, adjust. Look back and forth a couple times until you feel you're confident you're about right.

Now let's turn to negative shape. First, looking out through your viewfinder's window, trace around the upper negative in the air, then the lower one. Now work your way around the box. Break the complex negatives into manageable, bite-size pieces. Eyeball as you go. And adjust the proportions at each step. By following this method, you'll construct your box's silhouette. Once complete, eyeball all the pieces, and make any changes necessary to bring it closer to proportionality.

Now add the large negative in the center of the box that defines the bottom edges of the two rear flaps, then the negative surrounding the right front flap, and the negative surrounding the left side flap.

Now, one last line to express the change of plane in the interior of the box. Look out through your viewfinder and eyeball all the shapes, and adjust as needed. When you feel you're in pretty good shape, erase any of your construction lines in the negatives, do a little more eyeballing and correcting, and you should have a reasonably proportionate drawing of your subject.

These tools are all useful. With practice, they can provide us with good results, but they're rather general. Our next set of tools allow for greater specificity of measure.

The first of these is the gridded picture plane, the *velo* of Alberti. As we've seen, this helps us plot specific locations. Let's see how we could apply it to this drawing problem.

First, we'd fix the grid into our viewfinders. Then, lightly, with a well-sharpened 4H pencil, we'd draw the format shape and an identical grid on our paper. In our last drawing using the grid, we had five major planes and used eight points to construct them. Here, we have 10 planes, two in the tabletop and wall and another eight in the box. We'd need 21 points of intersection to make this drawing. We'd place a small mark on our gridded page for each location, check the locations against what we see through the viewfinder, make any changes needed, and connect the dots. If you like working with the grid, you could use it to check the drawing you just did using negative shape.

So those are our first seven tools. The next set was derived from what artists came to understand by analyzing what they were seeing using tools like the *velo*.

And that brings us to our next tool, number eight. It represents a means for quantifying those tricky angles. You'll need two pencils, new, full-length ones are best. Take the first and hold it out in front of you with your left hand, vertically, point up. If the screen you're using is vertical, you can hold the pencil flat against the screen the first time.

Now, closing one eye, rotate your pencil so that it comes into line with the angle of the box, like the pencil here. Now take a second pencil in your right hand and place it pointing straight up from the eraser end of your first pencil. Now I'd like you to imagine your pencils are hands on an analog clock face. Then tell the time. Here, about 13 minutes to noon. And that represents a way to quantify and remember an angle; makes it much easier to draw.

We just read this angle as an acute one. We could equally read it as obtuse. Depending on whether you're right-handed or left-handed, one way or the other may be more comfortable, so let's hold the first pencil in our right hand, but instead of holding it against the screen, hold it a couple inches away, but make sure it's vertical, point straight up. Close one eye, then rotate it so that it comes into line with the angle. Hold the second pencil up to 12 in your left hand. Imagine that clock face. Ask yourself what time it is. Here, about 12:18. Once you've done this a couple times, you can imagine the hour hand, and you'll only need a single hand and pencil to measure the angle.

Let's try it that way now. Look at the angle of the flap on the far right. Rotate your pencil to coincide with the angle. Imagine another pointing to 12. Then the clock face. And read the time. About seven minutes after the hour.

You might want to practice this a bit without drawing at all. Walk around your home or office, look at angles in your ceilings, windows, doors, kitchen cabinets, tables, anything that angles forward or back in space, and quantify it. Practice doing this with one pencil, it's going to make it much easier when you're actually working on a drawing if you've done some rehearsal. The most important thing to remember is to hold your pencil parallel to an imaginary picture plane as if it were held against a glass plane perpendicular to the floor or on a flat clock's face. You don't want to tip your pencil into space.

You've likely seen an actor portraying an artist doing this, holding out his arm, closing one eye, and looking out over his thumb. That's a version of our next tool, number nine. It allows us to measure vertically and horizontally across the picture plane, and it will help us measure proportions, amounts, and distances. This is how it works.

We want to identify some part of what we're seeing to use to measure everything else. We call this a standard unit of measure. In choosing the unit, there are a couple factors to keep in mind.

First is orientation. We want something that's parallel to the picture plane. We don't want anything that's tilting back into space. Anything receding will be less clear in terms of measure. In fact, it's best if what we choose is a self-contained unit and is vertical or horizontal.

There's a second factor to consider, scale. Measuring a person's height in feet and inches makes all the sense in the world, but for the distance between New York and L.A., feet and inches are too small. And while light years are good for measuring across the universe, they'd be too large for New York to L.A., so we use miles. The point here is that for any unit of measure to be useful, it can't be too big and it can't be too small.

Looking at our box on the table, the front edge of the box may be our best bet. While it's a couple degrees off true vertical, it will still work for our purposes.

This is what I'd like you to do. Take a well-pointed pencil, hold it vertically, point up, with one eye closed. Outstretch your arm fully. Align the pencil's tip with the top of this standard unit of measure. With your thumb and first finger, hold the pencil at the base of the standard unit of measure. You've now captured the unit on your pencil, and you can use it to measure across the picture plane. Here's how.

Continuing to hold the pencil in the same place between thumb and first finger, lift your arm straight up so the thumb and first finger come level with the inside corner of the box. That would be the top of our standard unit. We've stacked our measure on top of the unit itself. This reveals that the point along the back flap directly above the front corner of the box is just a little less than one standard unit above the unit itself. We'd also note that the point where the pencil traverses the hinge of the flap is a bit over half a measure from the top of the corner.

We can sum up what we've discovered about these locations. The top of the flap is a little less than one measure above the standard unit. The hinge of the flap is a little more than half a measure above the standard unit.

We can also turn our hand 90 degrees and measure right and left across the picture plane. Let's measure, from the standard unit, our box's corner out to the near corner on the left flap. This reveals that the distance is a little less than 40 percent of a unit.

The core idea is that, once we've placed our standard unit of measure in our drawing, we can measure from it to locate any other point we might need. We're going to elaborate on this method when we get into the drawing itself.

Our 10th tool is a straight line, either a horizontal level line or a vertical plumb line. Here's how they work. I can turn my pencil horizontally and line it up with any point, say, the far left inside corner of the box. Then I look to see if anything toward the right lines up with it. No perfect line up here, but what I do learn is that the far right inside corner is just a little bit higher than the left. So I can use this tool, a level line, to see how things line up and also to understand how different points or edges correlate.

Take a look at the corners of these two flaps. Try and guess which one's higher. Apply our level line, we find that the far left corner is higher.

We can also use this vertically as a plumb line. We don't have any clear vertical line ups in this setup, but placing my pencil vertically along the front corner reveals how the back flap should be positioned. The corner should be just off to the left, and I should have a large shape to the right and a much smaller one to the left.

We now have all the tools we'll need to make our second drawing of the box. Clock hands for angles, and a standard unit of measure, and level and plumb lines to locate positions. This time, we'll use charcoal on the 18 × 24-inch white paper. You want to draw from a fixed location with the same eye closed, and when taking measurements, extend that arm fully, so it's always in the same place. The directions here are very specific, much like a recipe.

I've put it together this way so you'll be able to follow the steps in clear succession.

In practice, once you've done this a couple times, you'll be able to work with the basic ideas with clock hands, a standard unit of measure, and level and plumb lines in a much more fluid and organic way. You'll find that these same procedures can be used in all kinds of drawings to draw just about anything. They can also be incorporated with the other tools we've studied.

So let's start by framing the box in your viewfinder. Our drawing's going to be 18 × 24 inches, so make sure your viewfinder is open in the same ratio, any 3:4 ratio. The most convenient ones would be three by four inches, four-and-a-half by six inches, like mine, six by eight inches, and 9 × 12 inches.

Once again, note the aggregate shape of the box, a rectangle that we imagine relative to the viewfinder's opening. We want to get a sense of the box's footprint, how much width does it have to its height. You can even do a phantom tracing of the aggregate shape in the viewfinder window, right over the box itself. Do it a couple of times with the goal of getting a clear sense of that shape. You'll also want to note the negative shape, the amount of frame between the edges of your aggregate shape and the edges of your paper.

Since your viewfinder is scaled in a 3:4 ratio, just like your paper, you can draw the rectangular aggregate shape lightly on the page. Then check the shape and its negative, a bit of eyeballing here. Ask yourself if it looks like what you're seeing through your viewfinder. Make any changes that are necessary.

Once you have your aggregate shape, you want to add your standard unit of measure. To do this, we have to know where to put it. Looking through your viewfinder, ask yourself, where along the bottom horizontal of the aggregate shape does the unit appear? Is it toward the center, the right, the left, and by how much? In my example, it intersects towards the right. It divides the horizontal with about 60 percent on the left and about 40 percent on the right. Once you've made this determination, make a small mark with your charcoal at this location on the page.

The next step is to draw the standard unit of measure in the drawing. We're going to do this in two steps. First, take the measure of your standard unit with your pencil, then draw that measure with your charcoal at the location you've noted. The second step is to scale the measure.

Our drawing is 18 × 24 inches. If your viewfinder opening is three by four inches, your drawing is larger by a factor of six; if four-and-a-half by six inches, by a factor of four; if six by eight inches, by a factor of three; and if 9 × 12 inches, by a factor of two. My viewfinder's open four-and-a-half by six inches, so my drawing is larger by a factor of four, and I'll scale up the standard unit of measure in my drawing by a factor of four. You should do this relative to your own viewfinder's opening. Then, check for accuracy. You're now looking at your unit of measure scaled up to your page.

What I'd like you to do now is to hold your viewfinder in one hand and your pencil, point up, in the other. As we did earlier, locate the standard unit of measure on your pencil with your thumb and first finger. Now, measure from the standard unit on the box to the top opening of the viewfinder, one unit, and about 80 percent of the unit. Now let's measure below. There we get half a unit. Even though we're drawing with charcoal, it's easier to measure with a pencil. The irregular shape of the charcoal simply makes it less precise.

So now, lightly with your charcoal, draw these units on your page. If you don't have enough room for 1.8 units above and half below, it means you've drawn your standard unit too large for the page. If there's too much room, the standard unit's too small. So take a little time to check for accuracy before moving on to the next step.

With our vertical measure in place, we want to add a horizontal one, too. Again, look out through the viewfinder, measure from the top of the standard unit out to the left. About two and a little over half a unit; 2.6 units all told. Then out to the right. Here we get one unit and a slightly larger fraction of a unit than on the left, about 1.7 units in all. Let's draw this on our page as well.

While more complex, this is similar to what we did when we drew a square and other construction lines to help us draw a circle. In essence, we created a structure that would help us see and draw a form. And you may be thinking that what we have here on our page resembles a partial grid, a partial *velo*, and you'd be absolutely right. And we could easily fill in the rest of a grid based on standard units. Just extend horizontals and verticals out from our existing intersections.

I'll let you try that in another drawing. For our purposes here, we'll continue measuring our way through the drawing without filling in the grid. And we won't need the viewfinder anymore for this project, so let's put it aside. Instead, we'll use the clock hand technique next.

Let's look at the bottom right diagonal of the box. Close one eye. Make sure the pencil is parallel to an imagined perpendicular picture plane and turn your pencil to line up with the angle. It's about seven minutes after the hour. And we'll draw a line at this diagonal moving out from the bottom of our standard unit. We haven't yet determined how long the line should be, so we'll turn to our standard unit of measure for an answer.

Place your thumb and first finger at the one unit measure. Then turn the pencil horizontally, with the pencil's point lining up with the box's front edge. Now, you want to ask yourself, how far do you have to travel to the right to reach the back corner of the box? About half a unit.

So return to the drawing and measure out half a unit to the right to intersect the diagonal, and you can erase anything extra. Then, repeat these steps on the other side. First, use the clock hand technique to determine the angle. Then, you want to use your pencil to measure its termination point in standard units. Last, draw the diagonal out to the left to accord with your measure.

Let's finish this long left plane of the box. From the top of the front corner, we'll use the clock hand technique to find the angle, then the standard unit of measure to find the length. Next, we'll use the clock hand to check the angle of the left side, and draw this edge as if we could see through the folded flap. Next, we'll do the same thing on the other side.

Now, there's a little divot connecting the two sides, but we can eyeball that and just draw it in. Since we have our standard unit stated in the drawing repeatedly, we can erase our first standard unit and draw the slightly angled line to express the front edge of the box.

This would be a good time to check the far right and far left corners using the level line. Check the lower ones, then uppers. In both cases, the right should be a little higher than the left. If anything's off, measure again using the three new tools and erase and correct.

Now we'll move to the box's open top and follow the same method we used for the base. We'll use the clock hand tool for the diagonals' angles, and use the standard unit of measure to calculate the length. As we did at the front corner, we can eyeball the divots where they occur.

Next, we'll add the line that creates the two interior planes, and we're ready to work on the flaps. We'll start with the front right diagonal, clock hand tool for direction, standard unit for length, then the rear diagonal, and next, the connecting one. Let's locate the point along this last diagonal where it intersects the back edge of the table and draw a horizontal here.

Now, we'll repeat these steps with the front left flap. Let's use the pencil as a horizontal level to check the alignments of the corners. Make any adjustments you need. We're almost done, just another six angles to measure for direction and length, three for each of the rear flaps. Then erase the construction lines and the lines we drew through. And we'll make a final level line check to make sure the corners correlate. And do the same thing with our vertical plumb line. Make any necessary changes and you're done.

Take a breath. We've covered a lot of material and I know it's a lot to absorb. We've been doing this in a very step-by-step, even mechanistic way, all about breaking down the processes into understandable pieces. But as you use them, they become more natural and they'll be embedded in the way you scan everything you see.

And I want to assure you, that this isn't about a style of drawing. With practice, it just all gets absorbed, and the knowledge lets you draw freely and gesturally. Whether you're drawing sleepy figures in a room like Degas, or a river and landscape like Monet, it just takes time and practice.

There's a related approach to what we just did, and you can try it at your leisure. Essentially, we start by using our pencil to sight and measure the height of the object, and we're doing that in relationship to its width. And we draw a vertical I-beam to represent the height, and a horizontal one to represent the width. In essence, this expresses the object's aggregate shape and locates it in the page.

Next, we'd calibrate the axes at the quarters. Depending on what we're drawing, we might want to find the eighths as well, in one or both axes. It would be very common to do this along the vertical axis if we're drawing a standing figure. The I-beams and quarter calibrations help us imagine an even grid over our subject. Holding our pencil so that we capture the measure of the half or quarter of the vertical or horizontal axis, we can measure our way through the drawing, finding the key points that help us draw proportionately. As with Alberti's *velo*, these points don't have to line up with the grid units, we just have to know where they are in relation to the units.

Our final tool, number 12, is linear perspective. For the moment, it just gets this mention. But, you'll soon learn it's a really powerful tool for understanding proportion.

As you're coming to see, drawing can be an interrogative process, we ask one question after another. How does the picture plane divide? What's the largest shape? What's the angle of that diagonal? How long is it? The drawing represents the sum of our responses.

Next, we'll talk about 12 principles that can guide us in creating the illusion of three-dimensional space on a two-dimensional surface, and then you're going to be primed to tackle a range of interesting and complex drawing projects.

Creating Volume and Illusionistic Space
Lecture 13

A central theme in our discussions about proportion revolved around the challenges of translating three dimensions into two. In this lecture, we'll look more broadly at how we create flatness, volume, and space. The surface we generally draw on—a piece of paper—is flat. In addition to controlling proportions, we often want to create the illusion of three-dimensional space on that flat surface. Broadly speaking, we can differentiate between two types of dimensionality: the volume of an object itself and the dimensionality of the environment that the object occupies—the space. Putting these two pieces together, we get volumetric form in space; we'll explore that process in this lecture.

Creating Illusionistic Space: 12 Principles

As we've noted, learning to draw is related to learning to understand what we see. A number of factors govern the way we perceive depth of space in the world around us, and these same factors correlate with ways we depict space on the page. The 12 primary factors are as follows:

- Overlap

- Diminishing size

- Position along the page's vertical axis

- Position relative to the format's edges

- Diagonals creating spatial depth

- Foreshortened shapes

- Cross-contours

- Value, light, and shadow

- Value and atmospheric perspective

- Level of detail

- Color and atmospheric perspective

- Subject matter of recognizable size.

Overlap
The first and among the most powerful factors governing our experience of depth is overlap. We know one person is in front of another because the first person partially conceals the second from view. Not surprisingly, overlap was one of the first factors artists recognized and used in their drawings.

Diminishing Size
A second factor here is relative scale. We look out into the world and see two things that we know are the same size. If one looks smaller than the other, we know that the smaller one is farther away. Similarly, if we see two things in a drawing that we know to be similar in size but one is drawn smaller than the other, we will, all else being equal, feel that they're in different spatial locations. This creates a volume of space between the two.

Position along the Page's Vertical Axis
Another factor affecting the sensation of depth of space is position along the vertical axis of the format.

In looking at a naturalistic drawing or a painting, as your eyes move up the vertical axis of the page, you are most often moving back in space. This imitates our experience in life. Look down at your feet; then, keeping your eyes focused downward, lift your head and allow your gaze to travel away from your feet into increasingly greater depth, until you hit the back wall of the room you're in.

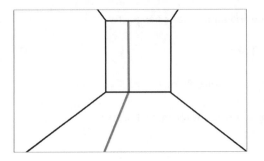

On reaching the back wall, if you continue to lift your head, you'll eventually reach the ceiling. Then, you begin to return back toward yourself, finally reaching a point on the ceiling directly above your feet—right where you started.

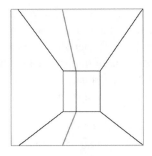

We find this spatial permutation in many works where we're looking into an interior and in certain landscapes.

Position Relative to the Format's Edges
The next factor has to do with the subject's relationship to the format's edges. Figures or objects that intersect the edges of the format shape can appear closer to us in space.

Diagonals Creating Spatial Depth
With regard to space, there are two types of diagonals: those that define the edge of an object or part of an object that is parallel to the picture plane and those that create the illusion of a recession in space.

It took human beings a long time—most of the 80,000 years that our species has been drawing—for someone to realize that a diagonal could also create the illusion of depth on a two-dimensional surface.

Foreshortened Shapes

As we've noted, not all shapes read as strictly flat, especially those that contain diagonals, which can pitch us back into space. We've referred to these kinds of shapes as *foreshortened shapes*.

A triangle can simply be a triangle—as flat as the piece of paper it's drawn on.

Or that same triangle could read as the top plane of a prism receding in space or a road receding back to the horizon.

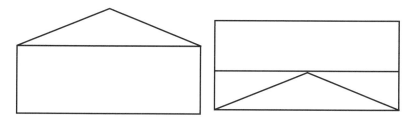

Trapezoids, which are essentially truncated triangles, function in the same way, as can parallelograms. The ellipse, a curvilinear shape, acts similarly.

Cross-Contours

As we discussed in an earlier lecture, cross-contours can be instrumental in creating a sense of three-dimensionality, turning shape into volume.

Value, Light, and Shadow

Value can affect our understanding of space and volume in a number of ways. First, a shift from light to dark can describe the play of light on three-dimensional form and indicate volume. If there's no light, we don't see any three-dimensional form. With a little light, we begin to see a modest amount of form. But a strong directional light gives the best evidence of volumetric structure. The planes of an object turned toward the light will appear lighter, and those turned away will appear darker. The shift from light to dark is evidence of the underlying planar shift, which translates to volume. The use of varying degrees of light and dark to simulate the passage of light over form and create volume is referred to as *chiaroscuro*.

In drawing, we speak about two kinds of shadow: object shadow and cast shadow. *Object shadow*, as the name implies, refers to the shadow on the part of an object that is turned away from the light and, as we've said, reveals form. *Cast shadows* describe the planar surface on which they fall and, thus, can reveal form, too.

Value and Atmospheric Perspective
Another way that value affects our perception of depth is through *atmospheric* or *aerial perspective*. This is what we experience when we see a distant mountain or building. The distant object looks less clear than when we're close to it. The darks get lighter, and many of the bright lights get dimmer. The object appears to fade somewhat into the atmosphere. Another way of saying this is that value contrasts can appear to diminish with depth. This is accompanied by changes in the way edges appear. Up close, they're clear and precise, but from a distance, they appear fuzzier. The use of atmospheric perspective not only gives us space but can also create the illusion of airiness or atmosphere on the page.

Level of Detail
The next principle is related to atmospheric perspective. It concerns the amount of detail we're able to see at any given depth. Clearly, we see more detail up close and less as something recedes from sight.

Color and Atmospheric Perspective
The next factor is color. We'll discuss this in much greater depth later in the course, but for now, suffice it to say that distance affects color similarly to the way it affects value.

We think of color as having three attributes: (1) hue (the color's blueness, yellowness, or redness), (2) saturation or intensity (the color's level of purity versus neutrality), and (3) value (lightness or darkness). Look at the water in the foreground of the Eakins watercolor and note the saturation. Now, compare that with the saturation of the water in the area behind Biglin's scull, extending to the horizon. The difference is marked: The color is much more saturated in front and much more neutral as we recede. Unsurprisingly, this is accompanied by a shift in value contrast, as well. There is more contrast in the foreground and less as we recede.

© Yale University Art Gallery.

A second effect regards the type of color, warm or cool. All else being equal, warm colors will tend to advance, and cool will tend to recede. However, greater saturation generally trumps the effect of warm advancing and cool receding. In other words, a saturated blue bowl—a saturated cool color— will advance easily against a neutral warm color, such as a beige wall or table. High value contrast can often override high saturation, too.

Subject Matter of Recognizable Size
The final principle has to do with subject matter. Space is more measurable if it contains something that has a more or less recognizable measure. If we see a boat on the ocean from a distance, we may not be able to tell its size, but if we see figures on the deck, we'll be better able to gauge the size of the boat and the space that contains it.

Suggested Reading

Pumphrey, *The Elements of Art*, chapter 7, "Space."

Rockman, *Drawing Essentials*, "The Illusion of Space and Depth on a Two-Dimensional Surface," pp. 46–51.

Sale and Betti, *Drawing*, Part II, "Spatial Relationships of the Art Elements."

Creating Volume and Illusionistic Space
Lecture 13–Transcript

A central theme in our discussions about proportion revolved around the challenges in translating three dimensions into two. In this lecture, I'd like to look more broadly at how we create flatness, volume, and space.

The surface we draw on, generally, a piece of paper, is flat. In addition to controlling proportions, we often want to create the illusion of three-dimensional space on that flat surface. Broadly speaking, we could differentiate between two types of dimensionality. The volume of an object and the dimensionality of the environment the object occupies—what we refer to as space. Putting these two pieces together, we get volumetric form in space.

As we've noted, learning to draw is related to learning to understand what we're seeing. There are a number of factors governing the way we perceive depth of space in the world around us. These same factors correlate with the ways we depict space on the page. There are 12 primary factors we'll discuss: overlap, diminishing size, position along the page's vertical axis, position relative to the format's edges, diagonals creating spatial depth, foreshortened shapes, cross contour, value, light, and shadow, value and atmospheric perspective, level of detail, color and atmospheric perspective, subject matter of recognizable size.

The first, and among the most powerful factors governing our experience of depth, is overlap. We know one person is in front of another because they partially cover the second person, concealing part of that person from view–nothing subtle about it at all. Not surprisingly, it was one of the very first factors artists recognized and used in their drawings. We even find it in cave paintings going back tens of thousands of years. In this example, dating from about 31,000 years ago, it's known as *The Panel of the Horses* from the Chauvet Cave in France, we see four horse's heads overlapping like dominos.

Now, whether this was intended as overlap with the goal of created space is another question. This could have resulted from a single individual drawing all four heads, just as we see them today. Or, it could have resulted from one person drawing a single head. And, then later, someone else, or several other people, coming along, adding others. Just like the way much contemporary graffiti occors. So, here, we can't say for sure.

Our Egyptian stele, which goes back close to 3,000 years ago, is clearer in this regard. It's pretty flat. But we get a hint of three dimensions where Ra's crook and flail overlap his chest and shoulders. We get a bit more, where his foot overlaps the object behind it. And we get our most developed sense of space where the kneeling harpist's arm overlaps the harp and strings, which then, in turn, overlap his other arm.

In the early 12th-century Court Ladies handscroll, overlap is one of the primary tools used to create a sense of space. The girl in white overlaps the stretched silk, which, in turn, overlaps the woman in the orange robe. And on the right side of the scroll, the woman in white, green and orange overlaps the box-like structure and the woman in blue and red. And the box-like structure then overlaps the woman in pink and white.

In "Two Lovers," there are many complex overlaps. The serpentine hose of the water pipe makes its way from the foreground into the midground overlapping the platform. Then, it twists back on itself so that the mouthpiece overlaps the flexible hose. The pillows overlap the young woman. Her hand, in turn, overlaps the man's right arm. His arm overlaps his leg, which, along with the woman's hand, overlaps the back edge of the platform.

And in the Schiele, the very structure of the drawing depends on overlap. The woman is closest to us. She overlaps her own reflection, which overlaps Schiele's. This creates a cascading depth of space.

In Norman Lundin's "White Doe at Home," the recession of space is dramatic. The woman's lower leg overlaps her thigh. The thigh overlaps her arm, which partially overlaps her rib cage and chest. The chest overlaps the collarbone to the point of obscuring it. As well as partially overlapping the neck. The head overlaps the pillow. The pillow overlaps the bed. The bed overlaps the change of plane between the floor and wall. That's a lot of overlap, and not coincidentally, a lot of space.

What we've seen in these six images, spanning 31,000 years, is an evolution of the use of overlap. We started out in prehistory where intention is unclear. We moved to some very modest uses in early historic times, then to a firmer understanding of the power of this tool in the Middle Ages. And, finally, to a full-throttle embrace in more recent times. As I'm sure you've noted, as the overlaps become more pronounced, the space opens up accordingly.

Our second factor is relative scale. We look out into the world and see two things that we know are the same size, but one looks smaller than the other. So, we know the smaller one's farther away.

Similarly, if we see two things in a drawing that we know to be similar in size but one's drawn smaller than the other, we will, all else being equal, feel that they're in different spatial locations. The bigger one closer, the smaller farther away–and, this creates a volume of space between the two.

This seems natural to us, but it may be learned. The anthropologist, Colin Turnbull, tells an interesting story in his book, *The Forest People*. It's about the Mbuti Pygmies, forest dwellers, in what's now the Democratic Republic of Congo.

He recounts a hike to the top of the mountain with a Mbuti tribesman named Kenge. Living in the forest, Kenge had never experienced a vista that stretched out and away for miles and miles. In the distance, he saw a herd of buffalo and he asked Turnbull what kind of insects they were. Turnbull explained that they were buffalo, far off in the distance. He records Kenge's reaction, "…he roared with laughter and told me not to tell such stupid lies."

Well, learned or not, we see scale at play in many drawings from diverse cultures. This is a section of a Yuan Dynasty, circa early 14th-century handscroll. It's by Zhao Mengfu and it's titled, *Twin Pines, Level Distance*. Look at the scale relationship between the large trees on the right, and the much smaller ones in the center, as well as the scale relationship between the central hills and those to the left. We see something similar in the Holbein, but here, with figures. Look over the shoulder of the man standing on the far right. The figures behind him are not only overlapped. But, in relation to him, they're diminutive, signaling our senses that they're well behind him.

Holbein's using multiple spatial signals to compound the illusion of depth. Here, overlap and scale work together. And we'll see this repeatedly. In the Eakins watercolor, we see Biglin and his scull relative to the nine tiny figures in the scull in the mid-left section of the page. That creates space. Van Gogh uses the same principle in his 1888 drawing of *La Crau*, though in a different way. The large divisions in the landscape diminish in scale as we move from the bottom of the page to the top.

Linear perspective, which we'll discuss in detail later, provides a method for precisely determining how much a set of equal measures should diminish as they recede in space. And this is just what we see in Eakins' preparatory drawing for the Biglin watercolor. The ever-shrinking parallelograms represent the same amount of surface but in different locations. And, this system will tell us exactly how the horizontal widths should diminish.

The distance represented by the lower line has to shrink to the size of the line above to represent an equal distance at that depth. In Schiele's drawing, as in the Holbein, overlap is accompanied by diminished scale. The woman is not only overlapping her reflection but her reflection is much smaller, compounding the sensation of spatial recession.

Now, if we don't recognize the subjects as being more or less equal in size, we won't feel spatial depth. For example, compare the small figure in the pink robe in *The Court Ladies* to the much larger figure to the right.

We don't read significant depth here because, among other reasons, we know the small figure's a child. She's small by nature, not by optical effect.

It's also worth taking a look at how scale plays out in the four horses from the Chauvet Cave. The horses' heads actually get bigger as they overlap creating a rather strange spatial sensation. If we flip them so that the smallest head represents the final overlap, the spatial recession feels more normative.

Another factor affecting the sensation of depth of space is position along the vertical axis of the format. We noted this briefly in the lecture on how artists compose. In this drawing by Leonardo the woods are located high in the page and feel distant. By repositioning the woods lower in the page, we change the sensation of depth. The mass of trees becomes much closer.

This imitates our experience in life. If you look down at your feet, well, they're pretty close to you. Keeping your eyes focused downward and as you lift your head, your gaze travels away from your feet into increasingly greater depth. That is, until you reach a wall. And this is just what we see in *Two Lovers*. As we move up the vertical axis of the page, we move back in space. And, with the exception of the two figures in the distant room, it's what we experience in the Holbein. And it's exactly what we see in Lundin's *White Doe at Home*.

In *The Court Ladies*, though the ground's flat, the principle applies. The higher up along the vertical axis of the page we encounter the base of an object or figure, the farther away from us it reads.

Our two landscapes, the Zhao Mengfu and the Van Gogh function similarly. You move back in space as you vertically ascend the page. In both drawings, the sky acts like an atmospheric back wall.

Here's a variation on the theme. If, on reaching the back wall, you continue to lift your head, you'll eventually reach the ceiling. Then you begin to return back towards yourself finally reaching a point on the ceiling directly above your feet right where you started. And we find this spatial permutation in many works where we're looking into an interior, like this drawing by Antonio Lopez Garcia.

Or, like some of the examples I showed of my students' hallway drawings. It's also the case in certain landscapes. Here, instead of the ceiling, the sky returns from the horizon and hovers over the land below. Like in this Rembrandt drawing, or this watercolor by Winslow Homer.

Even in the Eakins, once you reach the sky at the horizon, as you continue to travel vertically up the page, the sky returns forward toward Biglin and the picture plane. Just as we have a foreground, a midground, and a background, we can have a fore sky, a mid sky, and a back sky.

The next factor has to do with our subject's relationship to the format's edges. In this drawing by Norman Lundin, both the figure and the blackboard are cropped. Both intersect the edges of the format shape with the result they feel very close to us in space. Biglin is much farther away from us than the model on the Lundin. His scull is just gently cropped on the left. In contrast, Homer's sailboat is much farther away in space. It's located well within the page with space around on all sides.

To bring the point home, we can easily push objects or figures back in space. We don't have to do anything to the way they've been drawn. We simply create more distance between them and the edges of the format's shape—we zoom out. And, inversely, we could bring Sir Thomas More forward in space by closing the distance between him and the format's edges—just zoom in and crop.

In regard to space, there are two types of diagonals. Those that define the edge of an object or part of an object that's parallel to the picture plane. And, those that create the illusion of a recession in space.

The Egyptian stele has a number of diagonals. There's the angle of the harp. And, both the harpist's arms and thigh have diagonals. But, they're all parallel to the picture plane, nothing tipping back in space.

It took human beings a very long time, most of the 80,000 years that our species has been drawing, for some keen soul to realize that a diagonal could also create the illusion of depth on a two-dimensional surface. That must have been a great day. That guy must have been drawing diagonals for everybody showing off his new trick. The earliest really convincing examples I know of come from Pompeii and date back about 2,000 years.

We could draw the front face of the table, its width, and height, using two more or less horizontal and vertical lines—nothing new here. This could be Egyptian. But, once we draw its depth with diagonals, and then add the rear horizontal and verticals, we get a palpable illusion.

Being able to do this amounted to a major advance in drawing's history. And we see it put to work in the Song dynasty *Court Ladies Preparing Silk*. From left to right we note the diagonals of the long white piece of silk. Then, the diagonals of the stool the central woman's sitting on, then in the green mat on the floor and finally, the diagonals of the box between the women on the right. We find the same thing in our *Two Lovers*. The small table among the still life objects in the foreground and the side plane of the dais are constructed much the same way as the Pompeian table. And Holbein is using a similar convention to draw the footstool we looked at earlier. Though, here, the diagonals are no longer parallel, they converge toward a point beyond it. And this as we'll soon learn, is at the heart of linear perspective. The window and ornate doorway on the right are constructed using diagonals that converge toward a point too.

Eakins uses multiple converging diagonals to help him understand the receding planar surface of the river. And the diagonals need not be linear or obvious. In the Rembrandt, they're soft and gestural. Yet, these implied diagonals serve to create the illusion of depth in the landscape.

Though the feel of the Rembrandt's different than the feel of the Lopez Garcia, the use of diagonals to construct the depth of space is remarkably similar.

Removing diagonals can reveal how important they are. Here's one of my student's drawings of our library's staircase, very good sensation of depth of space—dramatic, even.

Here's what happens if we crop to a section of the staircase with no diagonals. Pretty flat, huh? As we've noted, not all shapes read as strictly flat, especially those that contain diagonals. Because diagonals can pitch us back into space. We've referred to these kinds of shapes as foreshortened shapes. A triangle, well, can simply be a triangle. Flat as the piece of paper it's drawn on. Or, that same triangle could read as the top plane of a prism receding in space, or a road receding miles back to the horizon.

Trapezoids, essentially truncated triangles, function the same way. There's one representing the small tabletop in the foreground in our Punjab Hills drawing, though this one expands in scale as it recedes in space. And the

Lopez Garcia is constructed of four large trapezoids defining the walls, floor, and ceiling of the room—a very common compositional device.

Parallelograms can function similarly. In *Court Ladies*, both the white piece of silk and green carpet pivot back in space. And, there are a number of shapes in the Van Gogh, which are related to trapezoids and parallelograms.

Triangles, trapezoids, and parallelograms are all angular. The ellipse is a curvilinear shape that acts similarly. In *Court Ladies*, the fire pit's elliptical.

In Zhao Mengfu's *Twin Pines, Level Distance*, the rocks in the foreground and the receding hills are all constructed using foreshortened shapes to create a planar structure suggesting volumetric form. And in the *Two Lovers*, there are multiple ellipses indicating the object's spatial orientation.

As we discussed at length in an earlier lecture, cross contour can be instrumental in creating a sense of three-dimensionality turning shape into volume. We also noted how artists, in a single line section, move from contour to cross contour and vice versa. The cross contour describes the 3D character of a form. And as we see in the official's robe, these kinds of lines can be organized to overlap one another—another example of compounded spatial signals.

We'll speak at length about value later in the course. For the purposes of this discussion, it's important to mention several ways values affects our understanding of space and volume.

First, the shift from light to dark describes three-dimensional form. One of the ways we know an object has volume is because of the way light plays on its surface. If there's no light, if it's pitch black, we don't see anything, there's no 3D form. With a little light, we begin to see a modest amount of form. But a strong directional light gives the best evidence of volumetric structure. The planes of an object turned toward the light will appear lighter. Those turned away, darker. The shift from light to dark is evidence of the underlying planar shift. The planar shift means volume.

This is referred to as *chiaroscuro*, it's Italian. "Chiaro," from the same Latin root as our word "clear", means light, "oscuro" means "dark," like our word "obscure". So, we can use varying degrees of light and dark, or *chiaroscuro*, to simulate the passage of light over form and create volume.

In drawing, we speak about two kinds of shadow–object shadow and cast shadow. Object shadow, as the name implies, refers to the shadow on the part of an object that's turned away from the light. We've just seen how object shadow reveals form. But cast shadows can reveal form, too. They describe the planar structure of the surface they fall on.

Here, in Norman Lundin's drawing, the object shadow on the left side of the arms, the breast and the rib cage and abdomen create the sensation of volume across the figure's horizontal axis. The vertical passage of the object shadow acts like a cross contour to reveal the volumetric shifts along that axis.

The cast shadows similarly inform our sensation of volume. The shadow of the left arm falling over the pelvis and abdomen reveal their undulating form. And the large shadow of the wall and windows reveal the contrasting flatness of the blackboard.

Another way that value affects our perception of depth is through what we term atmospheric or aerial perspective. It's what we experience when we see a distant mountain or building. The distant object looks less clear than when we're close-up. The darks get lighter and many of the bright lights, dimmer. It appears to fade into the atmosphere. Another way of saying this is that the value contrasts diminish. And this is accompanied by changes in the way edges appear. Up-close they're clear and precise, but from a distance, fuzzier.

It's one of the major guiding principles in the spatial recession in this 13th-century ink painting by Xia Gui. The landscape elements in the lower horizontal half have the highest contrast and darkest values. This diminishes in the upper right quadrant. And the most distant craggy peaks in the upper left appear as a whisper. Monet applies the same principle in his view of *Rouen*. We have the highest contrast in the boat and its reflection in the left foreground. Our next highest contrasts are in the midground. Right and left, we have a building, trees, and reflections. Moving back to the central buildings—that would be Rouen—the contrasts diminish. Receding to the hills and clouds behind them, the contrasts fade further. The final strip of gray clouds close to the top of the image gains in contrast relative to the lower clouds. Why? Because these are moving forward in space relative to those close to the horizon.

The basic principle could be summed up like this. Greater contrast and clearer edges equals forward in space. Less contrast and less well-defined edges equals farther away. The use of atmospheric perspective not only gives us space, but can also create the illusion of airiness or atmosphere on the page.

In this portrait, Ingres is using the same principle and applying it to line. He modulates the architectural events behind the figure so they fade back into an atmospheric depth. The lines get progressively lighter and thinner.

He accompanies this with a compositional use of value, striking his highest value contrast in and around the head, and next around the hand grasping the elaborate hat.

As we noted in an earlier lecture, Picasso, a great admirer of Ingres, uses a similar principle in his portrait of Apollinaire. He's also combining a compositional use of value to create focal areas in the head and forward hand. He uses diminishing line weights and discontinuous line in the far hand, shelf, and the objects and wall to push these into greater depth and deprive them of focus.

Artists will even use this same idea in a single head to make us feel that the eyes, nose, and front plane of the head are closer and the ears and hair toward the rear of the skull are farther away. While this isn't applied uniformly in this portrait by Ann Gale, I think you'll see what I mean. Do you see how the top plane of the head fades back into the distance just like Xia Gui's craggy cliffs?

This is what Norman Lundin had to say on the subject in an interview I did with him that was published in a catalog on his work:

When I compose, I consciously relate the rectilinear aspects of the imagery to the edges of the painting. But I'm interested in breathable air. So, I use geometric relationships in combination with atmospheric perspective.

Atmospheric perspective can give us that very sense of air.

The next principle's related. It concerns the amount of detail we're able to see at any given depth. Clearly, we see more detail close-up and less as something recedes from our sight.

If someone's close enough we can read what's on their t-shirt. If they're farther away, we still may be able to tell there's something on the t-shirt, but we may not be able to tell whether it's text or an image. Farther away yet, and we won't be able to tell if there's anything on the t-shirt. And, at yet a further remove, we wouldn't be able to tell what the person was wearing.

This principle's on display in Zhao Mengfu's landscape, the events in the foreground have the greatest detail, less in the midground, and least in the hills in the distance.

In the Holbein, the figure in the foreground is highly detailed, two figures in the backroom considerably less so. And if we look at the Eakins watercolor, we find the same thing.

We can tell just what Biglin's wearing. We see the play of light on his body and understand its planar structure. He's three-dimensional. We can even see his reflection. Compare that with the long scull in the distance. While we can count the number of people in the boat, we can't tell much more than that. They're specks without dimension.

Our next factor is color. We'll discuss this in much greater depth later in the course. Here, suffice it to say that distance affects color similarly to the way it affects value. We think of color as having three attributes. The first is hue. That refers to the color's blueness, yellowness, or redness. The second, saturation or intensity–referring to the color's level of purity versus neutrality. The last is the color's value. And this refers to its lightness or darkness.

Look at the water in the foreground of the Eakins and note the saturations. Now, compare with the saturation of the water in the areas behind Biglin's scull extending to the horizon. The difference is marked—much more saturated in the front, much more neutral as we recede. Unsurprisingly, this is accompanied by a shift in value contrast as well—more contrast in the foreground, less as we recede.

If we compare Biglin in his scull with the figures and scull in the distance, we find the same thing. And in the sky, we get the color version of what we saw in the Monet. At the horizon, the sky is at its most neutral, as we move higher in the page Eakins creates the illusion that the sky is moving forward toward the picture plane by increasing the saturation of the blue.

We could sum this up as follows: More saturated equals closer; less saturated equals farther away.

A second effect regards the type of color concerned. One way in which we categorize color is as either warm or cool. Warm colors are those associated with fire–yellow, orange, and red.

The cool colors are those associated with nature, water, sky and the like–green, blue, and violet–like most of the palette in the Homer watercolor.

The principle here goes like this, all being equal, warm will tend to advance and cool recede. But there's a caveat here. Greater saturation will generally trump the effect of warm advancing and cool receding. In other words, a saturated blue bowl, a saturated cool, will easily advance against the warm that's neutral enough. Say, a neutral orange, or beige, wall and table. And, high value contrast can often override high saturation, too. It's important to remember these aren't rules, they're principles.

Our final consideration has to do with subject matter. Here's a black circle on a page. We can imagine it located on the surface of the page. And we can equally imagine it in the depth of space of the page.

Swap a planet of the same size for the circle and the space becomes palpable—miles and miles, could be hundreds of thousands, like from the Earth to the Moon. Swap a marble for the planet. While it's still floating in the interior space of the page, we could grab it, it's at arm's length. Finally, swap the marble for a penny and most people will read the penny as sitting on the surface of the page.

Let's return to the Homer. Note the figures in the boat. Without the figures, we'd feel space, no doubt. There're many factors working to foster that illusion. But absent the figures, well, the boat could be a 20-footer or a 120-footer. So the space is less measurable without something that has a more or less recognizable measure.

Let's recap our 12 factors. They include: overlap; diminishing size; position along the page's vertical axis; position relative to the format's edges; diagonals creating spatial depth; foreshortened shapes; cross contour; value, light, and shadow; value and atmospheric perspective; level of detail; color and atmospheric perspective; finally, subject matter of recognizable size.

Using what you've now learned about proportion and space you're ready to take on some pretty complex drawing problems.

Six Complex Drawing Projects
Lecture 14

Thus far in the course, we've seen how line can make shape; how basic shapes, along with construction lines, can be used to construct objects; and how oblique shapes and cross-contour can turn flat shapes into three-dimensional volumes. We've also learned about composition. We've seen how we can create strong structures for drawings by relating the negatives to the positives and by relating large aggregate shapes to the even larger ground shapes that create the shape of the drawing itself. In addition, we've seen how artists relate what they draw to the armature of the format shape. We've learned how to use gestural line to do the work of contour, cross-contour, and construction line. We've also explored 12 methods for arriving at accurate proportions and learned another 12 principles that can be applied to create the illusion of volume and space on a two-dimensional surface. In this lecture, we'll take on some challenging drawing projects to begin to synthesize this knowledge.

Drawing Projects
To make the concepts and techniques we've discussed so far your own, in this lecture, you'll apply what you've learned to a number of intriguing and increasingly complex drawing projects: a still life of boxes, a still life of books, a translation of a complex figure painting, a complex interior with a staircase, a figure in an interior, and a self-portrait in an interior. As you work through these projects, ask yourself the following self-critique questions:

- Is the format shape defined?

- Are the ground shapes defined?

- Is there a large aggregate shape that makes sense in the format?

- Are the large positive and negative shapes well-organized?

- Are you composing well? Are you relating what you're drawing to the format's armature?

- Do all the planes read convincingly in space?

- Are you using line weight spatially? Are you able to use line weight to make some things appear nearer and others farther away?

- Are you using line weight compositionally? Are you able to use line weight to create zones of greater and lesser focus?

- Does the object or figure read convincingly in relation to the ground?

- Are the proportions accurate?

- Is the whole drawing activated? Are there dead areas?

Proportions

In each of these projects, you'll be working to arrive at accurate proportions. If something is eluding you, apply the tools we've learned to see if you can find a solution:

- Centerline

- Building-block shape

- Large ground shapes

- Aggregate shape

- Eyeballing

- Negative shape

- The gridded picture plane

- The clock-hand method of determining angles

- A standard unit of measure

- Level lines and plumb lines

- The technique of sighting the half.

Common Spatial Problems

Beyond proportion, much of the challenge in these drawing projects is related to creating a believable sensation of three-dimensional space. Again, recall the 12 principles we've discussed related to spatial illusion:

- Overlap

- Diminishing size

- Position along the page's vertical axis

- Position relative to the format's edges

- Diagonals creating spatial depth

- Foreshortened shapes (flat shapes that allude to planar structures)

- Cross-contours

- Value (light)

- Value (aerial perspective)

- Amount of detail

- Color (aerial perspective)

- Subject matter of recognizable size.

Pitfalls in Drawing Naturalistic Space

There are a number of pitfalls to avoid when trying to draw naturalistic space. The first has to do with carefully positioning your subject in the format's shape. Many beginning students position the subject or some part of it so that it lines up with an edge of the format. The result is generally a flattened image. To avoid this, think compositionally. Use large aggregate shapes to position your subject at the outset and work from the general to the specific. This way, you'll be able to control the locations of all the major components relative to the drawing's shape.

Another common problem is drawing what we know, not what we see. Our preconceived shape ideas of most things are limited and differ from how the shapes appear from a specific and often oblique point of view. Thus, it's a common error to draw the top planes of objects, such as tables and beds, too large; we know that these are relatively expansive surfaces, but from many common points of view, they can shrink to an oblique sliver. The way to avoid this is to use a standard unit of measure to gauge the vertical distance from the front edge to the rear and the clock-hand tool to gauge the diagonals of these kinds of planes.

Another common problem involves inaccurate diagonals and even diagonals going in the wrong direction. Again, using the clock-hand tool can help, as can looking out through the gridded viewfinder. This allows you to check the diagonal in reference to the horizontals and verticals of the grid. If something still eludes you, remember Leonardo's advice about tracing on a piece of glass, or do a phantom trace in the air. You could even take a picture of the problematic angle and trace over it with your finger on the screen.

There's a similar problem with flattening objects by drawing their curvilinear cross-contours as horizontals. This applies to everything from the curving top of a bowl to stripes on a shirt curving around an abdomen. It also applies to facial features, such as lips, that naturally follow the curving plane of the head. When drawing your own features, close one eye, look in the mirror, and trace over the curve with a pencil or your finger. Do this several times to get a good feel for the form.

Line weights are also crucial. Many beginners don't pay attention to the actual lines they're drawing—how light or dark or how thick or thin the lines are. And they don't pay attention to how lines relate to one another on the page. Take a look at your drawing and ask yourself which line or lines grab your attention. Which ones advance in space and which ones recede? Just look at the lines themselves, abstractly. Then, ask yourself which lines should be creating focal points and focal areas and which ones should be advancing and receding. Edit your drawing accordingly.

In addition to line weights, also pay attention to line overlaps. A line attached to something in the background that overlaps something in the foreground will confuse the spatial reading.

A last and common problem is something we might consider as the opposite of overlap. This occurs when something in one spatial location—something in the foreground, for instance—lines up with something in another spatial zone, such as the background. This can flatten the space in a drawing.

Suggested Reading

Review as needed Suggested Readings for Lectures 5 through 14.

Six Complex Drawing Projects
Lecture 14—Transcript

You're now acquainted with many of the basic concepts related to drawing's formal language. And you've learned about many of the essential techniques we use to draw a wide range of subjects. By taking on some challenging drawing projects, you'll begin to synthesize what you've learned.

Before we move ahead, I want to review the major topics we've covered. We've seen how line can make shape; how basic shapes, along with construction lines, can be used to construct many of the things we want to draw; and how oblique shape and cross contour can turn flat shapes into three-dimensional volumes. We've learned a lot about composition. We've seen how we can create strong structures for our drawings by relating the negatives to the positives; and by relating large aggregate shapes to the even larger ground shapes that create the shape of the drawing itself. In addition, we've seen how artists relate what they draw to the armature of the format shape.

We've learned how we can use gestural line to do the work of contour, cross contour, and construction line. And we've seen how this can really help us move through compositional ideas at an accelerated pace. We've learned about 12 different methods for arriving at accurate proportions. And we've learned about another 12 principles that we can apply to creating the illusion of volume and space on a two-dimensional surface.

In earlier lectures, we drew a deep room and a box. In many ways, these are the same form. A room is a box seen from the inside; a box, a room seen from the outside—a room turned inside-out. While drawing a room or a box may seem a minor thing, things like this eluded human beings for the overwhelming portion of our history on the planet. And, these are precisely the kinds of things that no one understood until people like Alberti, Dürer, Leonardo began figuring them out.

In fact, Leonardo's *Last Supper*—absent the figures—boils down to a box in a room, just like the example we've been looking at. And Van Gogh's *The Night Café* is a permutation on the same theme—a room with a box of sorts inside. The box we drew was sitting on a table that was pushed back against a wall. The table and wall are perpendicular planes, like the interior of a box, or like the floor and wall in Leonardo's *Last Supper*, or Van Gogh's *Café*. But close up, it would look like this. Which, at an abstract level, is like many of the artworks we've looked at, including this Eakins.

Coming to an understanding of this basic template gives you the tools to draw many diverse subjects because so many of things we want to draw involve a volumetric subject in a volumetric space. An interior, like a living room or an office, is nothing more than the inside of a box. The furniture, modified versions of blocks. A barn in a field or a car parked on a city street is just another permutation of volumetric subject in volumetric space. And, as we saw in the last lecture, a gestural landscape can share elements of box construction, too. Even the figure's routinely thought of in this way. This is a preparatory drawing for a last supper by Luca di Cambiaso. Like the Leonardo, he constructs his scene with a table in a room—a block inside a box. And the figures themselves are constructed out of smaller blocks. We'll see how useful this approach can be in the lectures on the figure, especially when drawing figures from our imagination.

But now your goal's to make the concepts and techniques we've discussed your own. Internalize them; personalize them so that they become second nature. And this takes practice, but, at this point, the practice should be fun. You'll be applying what you've learned to a number of increasingly intriguing and complex situations. The projects that follow vary. Some are technical, more like exercises to practice specific skills. Others are really about making a complete drawing—a sophisticated work of art.

The first project is a still life of boxes. This will really help cement your ability to measure complex angles. It's excellent practice for what we'll do next. You want to have at least three, and not more than five or six, boxes for the project. It's best if you have a variety of sizes.

Let some rest on their bases. Tip others up at angle. This will give you a range of problems to solve. Set the boxes on your table in front of a wall. Consider the aggregate shape in your point of view. Use your viewfinder to find a format shape and composition. Pay attention to where the edge of the table meets the wall. Ask what kind of ground division will this make.

Do three to five quick gestural compositional studies using different format shapes, then select the best one. Scale-up to the largest size that'll fit in your 18 × 24-inch paper, and follow the steps we used in the box drawing to select and scale your standard unit of measure. Freely combine the proportion tools we've studied. Checking with multiple tools is one of the best way to move toward accuracy.

Don't worry about anything written on the boxes. Getting in the proportions and the angles accurate is plenty. Here are some questions you can use to self-check your drawing: Is the format shape defined? Are the ground shapes defined? Is there a large aggregate shape that makes sense in the format? Are the large positive and negative shapes well organized? Are you composing well? Are you also relating what you're drawing to the format's armature? Do all the planes read convincingly? Are you using line weight spatially? Are you able to use line weight to make some things appear nearer and others farther away? Are you using line weight compositionally? Are you creating zones of greater and lesser focus? Do the figures—your boxes, in this case—read convincingly in relation to the ground? And of course, are the proportions accurate?

Here's a permutation on the still life of boxes: A still life of books. It's actually been a popular historical form. Type "still-life of books" into your search engine and you'll find many examples from the 17th century in the Netherlands to contemporary ones. For this drawing, follow the same steps as for the still life of boxes. Though, you could set-this-up on the floor instead of the table.

This next project's an excellent one, both for understanding composition and working with line weights. It involves translating a complex figure painting into a line drawing. The focus is on using line alone to convey the essential character of a complex visual situation. You want to translate what value and color are doing in the painting into contour and cross contour line. Select a large, good quality reproduction of a painting. Make sure it has a figure or figures located in a complex environment. Best if the figures are not cropped, and best if it's not a cast of thousands. Choose something naturalistic. Works by Botticelli, Vermeer, Velázquez, Ingres, Degas, Sargent, and Eakins all can give you good results. There are many other artists that would also work very well for this project. Here's one example based on Renoir's *The Large Bathers*. Use a good quality paper for this drawing. The 22 × 30-inch size gives you more room to work. Choose a paper with a not-too-soft a surface, it'll take erasure better.

The first step is to measure your reproduction and scale-up the format shape to the largest size possible within your 22 × 30-inch piece of paper. Do this lightly with a well-pointed 2H or 4H pencil. And do it carefully; you need to retain the relative proportions of the original. The next step is to study the composition. Imagine the painting without the figures. Note how the rectangle's divided into large ground shapes—the large constituent shapes that form the format shape. Next, I'd like you to analyze the aggregate shape or shapes of the objects or figures. Understand how they're arranged in relation to the ground.

Start your drawing by drawing the ground shapes then the aggregate shape or shapes. Do this lightly with a 2H or 4H pencil. These are all construction lines. Then you can check for proportionality and adjust. Next, you want to divide the aggregate shapes into sub-shapes to construct your figures and the environment where they're located. Again, check proportions and correct. Now, you want to begin to measure more precisely. Choose a standard unit of measure and use plumb and level lines to make sure you've located everything correctly.

If the proportions elude you, try this: Get a sheet of tracing paper and put it over your reproduction. Trace the format shape. And then with a straight edge, draw an armature or grid in the format. Lightly draw the same grid or armature on your drawing. This will let you compare placements.

Once the shapes and divisions are laid out proportionately you're ready to draw with contour and cross contour to describe specific forms. You can erase your construction lines as you go. Remember, contour makes shape, cross-counter creates the illusion of volume. Look at the woman on the left, her tricep is contour. As we move into the armpit, the line becomes a cross contour, overlapping the breast. The breast starts out as contour, but becomes cross contour as it moves back in to overlap the rib cage. The rib cage repeats this, returning to overlap the abdomen.

There are many internal cross contours as well. All contribute to the volumetric feeling of the figures. Be aware of line your qualities. Remember, lines can be thin or thick, light or dark, short or long, fragmented or continuous, slow or fast, and straight or angular or flowing. Ask what kind of line would best express the form in any part of the painting.

So use a range of pencils, and use line weight to translate the focal hierarchy in the painting. Ask yourself where you're led first, second, third, et cetera, et cetera. Also use line weight to translate the space and volume in the painting. In this example you'll note how the line weights take you to the central woman first. Specifically, to her eyes. Next we go to the two other women in the foreground. Then to the women and landscape in the mid-ground. And, finally to the depth of space. Note the way the short, light, discontinuous lines in the distant landscape create depth. This represents a combination of the scale of line and the principle of atmospheric perspective. This example embodies an excellent use of line qualities to establish compositional hierarchy and spatial depth.

Here's another challenging project: a staircase. It helps if you can find one that's structurally interesting, large, and ornate. You could try this project using a staircase in your home or office. Better yet, if there's a public building, a library, a university, or some other place you might draw where there's a grander, more intricate staircase, it would be well worth your while. Now, a staircase is like a set of blocks—one stacked on the next. And staircases sit in a volume of space bounded by walls and a banister or balustrade, kind of like a box. Some are quite dramatic; some highly ornamented. Many are comprised of complex planes that twist and turn in space.

This project will require you to: Use small compositional gesture drawings as the basis for a larger drawing; determine complex and difficult angles; measure relative widths, lengths, and heights of planes in space; use contour to create shape; use cross contour to create volume.

Let's take a look at a couple examples of my students' drawings of the staircase at the Suzzalo Library at the University of Washington. The overall goal is to create an exciting drawing, so I'd encourage you to frame from many different points of view. This will help you find a complex and compelling one that brings out spatial movement and planar change. Then do three to five compositional gesture drawings to get a sense of which point of view and which framing will produce the best result. Once you've determined the format's proportions, you'll scale-up to your larger paper and locate the scaled format shape in the center of the page.

As we've done previously, lay out the drawing in large ground and aggregate shapes: a large shape for the stairway; another for the wall; another for the balustrade. And now, at this point, check your overall proportions before moving-on to sub-shapes.

To control proportions remember to use: building-block shapes, large ground shapes, aggregate shape, eyeballing, negative shape. Determine your angles with the clock hand method. Make sure you use that standard unit of measure. And use those level lines and plumb lines.

You could also use the *velo*—the clear gridded picture plane—inserted into the viewfinder as a further check. As in the line translation of the painting, line weight has to be considered, both so that it applies to spatial illusion and to focal hierarchy.

Here're some helpful questions to use critique your own drawing: Is the format defined? Is there organization to the large positive and negative shapes? Is the drawing well-composed? Are the proportions accurate? Do the planes read convincingly in space? Are the line qualities used spatially? Are the line qualities being used to create zones of greater and lesser focus?

At this point, working with the figure is a great idea and a good next step. At the University of Washington I pose the model in a complex interior with furniture and a number of other objects. In most homes, a living room should work—a sofa, chairs, a coffee table, as well as paintings on the wall will all be interesting to draw. You'll need a family member or a friend to model for you. They can be reading a book or watching TV. Keep it simple, natural. Make sure your model's comfortable so that it's not too hard to keep still.

It's not a bad idea to use masking tape to mark their position. Put tape marks where parts of their bodies touch a surface—an arm or thigh on the sofa, feet on the floor. This way when they take a break, it'll be easier to get them back in position. You could also take a snapshot to use for the same purpose. We use nude models at school. No need for this at home. But simple dress will be easier to manage than something with extravagant folds. Now, here's the catch, when you draw the figure you may fall into a common trap. You may forget everything you've learned and practiced having to do with composition, proportion, measurement and the importance of abstract thinking.

Instead, you may start by drawing some detail. And then draw your idea of what that body part looks like rather than measuring. You may start with your idea of the nose, or a breast, or a leg. Little sense of measure, lots of figures falling off the page, all notions of composition and object/ground relations abandoned. This will throw you back to where you started.

So I'm going to direct you to draw the interior first. Start this project without the model. Decide where the model will eventually be. Ask someone to briefly sit or stand where the model will be, so you can understand how the figure's shape relates to the ground. But then proceed just as you did drawing the staircase. Gestural compositional sketches. Scaling-up. Measuring. Just drawing the environment—no figure.

Once you have the environment clearly established in proportion, invite your model into the set-up. Now you can move ahead following the same procedures you used to draw your boxes and your stairway.

I think you'll see in these examples how the figure is related to the environment and sits believably in space. The figure's approached the same way the chair or other objects approached, through measure. And that's the goal for this drawing: to create a believable interior environment—a depth of space—and then to locate and relate a figure to that environment.

After you've done this first figure drawing, try a self-portrait. The goal here is similar to the preceding drawing: to locate and relate a figure—basically, a full figure—in an interior space. But I also want you to think about a portrait as an opportunity to portray something about yourself because there's a difference between a likeness and a portrait. Just think about the word in its literary sense.

Pay particular attention to where you pose yourself. Consider how place and the surrounding objects can be expressive of personality; how place and objects portray character. Similarly, consider hairstyle, wardrobe, and stance. To activate the larger planes, it's useful to have something on the wall or on the floor. We often read these planes by the way objects sit on them. So there are formal considerations as well in how we set this up. At best, these choices serve double duty. They can function both formally and narratively.

This time, start with yourself in the environment, but I'd caution you to analyze the spatial situation in the same abstract way you would with an interior or still life. Find the large ground planes. Identify large aggregate shapes. Measure the positives and negatives. A common trap here is the face and features. When beginners get to their faces, instead of measuring, and constructing things using planes, they'll often draw childlike symbols for eyes, nose, and mouth. So think about the difference between a face and a head—head's three-dimensional.

This is a planar head. It's used to help art students understand the planar structure of the human head. You should also try tracing over your face and head with your hands. Feel the top plane, side plane, front plane, back plane. Feel the depth of the eye socket and the swell of the cheekbone. Feel the planes of the nose. Feel the planes of the lips. Try to forget you're drawing features. When drawing the head, these planes, angles, and distances should be stressed.

As in the other drawings we've done to date, the goal is to use line alone. Don't color in your eyes or hair, find a way to draw them with line. And once again, we want to be attentive to that line weight; it will assert hierarchy and space.

As before, I offer you a list of self-critique questions: Is the format defined? Does it make sense with the composition? Is the whole drawing activated? Are there dead areas? Is there a strong positive and negative shape structure? Are you composing well? Are the proportions accurate? Do the planes read convincingly in space? Are you using line weights and qualities to create space and volume? And are you using line weights and qualities to create focal areas and focal points? Does the figure read convincingly in relationship to the ground?

In each of these projects you'll be working to arrive at accurate proportions. If something's eluding you, it's a good idea to have the list of tools we've covered at hand. They include: centerline, building-block shape, large ground shapes, aggregate shape, eyeballing, negative shape, Alberti's *velo*— that gridded picture plane. We can determine angles with the clock hand method. We can measure distances with a standard unit of measure. And, we'll put those level lines and plumb lines to work. And we also have that method of sighting the half. If you apply one after the other, you'll likely find a solution to the problem facing you.

Beyond proportion, much of the challenge in these drawing projects is related to creating a believable sensation of three-dimensional space, so it's worth talking about some of the common problems and pitfalls. Again here, it's a good idea to have a list of the 12 principles related to spatial illusion. This way, when the sensation of space is not reading well, you can run the list. Ask yourself if the overlaps are clear, or if you've positioned the subject relative to the format's edges in a sensible way, or if you're taking advantage of diagonals and cross contours. Here's the full list: We have overlap, then diminishing size, position along the page's vertical axis, the subject's position relative to the format's edges, diagonals creating spatial depth, foreshortening—flat shapes that allude to planar structures, cross counter, value and light, value and aerial perspective, amount of detail, color and aerial perspective, and subject matter of a recognizable size.

A lot of the art here is in applying the principles, well, artfully. We don't need to use everything on the list in every drawing. Like in cooking we have the five taste sensations: sweet, sour, salty, savory, and bitter. Making sure that each dish has them isn't necessarily going to make delicious food. A lot of the art is in judging when to use what, and how much of it to use. But there are a number of pitfalls to avoid when trying to draw naturalistic space. The first has to do with carefully positioning your subject in the format's shape. Many beginning students will position their subject or some part of it so that it lines up with an edge of the format. The result is generally a flattened image. To avoid this, think compositionally. Use large aggregate shapes to position your subject at the outset and work from the general to the specific. This way you'll be aware, and be able to control where all the major components are located relative to the drawing's shape.

Another common problem is drawing what we know, not what we see. That's because our preconceived shape idea of most things is limited, and different from how it appears from a specific and often oblique point of view. You may do what Ugolino does in his *Last Supper*. Now, I love this painting, but it's a total spatial mash-up. The plates are seen as if we're floating in the air and looking straight down at them; the table as if we're looking down at an angle; and the small bowls as if we we're seated. It's a common error to draw the top planes of objects, like tables and beds, way too big. That's because we know they're relatively expansive surfaces. But, from many common points of view, they'll shrink to an oblique sliver.

The way to avoid this is to use your standard unit of measure to gauge the vertical amount, and the clock hand tool to gauge the diagonals of these kinds of planes. Another common, and often related problem, are inaccurate diagonals, and even diagonals going in the wrong direction. Again, using the clock hand tool can help us out here. Looking out through our gridded viewfinder can help, too, because we can check the diagonal in reference to the horizontal and verticals of the grid.

If something still eludes you, remember Leonardo's advice about tracing on a piece of glass. You can also phantom trace in the air, or even take a picture of the problematic angle and trace over it with your finger on your screen. There's no cheating, just learning. We're trying to help our eyes and brains understand what's going on out there. You use training wheels for a while, then you get rid of them—it's a process.

There's a similar problem with flattening objects by drawing their curvilinear cross contours as horizontals. This applies to everything from the curving top of a bowl, to stripes on a shirt curving around a chest, or abdomen, or rib cage. It's also applies to facial features, like lips, that naturally follow the curving plane of the head, and are not simply horizontals. So when trying to draw something like your lips, take it slowly, close one eye, look in the mirror, and phantomly trace over the curve with a pencil or your finger. Do this several times to get a good feel for the form, it will help you visualize the nature of the curve.

Line weights are also crucial. Many people when they're beginning to draw don't pay attention to the actual lines they're making. They don't pay attention to how light, or dark, or thick, or thin they are. And they don't pay attention to how they relate to other lines on the page. Take a look at your drawing and ask yourself which line or lines are saying, "Look at me, look at me". It's always obvious. Ask yourselves which ones are advancing in space and which one's receding—just the lines themselves, abstractly. Then ask yourself which lines should be creating focal points and focal areas, and which ones should be advancing or receding. And then edit your drawing accordingly.

In addition to line weights, you want to pay great attention to line overlaps. A line attached to something in the background overlapping something in the foreground will confuse the spatial reading. A last and very common problem is something we might consider as the opposite of overlap, and it can really flatten the space in a drawing. It occurs when something in one spatial location—say the foreground—lines up or hooks up with something in another spatial zone—say the background.

There are actually a couple instances of this in the Ugolino *Last Supper*.

Jesus' foot sits on a raised wooden floor. The side plane of the floor connects horizontally with the side plane of the disciples' bench, which is above and in front of it. That they connect along a horizontal causes the floor to pull up and forward, and the bench to pull back and down. When our goal is a naturalistic depiction of space, this is something we want to avoid. We'd want the diagonal edge of the bench to clearly overlap the horizontal of the raised side edge of the floor plane. We see something similar where the back edge of the bench connects with a horizontal edge on the floor, created by a change in color from a lighter to a darker earth tone. Here, either having the bench's edge overlap the change in color, or having a negative shape separate the two would solve the problem.

It's very common for this to happen when something in the background hooks up with something in the foreground causing spatial flattening. And that's just what we see in Morandi's still life, though here, it's quite intentional. The back of the table hooks on the edge of the bottle. The line of the bottle's cast shadow connects to the bases of the first two objects, then travels up the side and around the top of the second, and finally hooks up with the edge of the pitcher behind. On the right side, the back of the table attaches to the right side of the bottle. Then it loops around, pulling the negative forward. He's interested in a kind of space that only exists in drawings and paintings, a purely pictorial space. One where foreground, mid-ground, and background can open and close like an accordion.

And, as we'll see, playing with pictorial space has been one of the main threads in drawing and painting for well over a century. In the William Bailey still life he does just what I suggested you not do. You'll notice that all of his objects—all vessels which, in the real world, would be round—terminate at their bases and tops with horizontal lines. The stripes or bands on the objects are similarly horizontal. Like Morandi, he's playing spatial games with us. He insists on naturalistic proportions, and naturalistic space through his use of overlap. He confirms this in his use of value. It indicates the play of light moving over curving planes. But he compresses the objects into a bas-relief by denying them curvilinear cross contours.

So we can create or reinforce the illusion of space through the use of one or more visual signals, and simultaneously insist on flatness using other, or several other sets, of visual signals. When both depth of space and flatness are suggested simultaneously, we call this an instance of ambiguous space or equivocal space. We'll look at this more fully much later in the course. Having an understanding of this will likely change the way you see and understand much of the art that's been created since the late 19th century.

Linear Perspective: Introduction
Lecture 15

The next five lectures lay out the basics of linear perspective. We'll learn to apply many of the most important concepts and techniques related to perspective that artists have used over the centuries. Linear perspective calls on us to use our analytic abilities, and many people enjoy learning about it. But others believe that art should be all about emotion. For those people, it's important to bear in mind that even a seemingly spontaneous watercolor, such as Eakins's *John Biglin in a Single Scull*, is the result of deep thought about perspectival spatial construction. Even Vincent van Gogh, often mistakenly portrayed as running on manic genius, took great pains to learn perspective. He understood that it would free his expressive ability. In this section of the course, we'll cover many technical aspects of drawing, but the underlying ideas are all applicable to freehand sketching; they will help you understand what you're seeing much more rapidly and with greater clarity.

Defining *Perspective*

The methods we've studied—using plumb lines, units of measure, and other visual tools to create a convincing sensation of proportion and depth of space—are referred to as *empirical perspective* and *nonlinear perspective.*

Empirical perspective relies on observation, rather than a set of rules. And it works fine when drawing many things observationally. Nonlinear perspective refers to overlap and to manipulations of clarity of edge, value, or color to create the illusion of spatial depth.

Our area of study, *scientific linear perspective*, is a method of drawing that relies on geometric principles. It uses a set of rules regarding the way lines recede to vanishing points. Linear perspective enables us to create form in space and control proportions.

Linear perspective isn't new to you. You experience it every day, whether you're walking down a city street or staying at a resort hotel.

Our experience of linear perspective is generally unconscious, but it's at the heart of the way we understand and navigate our way through space. Becoming conscious of what you understand intuitively will be invaluable in helping you learn to draw.

History of Perspective
In an earlier lecture, we mentioned an Arab scholar, Ibn al-Haytham, or Alhazen, who wrote on many subjects, including optics and visual perception. His book, titled the *Book of Optics*, was translated into Latin in the late 12th or early 13th century and was later translated into other European languages. Many scholars point to this text as a foundation for the development of linear perspective in Europe.

Lorenzo Ghiberti, the Renaissance Florentine who designed the ornate doors of the Baptistery next to the Duomo, cited Alhazen frequently. And Ghiberti's sometime-colleague, sometime-competitor Filippo Brunelleschi is generally credited as being among the first to demonstrate how linear perspective worked. The knowledge then spread across Europe and, indeed, around the world and would maintain an enduring presence in art.

Terms to Know
Linear perspective depends on a fixed monocular view of the world, similar to looking through the viewfinder of a camera. The position of that one unmoving eye is called the *station point*.

The most common forms of linear perspective also assume that the single eye is looking straight ahead, parallel to a flat ground plane. This is called the *center line of sight*.

Another key concept in linear perspective is the *horizon*. That's where the sky and earth would appear to meet if the ground were perfectly flat and nothing, such as mountains or buildings, blocked the view. Note that the height of the station point, or eye level, of the person drawing is the same as the horizon. As eye level is elevated, the horizon rises and the ground plane appears to increase in area. As eye level is lowered, the horizon follows and the ground plane becomes foreshortened.

There are three basic types of perspective: *one point*, *two point*, and *three point*. The basic conceptual unit used to understand perspective is the block. In one-point perspective, we see the face of a block parallel to the picture plane, and all the horizontal edges receding away from us as diagonals would appear to meet at a single vanishing point. In two-point perspective, the faces of the block are angled away from the picture plane. The edge of the block is closest to the picture plane, and the edges of the block's planes appear to converge to two different points—one on the right and one on the left. Three-point perspective describes situations where the line of sight isn't parallel to the ground plane, that is, we're looking up or down. In addition to a right and left vanishing point, a third point placed below the object produces a sensation of looking down or a third point placed above results in the sensation of looking up.

One-Point Perspective Basics
One of the things the early developers of perspective noted was that we see different views or planes of an object depending on its height and lateral position. As an object moves along a vertical or horizontal axis, the planes we see shift.

In one-point perspective, there are three main kinds of lines. Horizontals describe width; verticals describe height; and diagonals describe depth. In Leonardo's *Last Supper*, we see this at play. Horizontals and verticals describe the front plane of the table; diagonals describe its depth. The height and width of the back wall are described by horizontals and verticals, while the depth of the room is described by diagonals.

Leonardo's painting has a mid horizon. The vanishing point is located on Jesus's right eye. If you remember, the horizon is a function of the eye level of the viewer. Pictorially, our eye is at the same height as Jesus's eye.

We see the same thing in Raphael's 16th-century *School of Athens*. Here, the horizon and vanishing point are a bit lower and coincide with the two central figures, Plato on the left and Aristotle on the right. We're looking up at them.

In both of these cases, linear perspective is used compositionally, as well as spatially. All the receding diagonals point to the main subject or subjects: Jesus in *The Last Supper* and Plato and Aristotle in *The School of Athens*.

Van Gogh uses a higher horizon in *The Night Café*, which gives us the sensation of looking down at the pool table and room. He also places the vanishing point off to the left, giving us a larger right wall and a smaller left one.

Summing Up One-Point Perspective

Let's list some of the most important factors governing one-point perspective:

- It's used to describe blocks that have one face parallel to the picture plane. To draw these kinds of objects, we use horizontals to express width, verticals for height, and diagonals converging to a vanishing point to express depth.

- In one-point perspective, all block-like objects reveal a front plane parallel to the picture plane.

- Opaque objects straddling the horizon reveal neither a top nor a bottom plane.

- Objects below the horizon reveal a top plane, and objects above the horizon, a bottom plane.

- Objects to the right of the vanishing point reveal a left side, and objects to the left of the vanishing point, a right side.

- Objects on a vertical axis straddling the vanishing point reveal no side planes.

- As planes get closer to the vanishing point, they appear more foreshortened; as they move away, they appear lengthened.

- One-point perspective looks most naturalistic when what we draw is relatively close to the vanishing point. When objects are placed too far away from the vanishing point, they begin to distort.

Suggested Reading

Norling, *Perspective Made Easy*, pp. 1–30.

Rockman, *Drawing Essentials*, pp. 140–151.

Linear Perspective: Introduction
Lecture 15—Transcript

The next five lectures lay out the basics of linear perspective. We'll cover many of the most important concepts and techniques that artists have used over the centuries. And we'll see how we can apply perspective to draw, both from observation and from our imagination.

Linear perspective calls on us to use our analytic abilities. And artists like Leonardo, Piero, Dürer, and Eakins are proof positive that honing these faculties bear fruit. Many students really enjoy perspective. Things that seemed like they'd require artistic genius, become a simple matter of knowledge and patience.

But, I've encountered some students who believed that art is all about emotion. And felt that studying perspective didn't really have a bearing on what they wanted to draw. If you list in this direction, I'd ask you to give this a chance. Because perspective's such a powerful tool.

In his book *Successful Drawing*, Andrew Loomis gives this advice, "It may be hard to see the connection between planes and vanishing points and the kind of drawing you wish to do. But there is a definite connection, for anything you draw is related to a horizon and vanishing points."

Many people looking at a fresh and seemingly spontaneous watercolor like Eakins' *Biglin in a Single Scull*, would be surprised to learn that it was arrived at through methodical study. A lot of thought was given to the perspectival spatial construction. Vincent Van Gogh, often mistakenly portrayed as running on manic genius, took great pains to learn perspective. He understood it would free his expressive ability. In an 1880 letter to his brother, Theo, he wrote, "There are laws … of perspective, which one must know in order to be able to draw well; without that knowledge, it always remains a fruitless struggle, and one never creates anything."

Loomis echoes Van Gogh, writing, "The difficulties of not knowing are always much greater than the effort of learning."

In this section we'll be getting into many technical aspects of drawing. But the underlining ideas are all applicable to freehand sketching, because you'll be able to understand what you're seeing much more rapidly and with greater clarity.

The word perspective has a number of different meanings, so let's start with a couple definitions.

The methods we just studied—using plumb lines, units of measure, and other visual tools to create a convincing sensation of proportion and depth of space—those are all referred to as empirical perspective and also as non-linear perspective. Empirical perspective relies on observation, not a set of rules. And, it works fine when drawing many things observationally. Non-linear perspective refers to overlap. And to manipulations of clarity of edge, or value, or color to create the illusion of depth of space. That would include atmospheric perspective.

What we're about to study, scientific linear perspective, is a method for drawing that relies on geometric principles. It employs a set of rules regarding the way lines recede to vanishing points.

Linear perspective enables us to create form in space and control proportions. And we can do this and draw from our imaginations. Taken together, empirical, non-linear, and linear perspective enabled artists to create images of astonishing verisimilitude. Well beyond anything human beings had been able to accomplish prior to their use.

Linear perspective isn't new to you. You experience it waiting for the subway, walking the streets of a city like Beijing, or at a seaside palm-treed resort. We experience it daily. Though, generally, unconsciously. But, it's at the heart of the way we understand and navigate our way through space. Becoming conscious of what you understand intuitively, will be invaluable in helping you learn to draw.

Though some scholars claim the Ancient Greeks knew about linear perspective, there are no extant artworks showing its use.

The Grove Dictionary of Art tells us, "The word perspective derives from the Latin *perspectiva*, which in the middle Ages came to denote the whole science of optics, including the study of the eye, reflections, and refractions." It was during the late middle Ages and the early Renaissance that the pivotal ideas began to gel.

In an earlier lecture, I mentioned the influence of an Arab scholar, Ibn al-Haytham, or Alhazen. He was born in Basra in 965, and lived most of his life in Cairo. He studied Euclid and Ptolemy, among others, and wrote on many subjects including optics and visual perception. His book, titled the *Book of Optics* was translated into Latin in the late 12th or early 13th century and was later translated into other European languages. Many scholars point to this text as a foundation for the development of linear perspective in Europe.

Lorenzo Ghiberti, the Renaissance Florentine who designed the ornate doors of the Baptistry next to the Duomo, cited Alhazen frequently. And Ghiberti's sometimes colleague, sometimes competitor, Filippo Brunelleschi, is generally credited as being among the first to demonstrate how linear perspective worked. Sometime around 1413, he made a small painting of the Florence Baptistry on a panel, using linear perspective. He drilled a hole in it at the central vanishing point's location.

To demonstrate the painting's accuracy he'd have someone stand across from the Baptistry in the doorway of the uncompleted Duomo. He'd have them hold the unpainted side of the painting with the hole to their eye. Looking through the hole they'd see the Baptistry. While they were looking at the Baptistry, he'd slide a mirror into their line of sight so his little painting of the Baptistry would be reflected replacing the actual Baptistry.

Brunelleschi would go on to design and build the monumental dome of the Duomo, a 17-year project. He was the archetypical Renaissance man, artist, architect, mathematician, and engineer. In any case, while his little painting of the Baptistry didn't survive, the illusion was apparently quite convincing. And the fallout from his demonstration radically changed the way artists would paint and draw ever after. As we've noted, before the advent of perspective, images like this were commonplace. After its discovery, images like this became much the norm

Later in the 15th century, there were a number of treatises written on linear perspective. And they contributed to the spread of these new ideas. Among the best known were those by two of Brunelleschi's Florentine contemporaries—*De pictura* by Leon Battista Alberti and *De Prospectiva pingendi* by Piero della Francesca. Later, in the early 16th century, Albrecht Dürer published his own work, *Underweysung der Messung*, also known as the *Four Books on Measurement*.

Using linear perspective, Raphael was able to properly scale his figures and construct the elaborate architecture in *The School of Athens*. And Canaletto used the same principles in his painting of the Piazza San Marco in Venice. The knowledge would spread across Europe, and indeed, across the world and maintain an enduring presence.

As we've seen, Eakins used it in the 19th century. And its use wasn't limited to highly naturalistic artists like Leonardo, Raphael, Canaletto, or Eakins. Daumier uses it in this quick gestural drawing. Van Gogh used perspective in *The Night Café*, as did the Expressionist James Ensor in works like this. Even Munch's *The Scream* depends on a vanishing point and receding diagonals.

These same 15th century ideas are found in contemporary art. Here, in this 1970s drawing by Anotonio Lopez Garcia. The use of linear perspective is ubiquitous. Many art-related professions employ it in myriad ways. It's been used routinely in comics, from their earliest days to the present.

The Simpsons' animators use it to construct, well, just about everything. Houses, rooms, furniture, you name it. Pattern on the floor in the Raphael, and on the floor in the Simpsons, same method. And video games, like Grand Theft Auto wouldn't exist without linear perspective. All these examples rest on the same core principles.

So, let's begin to learn about them.

And we'll return to one of the early pioneers of the subject, Albrecht Dürer, and his woodcut of an artist using Alberti's velo. When we looked at this earlier we noted that the artist closes one eye. The open eye remains in a fixed position. Linear perspective similarly depends on a fixed monocular view of the world. Like looking through the viewfinder of a camera. The position of that one unmoving eye even has a name. It's called the station point. The most common forms of linear perspective also assume that the single eye is looking straight ahead. Parallel to a flat ground plane. We call this the center line of sight.

All of this was new. It's in marked contrast to the world of Ugolino. Here, plates and food are seen from way above. The table from a lower vantage point, and the figures, lower yet.

Now, there's an irony here. We really don't see the way linear perspective assumes we do. We generally look out at the world with two eyes, and we're fidgety, generally in motion, and rarely looking straight ahead. So, in reality, we're often experiencing a mash-up of points of view, like in the Ugolino. I mean, even when we want to stay still it's difficult. That's why photographers need tripods. But our operating software creates the illusion that we're seeing something akin to a tidy still image.

Another key concept in linear perspective is that of the horizon. That's where the sky and earth would appear to meet if the ground were perfectly flat and nothing, like mountains or buildings, blocked the view.

In the Dürer, you'll note that the height of the station point, or eyelevel, of the person drawing is the same as the horizon. This will always be the case. As eyelevel is elevated the horizon rises and the ground plane will appear to increase in area. As eyelevel is lowered the horizon follows and the ground plane will become more foreshortened.

There are three basic types of perspective—one-point, two-point, and three-point. The basic conceptual unit that we use to understand perspective is the block. And, we'll use it here.

In one-point perspective, we'd see the face of a block parallel to the picture plane. And all the horizontal edges receding away from us as diagonals would appear to meet at a single vanishing point. Looking at the inside of a block is like looking into a room. The back wall is parallel to the picture plane and the diagonals of the side walls recede to the vanishing point.

In two-point perspective, the faces of the block are angled away from the picture plane. The edge of the block is closest to the picture plane. And the edges of the block's planes would appear to converge to two different points—one on the right, another on the left. If we're looking into a room, the walls are angled to the picture plane and the diagonals of the walls recede to two different points—right and left. And the corner of the room is located at the greatest depth.

Three-point perspective describes situations where the line of sight isn't parallel to the ground plane. Situations where we're looking up or down. In addition to a right and left vanishing point, an added point placed below the object produces a sensation of looking down, or a third point above, the sensation of looking up.

One of the things the early developers of perspective noted, was how we see different views or planes of an object depending on its height and lateral position. As an object moves along a vertical or horizontal axis, the planes we see shift.

In one-point perspective, we have three main kinds of lines. Horizontals to describe width, and verticals for height. Together they create a rectangle, a face that's parallel to the picture plane. Last are diagonals receding to a vanishing point to express depth.

To get a sense of how this works let's draw nine blocks in various locations relative to the horizon and a central vanishing point.

This is what we'll draw. We'll end up with three bocks above the horizon, three straddling the horizon, and three below. Vertically, we'll have three blocks centered on the vanishing point, three to the right, and three to the left. You'll want a range of pencils and/or mechanical pencils, and a sheet of 18×24-inch paper, your t-square, triangle, and ruler.

Turn your page in the landscape position and fix it parallel to the edges of your drawing board. We'll start by drawing a horizon line in the center of the page, nine inches from either horizontal edge. Then, a central vanishing point. I use crosshairs. It's more precise than a dot. We'll need some construction lines. I'm using a 5H pencil.

Measure three inches to the right of the vanishing point and draw a vertical construction line. Make it at least 10 inches long. We need at least five inches above and below the horizon. From this first construction line measure to the right another one-and-three-quarter inches, make a second vertical construction line, same length.

Now, one inch below the horizon, draw a long horizontal construction line across the page. Then, another one, an inch above the horizon. We're ready now to draw the front face of our first block. I'll be using a darker pencil, a B.

Look to the right of the vanishing point you'll see that your construction lines form a rectangle straddling the horizon. Draw over this rectangle with your darker pencil. This is the front face of your first block. Because of the camera angle, this looks like an elongated rectangle on your screen, but it's a true square. Now, using the 5H, half an inch to the left of the block's face, I'll add another long vertical construction line.

Back to the B. I'll line-up the top left corner of the block with the vanishing point, then draw a line back at a diagonal, stopping at the new construction line. Then, do the same thing from the lower left corner. And go over the vertical to complete the first block's exterior.

A tip here. We're using a construction line to define the depth of our blocks. In situations where you don't, you might be tempted to draw a line all the way back to the vanishing point. It's a good idea to avoid this. Get in the habit of stopping an inch or so short of it. If you touch the vanishing point, you'll make it bigger. As it gets bigger your drawing will be increasingly less accurate because you'll be drawing to different points within the vanishing point.

Let's draw a block on the left like the one on the right. Add a vertical construction line three inches to the left of the vanishing point. Then, another, one-and-three-quarter inches further left. We already have our horizontals.

So we can draw the block's face. Then, add another vertical construction line half an inch to the right of the of the block's face. And complete the block's side plane.

Let's note what we've got. For blocks to the right and left of the vanishing point that are straddling the horizon we see a front and side plane. But neither top nor bottom. To the right of the vanishing point we see a left side plane. To the left, a right side. Let's add some blocks below the horizon.

We'll start with a horizontal construction line two inches below the blocks we just drew. And another, two inches below the first. We already have verticals, so we can draw a front face for a block directly below our right and left blocks.

Let's complete the block on the lower right. Line up the upper right corner of the face with the vanishing point, and draw a line back to the construction line. Do the same on the lower left. Now, connect the diagonals with a vertical. We can estimate where a horizontal from this last point would intersect a diagonal receding to the vanishing point from the upper right corner of the face, and make a small mark. Then draw a horizontal to that point. Last, the diagonal from the upper right corner to intersect the horizontal. You get the idea. You can complete the block on the left following the same steps as on the right.

Here, below the horizon we see top planes. Let's add some blocks above the horizon. We'll need a couple more horizontal construction lines. The first, two inches above the first blocks, then another, two inches above the one we just drew. And we'll draw the front faces. One on the left. Another on the right. Let's start on the left. Line up the lower right corner of this face with the vanishing point and draw a line back to the vertical construction line. Repeat from the upper right corner. Then connect the diagonals with a vertical. Again we'll estimate where our horizontal from this last point would intersect a diagonal receding to the vanishing point from the lower left corner, and make a small mark. Then draw horizontal to that point, then a diagonal from the lower left corner toward the vanishing point to intersect the horizontal. Do the same on the right. What do we see above the horizon? A bottom plane.

Let's add three blocks in the center. Draw a vertical construction line seven-eighths of an inch to the left of the vanishing point. Add another, seven-eighths of an inch to the right. Draw the front faces.

Let's complete the block above the horizon. From the bottom corners draw diagonals receding towards the vanishing point. Then line up your straight edge with the bottom rear of the blocks on the right and left and draw horizontal connecting the diagonals. Use this same method to complete the block below the horizon.

And what do we learn here? Well, blocks located along the vanishing point's vertical axis don't reveal their side planes. And a block that straddles the horizon and vanishing point will appear as a flat rectangle. Let's up the complexity. We'll imagine that these blocks are transparent—made of glass—and we'll draw their interiors. It'll help to control the illusion, if you use a thinner, lighter line for this. I'm going to use an H pencil.

Let's start below the horizon with the block on the right. We'll draw a diagonal back from the lower right corner toward the vanishing point in the box's interior. We'll intersect this with a horizontal line starting at the left rear corner and moving to the right. Last, from this point of intersection we'll draw a vertical to the top rear right corner.

Let's do the same thing above the horizon on the left. From the upper left corner, draw a diagonal back toward the vanishing point. Intersect this with a horizontal from the rear, upper right corner of the block. Where these two intersect, we'll draw a vertical down to the rear lower left corner of the block.

Worth noting here that if we draw transparent blocks, we'll see all six planes of each block in each location.Try the rest on your own. Remember, if you get stuck, we're only using three kinds of lines. Horizontals for width, verticals for height, and diagonals receding to the vanishing point, to express depth.

Once you've constructed all nine transparent blocks, we can take this another step. We'll put a smaller block inside each of the transparent blocks we just drew.

Like the table in the room in Leonardo's *Last Supper*, or the tables, bar and pool table in Van Gogh's *The Night Café*. Though, I should point out that some of his objects are in two-point perspective. But the idea's the same. In terms of drawing, a room's just a transparent block. A block turned inside-out. And many of the objects we draw are just modified blocks of one kind or another.

By drawing blocks inside of blocks we're getting the tools we'll need to draw all manner of subjects.

We'll need some additional construction lines. We'll begin below the horizon by drawing a long horizontal a quarter of an inch above the bottom horizontal of these lower blocks. And we'll draw another an inch above this. Let's start in the interior of the center block. Along the first horizontal we just drew, measure in a half an inch from the receding diagonal on the left and make a mark. Do the same on the right. Extend long verticals up the page from these points. Use these new construction lines to draw the rectangular front face of a small block inside the larger bottom transparent block. Repeat this procedure to draw a similar rectangle in the blocks to the right and left.

Now we'll need another construction line to define the depth of these new blocks. We'll draw a horizontal quarter of an inch above the rectangles for this purpose. We'll draw lines from the top corner of the blocks towards the vanishing point and reiterate the connecting horizontal with a darker line. To complete the right and left blocks we'll draw a vertical down from the last intersection and meet this with a diagonal from the inner bottom corner aimed at the vanishing point. Let's move to the blocks above the horizon.

First, we'll draw a new construction line a quarter inch below the front bottom edge of the block. And another, one inch above this. Use these construction lines to draw the front faces of the three small blocks above the horizon. Return to the small block below the horizon on the left. Project the rear vertical up as a construction line through the blocks above. Do the same on the right.

Now, let's return to the small block above the horizon on the left and draw diagonals from the right corners to intersect this new construction line. Then, reiterate the vertical connecting them with your darker line. From the bottom intersection draw a horizontal to the left to intersect with a diagonal from the lower left corner aimed at the vanishing point. Then repeat this on the right. Project the depth from the right to the center to complete that block.

Moving to the center row we'll need a horizontal construction line to define the bottom edge of the small blocks. The plane they'll sit on is very foreshortened. So we'll place this ½ , of an inch above the bottom edge of the larger blocks. Draw another horizontal an inch above this. Then use your construction lines to draw the blocks. All three straddle the horizon. The center block will appear as a flat rectangle and on both right and left we'll only see a front and side plane.

You could take this a couple steps further. You could draw the interiors of the small blocks. You could also create separate variations on this drawing by moving the horizon up or down and moving the vanishing point left and right. But now, let's look at some artists' works in relation to what we just drew.

As we've noted, Leonardo's *Last Supper* is essentially a box in a box. We have our same three primary directions. Horizontals describe width, verticals height, and diagonals recede to the vanishing point to create depth. We can see the landscape out the window. We have a mid-horizon. The central vanishing point's located on Jesus's right eye. If you remember, the horizon is a function of eyelevel of the viewer. Pictorially, our eye is at Jesus' eye height.

Horizontals and verticals construct the front plane of the table parallel to the picture plane. Diagonals converge to the same vanishing point, describing the tabletop moving back into space. We see the same thing in Raphael's 16th century *School of Athens*. Here the horizon and central vanishing point are a bit lower and coincide with our two central figures. Plato on the left and Aristotle on the right. We're looking up at them.

Fast forward to the 18th century and Canaletto's having a bit of fun with this. The buildings on the right vanish to a point on the right, right of center. The buildings on the left, to a point left of center. And the pattern on the central pavement to a point in between. There are a couple other vanishing points as well. Goes to show that, if you know what you're doing, you can bend the rules quite a bit and still come out with a naturalistic result.

In each of these cases, linear perspective is being used compositionally as well as spatially. All those receding diagonals are serving to point to our main subject or subjects. In the *Last Supper*, Jesus, in *The School of Athens*, Plato and Aristotle, and in the Canaletto, the main points all point to the façade of Saint Mark's Cathedral. In the 19th century Eakins we have much the same thing, though with a somewhat higher horizon.

In all the above, the point of view is most like the central box-in-a-box we just drew.

Van Gogh gives us a higher horizon in *The Night Café*. This gives us the sensation of looking down at the pool table and room. Van Gogh also placed the vanishing point off to the left. This gives us a larger right wall and a smaller left one. This spatial situation relates to the lower-right block-in-a-block we drew.

Ensor's crowd also vanishes to a point a bit left of center and almost coincident with the top of the format itself. And Munch's bridge vanishes on the visible horizon, to a point we see all the way on the format's left edge. We can find Daumier's vanishing point and horizon by projecting the receding diagonals of the table in the front to the point where they'd meet off to the left. Lopez Garcia locates his vanishing point off-center, to the right. And he's also playing a game or two, curving what would normally be drawn as horizontal lines expressing the tiles' widths.

The Simpsons still is like the Leonardo, Raphael, Canaletto, or Lopez-Garcia. The bookcases are like side walls. In the Raphael, Canaletto, and Lopez Garcia we get a pattern on the floor tied to a grid pattern. We get the same in the Leonardo and Simpson's still, though in these two, the gridded pattern is on the ceiling.

To finish up, let's sum up the most important things we've learned about one point perspective. First, it's used to describe blocks that have one face parallel to the picture plane. To draw these kinds of objects we use horizontals to express width, verticals for height, and diagonals converging to a vanishing point to express depth.

In one-point perspective all block-like objects will reveal a front plane parallel to the picture plane. Opaque objects straddling the horizon will reveal neither a top nor a bottom plane. Objects below the horizon will reveal a top plane. Objects above the horizon, a bottom plane. Objects to the right of the vanishing point, a left side. Objects to the left of the vanishing point, a right side. Objects on a vertical axis straddling the vanishing point will reveal no side planes. As planes get closer to the vanishing point they'll appear more foreshortened. As they move away, the inverse.

I should note, there are limitations to the system in this regard. You'll remember in an earlier lecture we saw how reflected light rays converge toward the eye. In linear perspective, we conceive of infinite rays converging in the form of a three-dimensional cone, and it's called the cone of vision.

If you hold your arms out to the sides and look straight ahead you'll likely be able to make out your hands in your peripheral vision. That would indicate a cone of about 180 degrees, ninety degrees on either side of your centerline of sight. In linear perspective, if we want to avoid distortion, we're limited to a much smaller cone of vision. Most texts advise a cone of not more than 45–60 degrees. Practically, what this means is that when objects are placed too far away from the vanishing point they'll begin to distort.

In this example, extending forward from the back of the room, all the planes look pretty good. But, as we move forward in space, farther away from the vanishing point, we get some distortion. The tiles closest to us on all the planes appear to bend.

So, one-point perspective looks most naturalistic when what we draw is relatively close to the vanishing point. That's not to say that warping or distortion can't be visually interesting in a work of art. But you want to be aware of the fact. To get a sense of how this plays out you could add more blocks to the drawing we just did. Some on the far left or right, and some high or low in the page.

Linear Perspective: The Quad
Lecture 16

Now that we have a general understanding of one-point perspective, we'll use it to create a solid, believable, and complex architectural landscape—a drawing of two buildings on a ground plane. Then, we'll move inside the buildings and draw furniture in the interiors. You'll also have the opportunity to take what you've learned and add other things to the drawing, such as a kitchen, a bedroom, even a ping-pong table or a swimming pool. Once you get a good grasp on using one-point perspective, you can create all kinds of things out of your imagination.

Pointers for the Quad Exercise

In any complex perspective drawing, there are a number of points to keep in mind. For example, it's common to generate many construction lines that won't be included in the finished drawing. Part of the craft involves managing all these lines so that the drawing doesn't turn into a jumble. Keep the construction lines light and thin.

Keep in mind, too, that small inaccuracies in measurements become exponentially problematic as these kinds of drawings unfold. Take your time with the drawing. If something doesn't line up, erase and redraw. Doing so will save you time in the long run.

Finally, you need to learn to manage your graphite, which can easily get picked up on the sides of your hands, your T-square, or other tools. Check periodically, and if anything is getting dirty, give it a quick wash and dry.

The Quad

Our subject for this drawing is two similar buildings separated by a rectangular open space. As we proceed with the first building, you'll note that its front face is made of two simple shapes: a rectangle and a triangle. The building itself is made of two simple volumes: a block for the base and a prism for the roof. We will construct all this starting with line, turning line into shape and shape into volume. Although our goal may be to draw things that feel convincingly real, we make those things out of abstract elements: lines and shapes. We can't actually make a building. All we can draw are lines.

After you've completed the first building, you may want to pause the lecture and work through the construction of the second on your own, following the same steps. Working through those steps repeatedly will allow them to become second nature to you. For your reference, here's what the exteriors of the two buildings should look like:

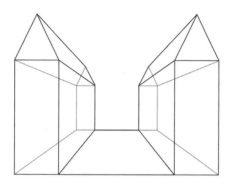

Once we've completed the exteriors, we'll add three equally spaced floors above the ground floor of each building and windows in the long foreshortened and receding planes facing the quadrangle. We'll then go inside the buildings and begin to construct some furniture. By the end of the lecture, your buildings should look like this:

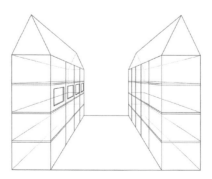

Auvil, *Perspective Drawing*.

Montague, *Basic Perspective Drawing*.

Linear Perspectives: The Quad
Lecture 16—Transcript

Now that we have a understanding of one-point perspective, we'll use it to create a solid, believable, and complex drawing of two buildings. This is a project I've based on one that a friend of mine, Jeffery Cote De Luna—an artist and professor at Dominican University—told me about.

We'll need a clean sheet of 18 × 24-inch white drawing paper; make sure the edges of the paper are parallel to the edges of the drawing board. We'll be using the T-squares, triangles, and straight edges. We'll be drawing both the exterior and the interior of the buildings. To do this, we'll need three line weights: One for the construction lines, these should be the lightest and thinnest; one for the buildings' exteriors, these will be the most robust; and a medium line weight, somewhat in between, for the interiors of the buildings.

We'll be drawing with graphite. If you use pencils, sharpen them regularly to maintain similar line thickness. Many people prefer to use mechanical pencils for this type of drawing; saves on the sharpening. If you want to go with mechanical pencils, it would be useful to have both a .3mm and .5mm. The .3mm for construction lines, and the .5mm for the drawing itself. Either way, draw construction lines with a harder lead, 2H–4H, and the main lines using HB–2H leads. You'll need your erasers; I'd suggest a pencil type, a pink pearl, and a kneaded. The last, as we've seen, is excellent for turning down the volume on a given section of line. Your drafting brush or a one to two inch chip brush and a kneaded erase will also be useful for all those erasure crumbs.

Before we get started, here are a couple tips. We'll be generating a lot of line, many construction lines that won't be part of the finished drawing. Part of the craft here is managing all of this so it doesn't turn into a jumble. Small inaccuracies in measurement become exponentially problematic as a drawing unfolds, so take time and care. If something doesn't line up, erase and redraw; it's going to save you time in the long run. We also need to manage the graphite. It's easy to pick it up on the sides of your hands, on the T-square, or your other tools; so you want to check periodically. If anything's getting dirty, give it a quick wash and a dry. There'll be a lot of step-by-step directions here. While this lecture is about 30 minutes, it can take longer than that to complete the drawing.

We'll be drawing an architectural landscape—two buildings on a ground plane. Then we'll move inside the buildings and draw furniture into the interiors. You'll also have the opportunity to take what you've learned and add other things to the drawing like a kitchen, or a bedroom, or even a ping pong table or swimming pool. Once you get the hang of it, you can create all kinds of things out of your imagination. We'll be drawing two similar buildings separated by a rectangular open space. You could conceive of it as something akin to a university's quad. Quad is, of course, short for quadrangle; literally four angles—basically a rectangular open space or courtyard surrounded or partially surrounded by one or more buildings. When you think about it, it's a lot like Canaletto's San Marco—a piazza flanked by buildings.

So let's get started. Paper in the landscape position—that's horizontal. irst, we'll make a 10-inch line 2 inches above and parallel to the bottom edge of the page. We're going to center that in the 24-inch width of the page. So you should have about seven inches on either side of that line. This will be the bottom center section of the quad—the rectangular open-space.

Next, very lightly, we'll draw a horizon line 6½ inches above and parallel to the 10-inch line. Remember, this is a diagrammatic line, so keep it light and thin. And give yourself a tiny vanishing point on this line; put it right in the center of the line at the 12-inch mark. Make it as small as possible—a single pin point or a crosshair. Vanish the two ends of your bottom line, the 10-inch line, back toward the central vanishing point. Remember, don't actually touch it; stop an inch or so away before reaching your vanishing point. If we continually touch it, it will become larger and larger—that means less precise—and that will negatively affect all of our angles.

Now, four inches above the bottom line, or six inches from the bottom of the page and parallel to both, draw a horizontal line connecting your converging diagonals. If you have some extra diagonal receding beyond this, erase what you don't need. You now have the quadrangle, represented by a trapezoid— same kind of shape as the piazza in the Canaletto, and the library floor in the Simpsons. Next, we'll draw the front face of the building on the left—a rectangle to start off. Make this 10 inches tall and 4 inches wide. Now we'll make a small light horizontal mark to note the height of the triangular roof that will extend above the rectangle—mine's four inches above.

We have our roof's height. But to draw a triangular roof, we need to locate a point centered above the rectangle at that height. Of course, we could measure with our ruler, but we want to find ways of calculating measure that don't depend on using our rulers. That's because we won't be able to use our rulers to measure into the depth of the page, into the illusionistic space of the drawing. Instead, we want to use the visual information we have to find the next piece. So how can we find this point deductively?

Let's take a detour. If I gave you a rectangle and asked you how to locate its center without measuring, I'm guessing you'd have no problem. You'd cross diagonal and say, "Voilà, center found." So, you're probably beginning to see how this applies here. Our building's bottom section is a rectangle. If you guessed that we could cross our diagonals to find the center and then extend this up vertically to the roof's height, you'd be right. And here's a point to remember: Crossing diagonals of rectangular shapes to find a center point is a common starting point to finding an answer to a problem having to do with measure in linear perspective; this will apply to trapezoids and parallelograms, too.

On another note, here's a tip on minimizing construction lines. Often we don't need to draw the whole line to get the information we need. In this case, we can just line up the straight edge with a rectangle's corners and draw two small crossing line segments near the center. Similarly, when we extend the center line up vertically, we only need position our straight edge on the center point; then draw a bit of line intersecting the horizontal associated with the roof's height. Once we have this point, we can extend diagonals from the upper corners of the rectangle to the center point to create the front face of the building's roof. We can get rid of our construction lines at this point, and brush away any erasure crumbs.

Now, let's shift to the building on the right. Using our straight edge or T-square, we can carry over a measure horizontally for the height of the building's rectangular section. Then intersect this point with a line from the bottom right corner of the trapezoid. This gives us the height of the first section of the building. We want the building on the right to be equal in width to the one on the left. Now here's a puzzle: How could we find the far right extension of our second building without measuring? Is there a way to figure this out deductively? I'm going to leave you to think about it a bit, but I'll give you a hint: It will involve intersecting diagonals.

So, let's move back to the building on the left and give it dimension. Just as we did with the blocks, we'll do this using our vanishing point. We already have the receding bottom edge of our building; it's synonymous with the receding left edge of the trapezoid of the quadrangle. We can complete the receding face of the building in two steps. First, we'll make a line from the top of the vertical representing the height of the building's base and take this back towards the vanishing point. Again, don't touch the vanishing point itself. Second, we'll extend a vertical line upward from the back corner of the quadrangle to meet the receding diagonal, and we'll erase any line segments that extend beyond their intersection.

Our next step's to complete the roof. We'll start by taking a line from the top of our triangle back toward the vanishing point. But where do we stop? We know we have to connect the back upper corner of the building's base to the roof, but to what point exactly? Now, the back face of the building is exactly the same as the front face except that it's zoomed back in space, so we should be able to apply the same set of procedures we used to construct the front to construct the back.

Think back to what we did earlier. We found the center of the bottom rectangle, then extended a vertical straight up to find the location of the center of the roof's apex. While we don't have the back rectangle or wall, we can certainly construct it. We'll draw the building as if we had x-ray vision, as if it were a building made of glass; like we drew the blocks in the last lecture. We call this drawing-through, and this is central to drawing itself. Imagining the three-dimensional form of things on a two-dimensional surface, making ourselves believe wholeheartedly in the illusion; that's part of the magic.

If you have a take on drawing the interior of the building, take it as far as you can. Find the floor, ceiling, back wall; find the center of the back wall, and all the pieces will fall into place. Once you begin to get a sense of how this works, it unfolds like the solution to a puzzle—each subsequent move naturally suggested naturally by the prior one, and it begins to be a good deal of fun. But I also know this can get confusing, so I'm going to take you through this step-by-step as well.

Let's start with that floor. The back edge of the floor is located along the same horizontal as the back edge of the quad, so we'll pull this line over into our building. And remember, we're now in the interior, so we want to modify our line weight relative to what we used on the exterior. It should be a bit lighter and/or a bit thinner, but not as light and thin as our horizon or other construction lines. To finish the floor, we'll take a line from the building's lower left corner and recede toward the vanishing point, stopping where we intersect the horizontal line representing the bottom edge of the back wall. Then, erase any extra line.

Here's a tip to make the exterior/interior illusion a bit stronger. There'll be places where the external lines overlap the internal lines; I often make the internal lines discontinuous at these junctures. If you've already drawn these as continuous lines, experiment with erasing a bit of the internal line at the point of intersection. It can often heighten the sense of overlap and depth of that space. We'll draw the ceiling following a similar set of steps.

We'll start at the back of the building at the upper right corner of the building's base, and draw a horizontal into the interior of the building. Next, we'll jump to the front to the top left corner of the building's base and draw a line receding toward the vanishing point, but we'll stop where we intersect the horizontal line we just made. We now have an interior floor and ceiling. We'll add one more line—a vertical connecting the left corners of the floor and ceiling. That will complete the interior of the base.

You now know how to find the center of the back wall intersecting diagonals. Using your straight edge, carry this measure up vertically to intersect the line representing the roof's peak, and you've found where the roof ends. Last, connect the upper left and right corners of the back of the building's base to this point and you'll have completed the basic form of the building. At this point, you might want to get rid of any unnecessary construction lines, any bits of diagonals or vertical extension lines; but make sure you leave the internal structure—the glass building view—because we're going to use it later.

There are a couple things worth noting here. The front face of the building is made of two simple shapes: a rectangle, and a triangle. The building itself is made of two simple volumes: a block for the base, and a prism for the roof. We constructed all this starting with line, turning line into shape, and then shape into volume. While a goal may be to draw things that feel convincingly real, we make it out of abstract elements—lines and shapes. We can't actually make a building, all we can draw are lines. It's like the novelist who arranges abstract elements, letters, into words and sentences on a page. And yet, we as readers come away feeling like we've experienced real three-dimensional people in actual places. So, it's time to return to the puzzle of the second building. How can we find its width? How can we predict this using diagonals? I'm sure many of you guessed right. Here's the thinking underlying the solution:

The shape formed by the interior vertical walls of the two buildings is a rectangle. The shape which will be formed by the external vertical walls will also be a rectangle, and it will be centered on the internal rectangle—you're seeing where this is going. Both rectangles will share the same center point. If I find the center of the internal rectangle by crossing diagonals, I can use that center point to construct the external rectangle. I can do this by lining up my straight edge with the upper left corner of the left building's base, and following this through the rectangle's center point to the place where it intersects an extension of my ground line. Then draw a vertical line up from that point, and then a horizontal across the top to complete the rectangular front face of my second building.

If you're working along with me, this would be a great place to pause the lecture and work through the construction of the second building on your own. Just repeat the steps we took in drawing the first building; this will help cement what we've just done. It's by doing these things repeatedly that they become second nature; instinctual; part of what becomes automatic in our seeing, thinking, and drawing. For your reference, here's what you should end up with, and then we can take it the next couple steps.

So, we've got two see-through buildings. Our next step will be to add three equally-spaced floors above the ground floor. We'll start with the building on the left and put a floor in the center of the structure. Remember to control the line weights; we're going to end up with lots of lines crossing one another. Controlling the relative weights will really help you see it all clearly. Once again, to find the center we'll use diagonals, and then draw a horizontal line. Now we'll draw the lines representing the long dimension of the floor receding into space. We'll start at both right and left sides of the horizontal, and draw lines back toward the vanishing point. We'll stop at the intersection with the vertical lines representing the back of the building. Connect the ends of the two receding diagonals to complete this part of the floor.

Now, let's add some thickness to the floor. I'm going to make it about an eighth of an inch on the front face of the building, then vanish back. We'll repeat this set of steps to create a floor below this one: Find the center, make a horizontal, vanish it back, and add the same thickness.

Now for an upper floor. Once again we'll find the center and draw a horizontal. This time we'll draw the thickness first and vanish both horizontal lines back toward the vanishing point. Then draw the underside of this plane.

You'll note, the three lower floors are seen below the horizon and we see their top planes. This last floor's above the horizon, so we see its underplane. Once you've done this, add identical floors to the building on the right.

Now we're just about ready to add windows to the receding plane of our building. But before we do, and since we're talking about space, let's do a little more work on managing line weights to make the drawing more compelling; more clearly readable. As we've seen before, the kneaded eraser will do a good job of incrementally diminishing a line's weight. We can drag it over certain lines, or sections of lines, varying the pressure to control how much graphite we remove. The twin keys are thinking spatially and hierarchically at the same time; balancing the two is where a lot of the art comes in. Thinking spatially, thinking in terms of atmospheric perspective, and applying this to line, tells us to adjust the things farthest away so they have the least contrast.

The contrast here is that of the line relative to the white of the paper. The lighter the line, the more similar to the paper, the less contrast; this equals farther away. The darker the line relative to the paper, the closer. We have to integrate this way of thinking with thinking hierarchically. The higher the contrast of line to paper, all else being equal, the more it will attract the viewer's eye; higher contrast gets more attention. Part of the question here is what should be more prominent and what less so based on spatial and hierarchical considerations? So take a look at your drawing. Ask yourself are any of the lines too prominent? Are any not prominent enough? And you can make adjustments back and forth.

Now we're ready to construct our windows. We'll create four vertical bays for windows in the long foreshortened and receding plane facing the quadrangle. And we'll make a brief detour to learn how to draw regularly repeating shapes that appear to diminish in size as they become more distant from the viewer—things like the tiles on the ground in the Raphael, or the windows in Canaletto's painting of San Marco.

Here's the basic principle; hold off drawing here. We know that we can locate the center of a rectangle by finding the intersection of the rectangle's diagonals. What really helps us in linear perspective is that this will also work in a foreshortened shape, like the side plane of our building. Crossing diagonals will yield the perspectival center of the shape. So to create four vertical bays of windows, we could draw a vertical through the center point and repeat on either side to create quarters; and voilà, four bays for windows. But there's a more sophisticated way of doing this, which will open up a range of further possibilities. Let's come back to our front view again. If we have a rectangle divided along the horizontal half and traverse it with the rectangle's diagonal, the point of intersection will similarly be the center point of the rectangle. And this will also work in foreshortened shapes like trapezoids; it will locate the perspectival center.

Now, back to the rectangle. If it were divided into four vertical sections or stripes, the rectangle's diagonal would traverse these lines at four quarters—

the half included. And this will work in perspective, too, if the trapezoid's divided into regular horizontal intervals. They're diagonals, of course, receding into a vanishing point, but they represent what would be horizontals seen face-on. So all we need to do is draw a diagonal from corner to corner, and the points of intersection will indicate where our divisions should be; and that's how you get all those receding windows in the Canaletto.

Now, let's return to our building and apply this. The side plane is already divided in quarters, so we'll draw the diagonal. In the example, I drew the diagonal all the way across, but all you need in your drawing are the bits where it traverses the floor lines. Then extend verticals through the intersections, and erase any extra construction line to reveal the four bays for windows.

It's a good idea to check your drawing at this point. Ask yourself if the four vertical bays are getting predictably smaller as they move back in space. If the third bay's the same size or larger than the second you'll want to retrace your steps. It's easy to get confused and draw the wrong diagonal; take care to extend it across the whole trapezoid. Another common error is to draw the vertical in the wrong place. We have lots of intersecting lines to choose from, it's easy to make an error.

Now some of you are probably thinking, "But what if I wanted five bays of windows or, like Canaletto, 14 bays of windows? How do I do this?" No problem, it's all about how we divide the vertical axis. It's a function of how many stripes we start out with. Four initial divisions of stripes give us four vertical columns, five divisions or five stripes would give us five bays of windows, and 14 stripes would yield 14 columns.

So let's play with this a bit. We have a second building to experiment with. In the building on the right we'll create five bays for windows. First, you'll need your ruler. We want to divide the vertical axis—that's the front vertical of the building on the right—into five equal units. It's 10 inches, so make small marks at 2-inch intervals. Lightly vanish these back, just line up the tick marks with the vanishing point to make five receding stripes. Place the straight edge on the diagonal, corner to corner over the receding plane, then make tick marks where this diagonal traverses the receding lines.

At the points of intersection, draw your verticals. Get rid of some of your construction lines and you'll have five bays or columns for windows. Again, check to make sure that each receding bay is smaller than the preceding one.

We can apply what we've learned, and further cement the idea, to draw windows of a specific size within the bays. Let's say I wanted the window itself to be centered in the bay and framed by an amount equal to one-fifth of the total height and width. Start by dividing the vertical edge of the bay into five equal measures. Next, I'll vanish my divisions back toward the vanishing point, and position my straight edge across the diagonal. Now, I could draw five vertical divisions in each bay, but all I need are two to show where each window will begin and end—front and back. So I'll make two tick marks, then two verticals. I now have the placement for my windows, and I can erase my construction lines.

Now, we'll give the windows dimension. Let's start with the window closest to us in space. You can decide for yourself what kind of thickness you want here and draw a vertical to indicate the amount. Next, we'll draw a horizontal from the window's bottom corner to intersect that vertical. Some people have a tendency to want to draw a diagonal here; make sure you stick with a horizontal. Remember, most of our lines will be horizontal, vertical, or diagonals going back to our vanishing point.

This point of intersection between the horizontal and vertical's important; it will let us carry the measure to the other windows. We'll line this point up with our vanishing point and draw a construction line forward and back across all four windows. We now know where the interior edge of the window recess is, and we can erase any extra diagonal line—we only need it where the windows will be. To get the same measure in the rest of the windows, we draw a horizontal from the corner to the receding diagonal and a vertical up from their intersection; and we'll draw a horizontal from the corner at the top of each window to intersect the vertical, then a diagonal related to the vanishing point. You can finish the remaining windows at your own speed.

But now, let's go inside the building on the right and construct some furniture. We'll put a bed on the third floor.

Well start by drawing the side view of the bed's base—a rectangle. Vanish the corners back toward our vanishing point. Then draw another horizontal and vertical to indicate the far edge of the bed. Then do a little erasing to get rid of the extra bits of diagonal going back into space, and to eliminate the line representing the intersection of the wall and the floor.

Next, we'll put a mattress on top of the base. Start with two verticals and a horizontal. Then vanish back the corners. Then draw another vertical and a horizontal. And erase back our diagonals, and we'll erase some of draw-through lines to make our bed more solid. And to begin to make things more naturalistic, we can add a blanket folded down.

That's all we have time for in this lecture; we've gotten a good start on this project. You're employing many of the basic procedures used in linear perspective. We'll learn some new techniques and take this drawing a couple more steps in the first part of the next lecture, as we continue our exploration of linear perspective.

Linear Perspective: The Gridded Room
Lecture 17

I n this lecture, we'll focus on perspectival grids. First, we'll draw one into the quad we started in the previous lecture. We'll also talk about further possibilities for that drawing. Then, we'll look at some of the ways we can use grids to measure the depth of space in a drawing.

Drawing a Receding Grid in the Quad
We'll begin this lecture by adding a grid in the open space of the quad drawing from our previous lecture. From there, we might add a path and doors.

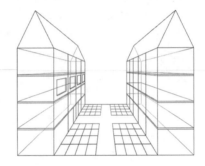

Working through the quad drawing will give you a grasp of many of the basic principles used in one-point perspective. You can make it your own by spending more time with this drawing, repeating and embroidering on the procedures we've used. For example, you can add more interior furnishings. On the exterior, you could construct volumetric doors or create windows of varying sizes, thicknesses, and types. On a grander scale, you could extend out on either side of the buildings we've constructed or extend from the buildings and quad both forward and backward in space.

Using a Grid in Perspective

For our next project, we will take the perspectival grid a bit further. If we grid all the planes in a drawing, we're able to make specific measurements in space. This can be particularly helpful in drawing from the imagination. It allows us to scale all the elements we want to draw. We can easily place a table that's 2½ feet tall, 3 feet wide, and 6 feet deep in the center of a room. We can draw a 7-foot-tall man standing on top of the table and place a 6-foot-tall woman standing 15 feet behind him. We can even draw things in specific locations in midair, such as a 2-foot cube floating 6 feet off the floor.

We've seen how we can create a grid on a receding plane, such as a wall. We used this to create bays for windows and to construct a gridded pattern in the quad. Although this method allows us to control the number of receding grid units, it doesn't allow us to control their shape.

With this method the grid units' shapes are a function of the larger trapezoid they sit in and the number of receding diagonal divisions. Having fewer divisions along the axis, or ground line, results in less-foreshortened grid units. Having more divisions results in more foreshortening.

If we want to determine the number of grid units along the ground line and want to control the shape of the grid units, we must adjust the procedure for creating the grid.

Using this new method, we estimate the first recession—the vertical height of the first row—based on the height of the horizon.

With a high horizon, we'd make the first recession taller. With a low horizon, we'd make it shorter.

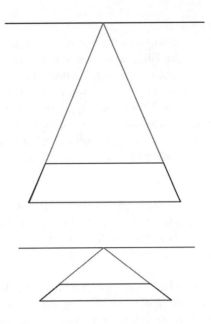

Then, we'd draw a diagonal, very light and thin, through the opposite corners of one of the bottom foreshortened squares and carry that diagonal across our receding lines.

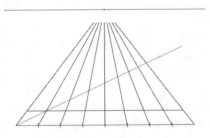

Next, we'd draw a horizontal at each of the points where this diagonal traverses those receding to the vanishing point.

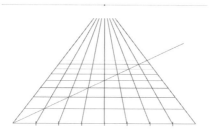

Drawing a Gridded Room

Our next project is to draw a gridded room. As we work through the drawing, keep in mind that all the lines here are construction lines. In other words, we're drawing the grid so that we can locate other things later, and we're using construction lines to create the grid itself. You'll want the horizon line and the construction lines used to generate the grid to be the lightest and thinnest. As we did in the quad drawing, keep your pencils well-sharpened to control line thickness. And take time with each step; small errors can compound, resulting in major headaches.

We'll then add basic shapes for a door, a bulletin board, a light fixture, and a box. You'll use what you've learned about perspective to make the objects feel three-dimensional and specific.

Suggested Reading

Mendelowitz, Faber, and Wakeman, *A Guide to Drawing*, "Perspective and Forms in Space," pp. 161–171.

Norling, *Perspective Made Easy*, "Dividing a Surface," pp. 144–154.

Linear Perspective: The Gridded Room
Lecture 17—Transcript

In this lecture, we'll focus on perspectival grids. First, we'll draw one into the quad we started and talk about further possibilities for that drawing. Then we'll look at some of the ways we can use grids to measure the depth of space in a drawing.

Let's return to Raphael, Canaletto, and The Simpsons animators. In all three examples, a pattern based on a grid recedes along the ground plane. We'll add one now in the open space of the quad.

We'll start by dividing the front edge, the very first line we made, into 10 one-inch increments. Next, we'll vanish these back. Try adjusting the pressure as you draw these lines—greater line weight forward, less as you recede.

Then, place your straightedge, corner-to-corner, across the quad and make tick marks where the diagonal traverses the receding lines. Then, draw a horizontal at each one and erase the tick marks. You now have a receding gridded floor plane. We can create a broad path leading back through the quad by erasing the central vanishing line and the horizontal line segments within the path. We'll create a second path, intersecting this, by erasing the center two rows—five and six. Let's draw a central door for the building on the left. Carry the vertical lines up from where the path intersects the building. And, lastly, erase the prior vertical.

You now have a grasp of many of the basic principles used in one-point perspective. You'll really make it your own by spending more time with this drawing. It's all about repeating and embroidering on the procedures we've used.

You could do a lot more with the interior furnishings. Take the bed further. Try constructing a couple pillows on top of the blanket. Or turn the block-like base of the bed into a four-legged base. You could try adding bedside tables on either side of the bed. And, put a painting on the wall. If you do, make sure to give it thickness. And, you could throw a rug on the floor under the bed. Slightly softening the hard corners of the bed, and other objects, will lend them a much more naturalistic feel.

Moving through the buildings you could construct a range of things. Desks, chairs, bookshelves, a sofa, kitchen counters, a sink, stove, a refrigerator, or a ping-pong table or swimming pool. On the exterior, you could construct volumetric doors. You could also create windows of varying sizes, thicknesses, and type. Some might be recessed and others protrude with a ledge. Others, yet, might have additional molding. You could also try drawing some benches or additional elements outside in the quad. On a grander scale, you could extend out on either side of the buildings we've constructed. And extend from the buildings and quad both forward and backward in space.

It's important to know, though, that it's possible to run into distortion as I mentioned in an earlier lecture. But, we're experimenting here. So, if you do, just take note of it. Distortion's built into the perspectival system. It kicks-in as you get farther away from the vanishing point. As we move out to the right or to the left, or above and below, things will eventually distort. Of course, some artists use perspectival distortions, fish-eye warping, and spatial ambiguity purposefully. M. C. Escher comes readily to mind. The essential factor is to be aware of the fact.

In any case, over the coming days, pay attention to all the things you see that you could use in your quad drawing—buildings, furniture, mailboxes, street lamps, utility poles, and the like. Also, pay attention to paintings, drawings, cartoons, and video games that make use of one-point perspective. They're ubiquitous. And, they'll suggest things to ignite your imagination.

You just constructed a perspectival grid. And, I'd like to take this further because grids can be very useful to us in measuring space. Here's a 10×10-inch square. Let's imagine it's a drawing of a 10×10-foot wall. I want to draw a three by four foot window in the wall. And I want to locate it five feet off the ground, and centered in the wall. No problem. I know the scale, one inch equals one foot. I measure with my ruler and draw my window. Let's also imagine I have a floor. Say, I wanted to draw a carpet centered in the floor and I want its front edge one foot from the picture plane. And, I want the carpet itself to be eight feet wide by seven deep. Well, now, I've got a problem. I can't measure into the illusionistic space of the drawing with my ruler.

Let's return to our back wall. If it had been tiled with one-foot square tiles, I wouldn't have needed the ruler. Count tiles, or grid units, and I can draw the window. And this solves the carpet problem. We can't push a ruler through the picture plane. But, we can draw a perspectival grid that will serve the same purpose—count back one tile to find the front edge of the carpet. Center an eight-unit width. Count back seven feet in depth. Draw the carpet.

If we grid all the planes, we're able to make specific measurements into space throughout the drawing. And this is very useful, particularly when we draw from our imaginations. It allows us to scale all the elements we draw. Place a table that's two-and-a-half feet tall, three feet wide and six feet deep, three feet from the picture plane in the center of the room, no problem. Draw a man, seven feet tall, standing on top of the table, again, no problem. And, if we want a woman, six feet tall, 15 feet behind him that's all doable. We can even draw things in specific locations in mid-air. Here's a two-foot cube floating six feet off the floor, it's four feet back from the picture plane and two feet from the left wall. So, this is very useful when you draw from your imagination, especially when you want to tie everything together in specific proportion and measure.

Our next project involves drawing a gridded room similar to the one in the example. You'll also draw objects in the room. Each will have a specific measure. And, each will be drawn in a precise location in space. For this to work, the grid units just can't be any kind of foreshortened rectangle. They have to look like foreshortened squares. So, we'll have to dig a little deeper into grid construction.

Before we do, let's recap what we've learned so far. We can grid a receding plane, like a wall—first we divide its vertical edge into equal units and vanish these divisions back to a vanishing point.

Then, we draw a diagonal line across a plane from one corner to its opposite. Where this diagonal traverses the receding lines, we draw verticals. This produces a grid with as many receding divisions as there'd been divisions along the wall's front edge. Four divisions along the vertical edge mean we'll get four receding units.

We found the same thing holds true for a floor plane. In the quad's ground plane, we had 10 divisions along the horizontal axis, receding into space, toward the vanishing point. We drew a diagonal construction line, corner-to-corner, traversing the plane. We noted the points of intersection and drew a horizontal at each traverse, then, erased the construction lines to reveal a proportionate diminishing grid.

While we've been controlling the number of receding grid units by controlling the number of divisions on the axis, we haven't controlled their shape. Instead, this was the result of the number of original divisions on the plane's horizontal or vertical axis. It's also a by-product of the overall shape of the plane. The floor or wall itself.

Let's compare our two examples. I've rotated the wall 90 degrees to make this clearer. Four divisions and a less-foreshortened plane clearly result in taller grid units. To isolate the effect of the number of divisions on the ground line let's use identical floor planes. Same thing, though, less pronounced. Whatever the degree of foreshortening of the original plane, fewer divisions along the axis, or ground line, will result in less-foreshortened grid units—more divisions, more foreshortening.

So, if I had 20 divisions along the ground line, the individual grid units would all be even more foreshortened.

Here's the point. I want my receding grid units to look like receding squares. If I want to determine the number of grid units along the ground line and also want to control the shape of the grid units, I'll have to adjust the procedure. To help make this clearer, let's imagine a grid—10 × 10 squares centered and paralleled to the picture plane. Now, let's add a second grid on top of the first, and lower it down to the ground plane. The diagonals of the second grid are now receding to a central vanishing point on the horizon. That equates with eyelevel. In this case the height of the center of the camera's lens. Take a look at the first row of tiles and note their height relative to the upright grid—smaller, got to be, they're foreshortened.

Now, let's raise the camera. The horizon and vanishing point move up, too. And look at the vertical height of the first row of grid units, taller than before, less foreshortened, though still less than the upright grid.

Let's take the camera lower. The first recession gets shorter—more foreshortened. As we lower eyelevel on the horizon, the grid units get smaller and smaller. More and more foreshortened.

If we cut a hole in the floor and could get the camera all the way down to the ground level, we'd see the floor and the grid compressed into a single line—it'd disappear.

And this is the key we'll use to construct a grid that feels like a square. We'll estimate the first recession, the vertical height of the first row, based on the height of the horizon—high horizon, taller, low horizon, shorter.

Let's say I'm marking off two-inch units on my horizontal axis with the goal of creating a perspectival grid of squares going back into space. A non-foreshortened square would be two by two inches. If I had a high horizon, I'd make my first recession closer to two inches, say one-and-a-half to one-and-three-quarter inches above the ground line. If I had a mid-horizon, I'd try an inch to an inch-and-a-quarter above the ground line. A lower horizon yet, and I'd go down to three-quarters or half an inch to start.

In each case, eyeball that first recession to make sure it looks like a square in a foreshortened view. And, as mentioned earlier, be alert to distortion that may occur as you move far right and far left as well as when you're projecting well forward in space. My students get good results using this intuitive method. There's a much more precise way to assess the first recession it's part of what's termed mechanical perspective. It involves drawing a plan, a view seen from above. You locate both what's being drawn and the location of the person drawing it. That's that station point. We're not going to cover this method here. But, if you're interested, you'll find this explained, step-by-step, in many books on linear perspective.

We've now gone over most of what we'll need to know to move forward with the drawing. So, take out a new sheet of 18 × 24-inch paper, fix it to your drawing board in the vertical, or portrait, position. One caution: All the lines in our gridded room are construction lines. In other words, we're drawing the grid so that we can locate other things later. But we'll also be using construction lines to generate the grid itself. So we have a couple layers of construction lines.

You'll want your horizon and the construction lines used to generate the grid to be the lightest and thinnest, say, 4H. The grid could be H or 2H. This leaves you a lot of room, from F to 10B, to draw things later. As we did in the quad drawing, keep your pencils well sharpened to control line thickness. Or, use mechanical pencils. And check your hands and tools for graphite residue. Wash and dry as needed.

We'll start out with a 16-inch horizontal line—the ground line—two inches above the bottom of the page. This will also be the bottom edge of the drawing's format shape.

Next, draw a horizon line 10 inches above the ground line. Locate a central vanishing point, or crosshairs, at the nine-inch mark on this line.

Now, we'll divide the ground line into two-inch increments. Make these marks as small as possible.

Our scale, at the picture plane, is two inches equals one foot. If the finished grid were tilted up from the ground plane so that it was pressed up against the picture plane, we'd see that each grid unit, each square, measured two by two inches. And, the only place that this true measure will reveal itself will be on the picture plane, or at the edge of the format shape—same thing, really. Take time with each step. Small errors can compound resulting in major headaches.

Now, we'll line-up these marks with the vanishing point and draw receding lines. As we did before, change pressure, meaning line weight with spatial depth. This will lend a sense of atmospheric perspective to the lines and aid in the illusion of depth. Remember, don't touch the vanishing point—keep it pristine.

You can erase any extra measure marks you have at the two-inch intervals on your ground line. And we're ready to set the first horizontal recession in our grid.

We have a midish horizon. So, we'll locate the first recession at one-and-a-quarter inches above the ground line.

Eyeball it to see if these look like foreshortened squares. I think they're pretty good.

We're ready to draw the grid. But here, our situation is different than it was in the quad. In that drawing we'd already defined our large ground plane and used the diagonal of the whole plane to locate the recessions. Here, we haven't decided where the plane ends. We'll be drawing a floor with 12 rows of tiles. But we don't know yet where the back of the 12th row will be. Let's take a little detour to figure this out. If we tilt-up the grid to an upright position, flat against the picture plane, it'll help us understand what we need to do.

If we had the first row of squares in this position, we could use our ruler to measure two-inch increments all along the vertical axis and complete the grid. But there's another way that doesn't entail measuring. Think about it for a moment, you might want to pause here.

Many of you likely got it. The solution involves drawing a diagonal through the opposite corners of one of the bottom squares, and then projecting that diagonal across the vertical lines. We note where the diagonal crosses the verticals, and draw a horizontal at each traverse to create the grid. And this will work precisely the same way in the foreshortened position. We draw a diagonal, very light and thin, through the opposite corners of one of the bottom foreshortened squares. We carry that diagonal across our receding lines. Actually, it's better not to draw the whole line. I've done it to make the example clearer. But, you can just make small marks on each receding line where the diagonal would traverse it. It saves some erasing. At each traverse, draw a horizontal. Make the lines lighter and thinner as you recede.

We're at a crucial point here. Check your grid and make sure each of the horizontals is really horizontal, not angled. Also, check to make sure that each successive row is smaller than the one preceding. When everything checks-out, you're ready to move on.

We have eight rows equaling 8 feet of depth—we want 12. So, we'll use the diagonal again to get four more receding rows. Project the diagonal across the first unit on the left of the last row, mark where this traverses the receding diagonals.

You may have noticed that our two diagonals appear as if they would intersect if they were extended. And, they would. They'd meet on the horizon at a place called the right diagonal vanishing point. If we'd drawn our diagonals from right to left, these diagonals would have terminated at a left diagonal vanishing point. All the diagonals we could draw through opposite corners of the floor's grid units would terminate at one of these points. In this drawing, they're off the page. But they can be useful for checking to make sure that everything is lining-up correctly.

In any case, we have what we need to finish this gridded plane. Draw in four more horizontals, then check for accuracy. Erase the tick marks on the receding lines as well as any receding lines beyond the final row.

Now's a good time to check your line weights. We're trying to achieve a sense of atmospheric perspective to enhance the effects of linear perspective. The lines should be getting lighter and thinner as they recede—closer, more contrast, farther away, less.

Complicating matters and due to foreshortening the lines representing the more distant tiles wind up closer together. This has the optical effect of making the overall line grouping seem darker than it would be if the lines were spaced farther apart.

You can use your kneaded eraser to great advantage to lower the volume on individual lines and groups of lines that are too dark. Pull the eraser across with a small amount of pressure to adjust the contrast. Repeat as needed.

Check everything one more time. If it looks good, this part's done.

We'll add a right wall, left wall, back wall and a ceiling. Each new plane should go more quickly because we'll be able to carry information from one plane to the next. Assuming what you've got so far is accurate.

We'll start with the right wall. From the bottom right edge of the ground line, draw an 18-inch vertical line. This will define the right edge of the format shape. This, like the ground line, is on the picture plane. This means we can use our ruler to measure here, just like we did with the ground line. Mark off two-inch increments along this vertical axis. Since we now know where the wall will end, draw a vertical to define its far edge. We can vanish, the two-inch increments back toward the vanishing point. This time we know where they should end, at the wall's back edge.

Next, we'll carry the measure of the first horizontal recession vertically up along the right wall. Line up your straight edge along the diagonal of the bottom foreshortened square, then, mark the traverse of the extended diagonal on the receding diagonals. Once again, I've used a continuous line so it's easier to see.

You can use both the horizontal recessions on the floor, and the diagonal to draw the vertically receding rows of tiles. They should agree. When you get to the eighth row, you can repeat the use of the diagonal to find the final four recessions. These two diagonals would meet directly above the central vanishing point that would be the upper vertical diagonal vanishing point. And, as you may have guessed, if we'd drawn the diagonals in the other direction, upper right to lower left, they'd have met at a point below the horizon that would be the lower vertical diagonal vanishing point.

Finish this wall and erase any extra construction line. Using your kneaded eraser, adjust the line weights. You want the wall and floor to feel the same at equal depths. If you've been conscientious, it'll get pretty easy now.

Follow the same steps to build the left wall.

As you're making your way through this, check to make sure that the left side is level with the right. Pick two points that should correspond. Use your T-square to verify that they're level. Once again, use your kneaded eraser to adjust line weights on the left. If all this is right, drawing the back wall's simply a matter of connecting horizontals from the two sidewalls, then extending verticals up from the floor.

Now, we can identify the viewer's eyelevel. We just count up the back wall to the horizon. The scene is being viewed from a height of five feet. And, adjust the line weights on the back wall.

Drawing the ceiling involves repeating what we did on the floor. This time, though, we can pull placement information from the three planes that abut, and are already completed. Using the diagonals provides another way to check that we're getting our lines in the right places. You don't actually have to draw the lines, just line up your ruler and make sure things are falling where they should. The ceiling diagonals should vanish to same point as the floor diagonals. When you've finished drawing the ceiling, check the line weights all around. At each depth of space, there should be a general correspondence. Congratulations, you've drawn a gridded room.

Now, you're ready to draw objects of specific measure in specific locations. We'll draw a door, a bulletin board, a light fixture, and a box on the ground. We'll block these in with simple shapes to mark the locations. Then, turn them into specific objects.

First, let's draw a six by three foot door in the right wall. We'll locate this at a depth of four feet from the picture plane. Where the right wall meets the floor, count back four feet. Make a small mark here, then, up six. Another mark, then back three, another mark, and down to the floor. Lightly outline the door's location.

Let's draw a bulletin board next. We'll make it three feet tall and eight feet wide. That's eight feet receding into the room. We'll put it on the left wall at a height of four feet, and a depth of two feet from the picture plane.

Start at the left edge of the ground line. Count up four feet, then two feet in. Make a mark. Now, up three feet. Make a mark. And back eight feet. Make a mark, down three. Last mark, and then you can draw the board's shape.

Next, we'll draw a light fixture that's six feet wide and two feet deep. We'll put it in the center of the ceiling. It'll straddle the sixth and seventh rows of tiles.

Last, we'll draw a box on the floor. The box is four feet tall and two feet in both other dimensions. We'll locate it at a depth of one foot from the picture plane and two feet from the left wall.

Now this is a little trickier. So, let me take you through it step-by-step. We'll need to draw a series of construction lines to understand the box's placement.

First, we'll draw its footprint—two feet by two feet. Locate this two feet from the left wall and one foot in from the picture plane.

Next, on the left wall, at a depth of one foot from the picture plane, note the box's four foot height with a vertical line.

Now, carry the height measurement over the footprint with a horizontal construction line. This locates the box's front face and you can draw it in. Then, erase all the construction lines except for the footprint.

To finish the box, draw receding lines toward the vanishing point from both top corners. Then, bring a vertical up from the footprint's rear left corner. Let this intersect the diagonal above it. This point defines the box's back edge.

Now you can draw the back edge of the top of the box. And erase the last construction lines.

You may have noted the unusual position of the right side of the box. It falls in line with the vanishing point. It means that the line defining the right edge of the top plane is not a diagonal. Even though it's receding to the vanishing point, it's a vertical. The same is true of the bottom right edge of the box. That was part of the footprint sitting on the floor. And both these lines are identical to the vertical right side of the box—all fall in line together. Generally, when artists are trying to create an unambiguous depth of space they'll avoid lining things up like this. On the other hand, many artists, especially in the west starting in the late 19th century—like Bonnard and Matisse—were interested in playing spatial games, and would embrace this kind of alignment.

This vertical is part of a larger x-y axis that straddles the room. Let's look at the central grid line, which passes through the vanishing point. First, it appears to recede from the ground line to the back wall. Then climbs up the back wall, and finally, comes forward in space, along the ceiling returning to the picture plane.

The grid line that passes horizontally through the vanishing point has a similar quality. It appears to recede into space back along the left wall. At the back of the room, it traverses the back wall, then, returns forward to the picture plane along the right wall. But, both the first and the second are nothing more that straight lines—a vertical and a horizontal making a big plus sign on the surface of the picture plane. But, they also appear to pivot into the 3D space of the drawing. That's a clear ambiguity.

Returning to our drawing, what we've done so far is to create a base for a drawing.

Here's one of my student's drawings. Though, the proportions of the room, the horizon height are slightly different, you should have something akin to this on your own drawing board. The goal now is to work into this. Embroider. Use what you've learned about perspective to give everything dimension. Make the objects feel three-dimensional and specific. Note, in this drawing, how the door, the corkboard, and the light fixture have been given thickness and dimension and projected into the space of the room. The door has a volumetric doorknob and volumetric hinges, too, built out of little cylinders. The corkboard has both internal and exterior planes. You'll also note that the objects standout from the construction lines. That's because they're handled with a stronger line weight.

Here we get some notices posted on the corkboard, a mat on the floor, and a volumetric bench.

And, here, we get a recessed door, a palpable handle, and other details. We also get a corkboard with notes posted on it, as well as an elaborate light fixture. And, even a staircase leading to a second door.

You now know how to create the illusion of depth using many of the same tools Raphael, Canaletto, and professional animators use. And you'll be able to experiment with all this to draw from your imagination.

Linear Perspective: Ellipses and Pattern
Lecture 18

Your next major project will be a complex drawing from your imagination using perspective, but before you undertake that, we'll add to our knowledge base. We'll begin with a further discussion of vanishing point placement. From there, we'll learn how to draw curvilinear forms and pattern in perspective. You'll then begin drawing an imagined room, putting together many of the ideas we've discussed, including format shape, composition, line weight, and space and volume.

Moving the Vanishing Point: The Quad

The same frontal view will produce different drawings as we position the vanishing point at varying heights and in different positions laterally. For example, this is a front-face view of the quad:

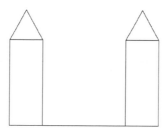

The horizon height and central vanishing point we used produced this result:

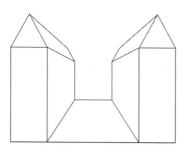

Leaving the front face but elevating the horizon gives us a different view, as does lowering the horizon or moving the vanishing point to the left or right. Thus, the vertical and lateral placement of the vanishing point is an important choice.

Curvilinear Forms in Perspective

As noted earlier, certain shapes are ambiguous. Ellipses are like trapezoids and parallelograms and fit into this ambiguous category.

An ellipse could be the shape of a mirror hanging on the wall or the shape of a serving platter seen from directly above. Both of these are flat shapes parallel to the picture plane. In contrast, an ellipse could be the shape of a car's tire or a round table seen at an angle. Both objects represent a plane receding in space.

We have many circular things around us—cups, plates, bottles, clocks, tires, coins, and so on—but we rarely see them as circles. Most of the time we see them foreshortened—as ellipses. Thus, learning to draw ellipses is useful. Here are a some points to keep in mind as you practice drawing ellipses, whatever their size, shape, or position in space:

- They fit neatly into rectangles.

- They're symmetrical along each axis.

- Their quadrants are identical.

To get started, draw four different rectangles with simple internal armatures, then draw each rectangle's ellipse. Here are some tips for this exercise:

- Make sure your lines are touching the proper points. You may find it helpful to rotate the page as you draw. That's also a good way to refresh your view and check proportions.

- Make sure to check the rounding at the end of the long axis. It shouldn't be pointy.

- Check for flattening on the long curves of each ellipse.

- Symmetricality is vital. Use the negative shapes in the rectangle as aids; they should be identical.

- If you get stuck, make a tracing of the ellipse and rotate the tracing above the original drawing. That will give you a read on symmetry.

The Foreshortened Ellipse
As we've seen, a circle fits into a square, and a flat ellipse fits into a rectangle. But an ellipse that's representing a foreshortened circle can also be thought of as fitting into a foreshortened, or perspectival, square.

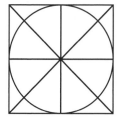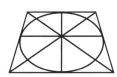

In other words, if we draw ellipses into trapezoids that represent squares in perspective, we'll produce perspectival circles. We can use the same kinds of construction lines that we used to draw a circle in a square to help us construct an ellipse in a foreshortened square.

Note that in the foreshortened view, the major axis divides the ellipse into perspectival halves—larger below and smaller above. The reason for this is that equal halves do not appear equal in a foreshortened view. The half that's closer looks larger, and the half that's farther away looks smaller.

Cylinders, Cones, and Spheres
Paul Cézanne once wrote: "Treat nature by the cylinder, the sphere, [and] the cone, everything in proper perspective so that each side of an object or a plane is directed towards a central point." Although Cézanne was a revolutionary artist, the sentiment he expressed here is traditional. He's saying that we should draw using basic geometric volumes and that we

need to relate them to a vanishing point. Following Cézanne's advice, we'll build on the ellipse to draw the basic curvilinear building blocks (the cone, cylinder, and sphere) in perspective.

Pattern and Perspective

As mentioned at the beginning of the course, our ancestors enjoyed the beauty of pattern tens of thousands of years ago. To this day, we have pattern on our clothes, on floor tiles, and on drapes and wallpaper. It's ubiquitous. With the advent of perspective, artists found that they could adapt pattern to perspectival grids, as Raphael did in the ground plane of *The School of Athens*.

© Photos.com/Thinkstock.

Beyond its aesthetic appeal, one of the reasons artists use pattern in perspective is that it acts like cross-contour. It makes planes take on spatial orientation. There are three main reasons for this:

- Pattern consists of repeating units. In perspective, these units diminish in size as they recede, giving the viewer a clear depth signal.

- Pattern placed in perspective either has or implies diagonals, which create spatial depth.

- A pattern wedded to a perspectival grid exhibits foreshortened shapes.

Patterns can range from highly repetitive and regular to extremely varied. Generating patterns becomes complex very quickly, but looking at some of the basic methods can stimulate your imagination. After generating patterns, you can also tessellate them, that is, put one patterned tile next to another. In addition, assigning value or color to a grid or pattern will bring out different groups of shapes and different object-ground relationships. Try generating some pattern studies by drawing on graph paper.

Transferring a pattern to a perspectival grid is a matter of remembering the steps you took to generate the pattern and repeating them in the foreshortened grid. Once you've created some patterns, return to your drawing of the gridded room. Look through the pattern studies you just did, and apply the best ones to the different planes of the room.

Drawing Project: A Constructed Space in One-Point Perspective
As a project for this lecture, you'll make a line drawing of a room using one-point perspective to construct a believable and measurable space. The under-drawing here will be a fully gridded room, with grid units that are foreshortened squares. The lines that structure the drawing will be of three primary types: horizontals to express width, verticals to express height, and diagonals to express depth. Of course, you could use curvilinear structures, too.

As you work on this drawing, keep in mind the topics we have discussed previously, including the importance of the format shape, of thinking compositionally, and of paying attention to line weights. Begin with some quick gestural drawings of an imagined room. Think about the major planes in the room—the back wall, floor, ceiling, and two side walls—and the rectangle they form; this will be the format shape. Then, consider your grid unit and scale, but again, work quickly and gesturally. You can work out the specifics when you scale up your drawing.

Suggested Reading

Rockman, *Drawing Essentials*, "The Illusion of Space and Depth on a Two-Dimensional Surface," pp. 51–187.

Stevens, *A Handbook of Regular Patterns*.

Linear Perspective: Ellipses and Pattern
Lecture 18—Transcript

You're headed toward your next major project: a complex drawing from your imagination using perspective. But before we get to it, let's add to our knowledge base. And we'll start with a further discussion of vanishing point placement.

We'll use the quad as an example. The same frontal view will produce very different drawings as we position the vanishing point at varying heights and in different positions laterally. This is the front face view of the quad. The horizon height and central vanishing point we used produces this result. Leaving the front face but elevating the horizon gives us this view; and lowering it, this one. Moving the vanishing point to the left gives us this; and to the right, this. Though all five of these share the identical front view, they looked markedly different. And that's all tied to the vertical and lateral placement of the vanishing point, so it's an important choice.

So far, we've drawn rectilinear forms in perspective. Let's take a look at how we can draw curvilinear forms using this system. Objects, like these tin cans with a circular end parallel to the picture plane, will appear truly circular. Here, they're shown lined up horizontally, but it would be much the same thing along a vertical axis. So circles parallel to the picture plane don't pose a problem. But a circle viewed perpendicular to the picture plane will never appear circular.

Earlier in the course you did an ellipse exercise. You filled a clear cylindrical vase with water, and drew the shape of the top plane of the water. Then you repeatedly poured off an inch or two of water, and successively drew the new shape. This exercise is designed to bring out a crucial recognition about the relationship of circles that are perpendicular to the picture plane and their relationship to eye level.

The shape of the top plane of water in a cylindrical vase is a circle. But viewed perpendicular to the picture plane, that circle will appear as an ellipse. There's one exception. You may have noted that at eye level, the ellipse was reduced to a single horizontal line. As the ellipse diverged from eye level, either up or down, it got progressively fatter the greater the distance. Below eye level, the front edge of the ellipse became more and more of a smile; above eye level, more and more of a frown. If we could have rotated the vase 90 degrees without losing the water, we'd have seen the same thing. The circle that's centered in our line of vision would look like a single vertical line, as we diverge from the center the circles would become progressively wider ellipses as their distance increased from our central line of vision.

So, let's draw some ellipses. As we saw in an earlier lecture, we can use a square and its armature to construct a circle. Ellipses are circle relatives, and we can draw an ellipse in a non-square rectangle. Cross the diagonals, then draw the horizontal and vertical center lines and, we have four points to use as guides. The ellipse's widest point should touch each side of the rectangle at its center point.

The circle and ellipse share the quality of being continuously curvilinear. But on a circle, every point on the circumference is equidistant from the center. On an ellipse, every point in each quadrant is located at a unique distance from the center. Both evidence a high degree of symmetricality; this echoes the symmetricality of the underlying rectangle. A square is vertically symmetrical, horizontally symmetrical, and its horizontal half is identical to its vertical half. The circle shares this.

A non-square rectangle is vertically symmetrical and horizontally symmetrical, but the horizontal and vertical halves are not. And ellipses share this—vertically symmetrical, horizontally symmetrical, but the vertical and horizontal halves are not equal. Though, like the underlying rectangle, and circle, and square, all quadrants are equal.

The ellipse's center lines are termed axes. They're referred to as the major or long axis, and the minor or short axis. The major and minor axes meet at a 90 degree angle in the ellipse's center. These principles govern all ellipses whatever their size, shape, or position in space. They fit neatly into rectangles, they're symmetrical along each axis, their quadrants are identical. Being aware of these attributes helps in drawing them. To get started, draw four different rectangles with simple internal armatures. Then draw each rectangle's ellipse. Here are some tips: Make sure you're touching the proper points. You may find it helpful to rotate the page as you draw. That's also a good way to refresh your view and check proportions. Make sure to check the rounding at the end of the long axis; it shouldn't be pointy. And make sure to check for flattening of the long curves of each ellipse; it should be continuously curving. Symmetricality is vital. Use the negative shapes in the rectangle as aids; they should be identical. If you get stuck, make a tracing of the ellipse and rotate the tracing above the original drawing; that'll provide a read on symmetry.

There's several mechanical ways to draw a perfect ellipse. And while they have applications in many fields, they're not practical for most of the drawing we do. But if the subject interests you, you'll find explanations in many books on perspective and online.

So far we've discussed the flat ellipse. As we noted earlier, certain shapes are ambiguous. They can appear flat, parallel to the picture plane; but they can also appear dimensional, angled to the picture plane. Ellipses, like trapezoids and parallelograms, fit into the ambiguous category. An ellipse could be the shape of a mirror hanging on the wall or the shape of a serving platter seen directly from above; both of these are flat shapes parallel to the picture plane. In contrast, it could be the shape of a car's tire or a round table seen at a angle; both objects representing a plane receding in space. We have many circular things around us—cups, plates, bottles, clocks, tires, coins et cetera—all are all measurably circular, 360 degrees. But we rarely see them as circles; most of the time we see them foreshortened as ellipses, so learning to draw ellipses is very useful.

As we've seen, a circle fits into a square, and a flat ellipse fits into a rectangle. But an ellipse that's representing a foreshortened circle can be thought of as fitting into a foreshortened or perspectival square. Here's a square with a circle and the circle's construction lines. It's presented parallel to the picture plane. Let's leave its left vertical edge where it is and rotate the right one back in space 15 degrees, then 30, then 45. Both the square, now a trapezoid; and the circle, now an ellipse, become progressively slimmer, more foreshortened. Now we'll let's go 60 degrees, then 75, and at 90 it's all reduced to a single line.

And let's try that again, but this time we'll keep the tile's bottom edge anchored to the ground and angle the top edge back. Again, 15 degrees, then 30, 45, 60, 75 degrees, and finally 90; all reduced to a single flat line. So if we draw ellipses into trapezoids that represent squares in perspective, we'll produce perspectival circles. And we can use the same kinds of construction lines that we used to draw a circle in a square to help us construct an ellipse in a foreshortened square.

So let's try this on a clean sheet of paper in the landscape position. Start with a nine inch horizontal line centered in the page and two inches from the bottom. Next, place a horizon line with a central vanishing point 12½ inches from the bottom of the page. Now, vanish the two ends of the nine inch line back toward the vanishing point. Locate the back of the trapezoid five and a half inches off the bottom of the page, then erase the extra. Cross the diagonals, and add the horizontal. Then line up the center of the tile with the vanishing point, and draw a line through the tile. Here it will be vertical because we're centered on the vanishing point. We have four points and a guide shape; use both to draw an ellipse.

It's important to note in the foreshortened view, the major axis divides the ellipse into perspectival halves—big below, small above—that's because equal halves do not appear equal in a foreshortened view. The half that's closer looks bigger; the half that's farther, smaller. So, here the quadrants will not be equal. But superimposing the flat ellipse on the perspectival circle shows they're identical. So everything we've learned about drawing a flat ellipse can be applied here, too. Interpolate the major axis of the flat ellipse and the shape should be symmetrical along each axis, and each quadrant should be identical.

In an earlier lecture, I shared part of a quote from Paul Cézanne about cylinders and spheres. The complete quote goes like this: "Treat nature by the cylinder, the sphere, and the cone, everything in proper perspective so that each side of an object or a plane is directed towards a central point."

While Cézanne was a revolutionary artist, the sentiment he's expressing here is very traditional. He's saying we should draw using basic geometric volumes and that we need to relate them, like Leonardo, to a vanishing point. If not, we'll wind up with a mash-up like in the Ugolino. Using the ellipse we've just drawn, we'll do just that. We'll draw a block; then inside; a cylinder; next a cone; then a cube; and last a sphere.

Through this exercise you'll learn how to draw basic curvilinear solids in perspective. I've included this preview because we'll be generating a lot of construction lines, so it'll be important to control your line weights as we go. Draw the construction lines with a well-sharpened 3–5H pencil or mechanical pencil, and be conscious of line weights as you draw.

Let's start with the block. Draw a 14-inch vertical line starting at the each of the front corners of the tile. Vanish these lines back toward the vanishing point, and make these lines a little lighter and thinner as they recede. Then, we'll draw verticals up from the back corner of the tile to meet the diagonals. Erase any extra line, and draw a horizontal to connect the corners. Add a final horizontal, connecting the two top corners. The block's done.

Now we'll use the ellipse and block to construct a cylinder. As you've likely guessed, we'll need to draw an ellipse on the top plane of the block. We'll start with some construction lines. Cross the diagonals, and draw the horizontal and vertical perspectival halves. Then draw the ellipse. Then erase the construction lines, but leave a small mark at the center point; we're going to use this very soon. After erasing, check your ellipse for symmetry. When you're ready, add a vertical on either side to connect the two ellipses at their widest points. Then adjust your line weights; if you lighten what would be the interior of the cylinder the illusion will be strengthened.

The cone's next. We'll use the center point in the top ellipse and draw diagonals to meet the right and left extremes of the lower ellipse. That's three down, two to go.

Next up, the cube; we'll draw it in the center of the block. The front of our tile is nine inches, so draw a horizontal line two and a half inches above the bottom of the block and another two and a half inches below the top of the block. This will create a nine inch square centered on the face of the block. Then, vanish the top and bottom front corners back toward the vanishing point. This time we know where to stop, at our back wall. So draw horizontals to complete the cube—done.

To draw our last solid, the sphere, we'll need to place an ellipse in the center horizontal of the cube. To draw that ellipse, we'll need the central horizontal plane of the cube. To draw that, we need to locate the horizontal midpoint of the cube. And to get the midpoint, we need to cross some diagonals. We'll do this on the cube's rear plane. Then, extend a horizontal through the center. Now, erase the diagonals and project the halfway measurement forward along the right and left planes. And we'll complete the midplane with a horizontal connecting the two front points.

Next, we need an ellipse in this plane, but you know how to do that— construction lines, then ellipse. Then erase the construction lines to reveal an ellipse that's the center plane of the sphere. We'll use the width of the ellipse to define the measure of the circle's diameter, and we can erase these last construction lines. You're done.

One note here: If you want to draw a hemisphere, it's often helpful to draw the full sphere first. You get a better sense of the proportions seeing it whole. If you'd wanted to draw a lower hemisphere, you could do just as we did and then erase the top portion. If you'd wanted an upper hemisphere, you'd do the inverse.

Our next topic's really a lot of fun: pattern and pattern in perspective. You'll remember this etched piece of ochre from the Blombos Cave in South Africa. Our various ancestors enjoyed the beauty of pattern for tens of thousands of years. To this day we have pattern on our clothes, on floor tiles, and on drapes and wallpaper—it's ubiquitous.

With the advent of perspective artists found they could adapt pattern to perspectival grids, like the ground plane in Raphael's School of Athens, or the pattern in the *Piazza San Marco*, or in Antonio López Garcia's drawing, or this tour-de-force of pattern by Jan Van Eyck. By the end of this lecture, you'll have a good idea about how you go about doing something like this. Even *The Simpson's* kitchen gets adorned with a pattern, though a much humbler one than in the Van Eyck.

Beyond its aesthetic appeal, one of the reasons artists use pattern is that it acts like cross-contour. It makes planes take on spatial orientation; makes a ground plane sit down; and a wall, well, feel like a wall. There're three main reasons for this; we discussed them earlier when we identified the principles that contribute to the illusion of three-dimensional space on a two-dimensional surface: First, pattern's repeat units. In perspective, they diminish in size—clear depth signal. Second, the pattern either has, or infers, diagonals which create spatial depth. And third, a pattern wedded to a perspectival grid, exhibits foreshortened shapes. So patterns in perspective do a lot of work.

Pattern's a subject in and of itself. There are many fine books that provide instruction and analysis at great length. Patterns can range from highly repetitive and regular, to extremely varied. Here we'll look at some of the basic ways we can generate patterns. It becomes very complex very quickly, even with a couple brief moves, but I think it'll stimulate your imagination.

We've actually already done some of the groundwork for this when we drew the rectangle's armature. Let's look at some of those same relationships inside a square. Perhaps the simplest pattern is one based on the repetition of the square itself at diminishing scales—a grid's really a fractal in this case. If we'd divided our square along diagonals, we'd approach a version of the Blombos Cave pattern. We could superimpose a square on the diagonals, then draw a large central triangle facing up, and repeat rotating 90 degrees each time—that's getting interesting. But we could also remove some of the lines to reveal a sparser star shape.

Let's go back to our simple armature, and take it in another direction by drawing a central diamond. Next, by removing the squares and some of the diagonals we get a very common pattern—a diamond in a square. If we add back in the lines we took out, we're back to this pattern. If we add the vertical and horizontal quarters, essentially a 4 × 4 grid, we get this. And if we add the missing diagonal to each small square, we get this. By removing the horizontals and verticals, we get a pattern of small diamonds. And we might draw staggered squares within this grid of diamonds. By repeating the squares in the corners at a diminished scale, the pattern gets even more elaborate.

Putting tiles one next to the other is referred to as tessellation, and we can tessellate any of these patterns—from a fairly simple one like this to a more complex one, like this. All we have to do is to repeat the lines in each grid unit. With certain patterns, some lines may go through multiple grid units. Once you get a sense of how the pattern works over a 2 × 2, 3 × 3, or 4 × 4 group, you can often draw across the grid units to create the pattern in a much more efficient way.

Soon we'll be making a full inquiry into the use of value and color. Suffice it to say here that assigning value or color to a grid or pattern will bring out different groupings of shapes and different object and ground relationships. Here I've applied value, a mid-gray, to the simpler pattern, and applied color to the more complex one. Here, the linear pattern is the same, but I've changed the ground color. You'll note how you read the figures differently. The red centers now project more; that's because the blue central squares are more like the ground color. That's foreshadowing a discussion we'll have about the importance of color contrast in reading visual hierarchies.

We can make one shape or group of shapes feel more like a positive, and others more like negatives. We can also inflect the rhythm of the pattern through a consideration of value and color. Incidentally, since our simpler and more complex patterns are based on the same underlying grid, we can superimpose one on the other to get an even more complex one. Here, the light color version; here, the darker. Like I said, it can get complex pretty quickly.

Stripping out the value and color for the moment, what we've done so far is nothing more than connecting points within a square—like when we drew the armature of our rectangle. A good way to get started with pattern is to draw on top of simple gridded graph paper. If you don't have any around the house, you'll find plenty online to download. Type "graph paper" into your search engine and look at the image results. Drag some to your desktop, print them out, and you're set to go. Either way, draw some patterns now. And if you can't help yourself, and want to throw in some value or color, go ahead. For color, colored pencils are great; so dive in. And since you know how to draw circles and ellipses, you could try curvilinear shapes like these in your patterns, too.

Transferring a pattern to a perspectival grid is a matter of remembering the steps you took, and repeating them in the foreshortened grid. Just earlier, we connected points in an upright square. Now we'll connect the same points in a foreshortened square. For the simpler pattern, I'll use four grid units as construction lines to draw the central diamond in the pattern. I note that the diagonals of the diamond will extend over multiple grid units—this means I don't have to draw each diamond individually. Instead, I can draw long diagonals cutting across underlying grid.

If I were doing a value drawing I could follow my basic plan here, then I'd erase my construction lines to reveal my pattern in perspective. If I wanted to use the more elaborate pattern overlaid on the simpler one, I'd draw it in the same way. It'd take some time and care, but it involves nothing more than connecting lines within the perspectival grid. And I could apply color, too.

As we'll soon learn, if I were doing a value or color drawing I'd inflect the value and color in relation to the drawing's overall hierarchy. I'd also be thinking about atmospheric perspective in this regard. I'd likely want to tune down both the value contrasts and the saturations as we moved back in space. Once you've created some patterns, take out your drawing of the gridded room. Look through the pattern studies you just did; apply the best ones to different planes of the room. And don't be shy about drawing ellipses.

You're just about ready to take on a complex drawing project—it's a line drawing using one-point perspective to construct a believable and measurable space. The underdrawing's a fully gridded room, the grid units are foreshortened squares. The lines which structure the drawing will be of three primary types: horizontals to express width, verticals to express height, and diagonals to express depth. Of course, you could use curvilinear structures, too.

Let's take a look at some excellent examples from my students at the University of Washington. Before we do, I should note that planning went into these drawings. We used small gestural compositional studies to move through compositional ideas before starting the larger scale drawings. And we'll talk about that aspect of the project a bit later. But first, let's take a look at the drawings, themselves. I think it will whet your appetite for the project.

Some individuals take this as an opportunity to construct a version of a normative room—here a kitchen, or a bedroom. Others build a more imagined kind of room. This example takes real advantage of the way pattern can enliven plane. In this drawing, we have both an interior and an exterior—a seascape—where you see the horizon. Here's another, a bit more fanciful, where we also get the open water and our horizon through windows on both the right and left walls. Others yet, combine diverse elements. Here again, we have pattern melded with the grid. We have curvilinear structures, including an elaborate curved ceiling light fixture; we also have a draped cart and a basket of full of laundry.

You can construct all kinds of things. Here, arched windows and doorways, and very specific furniture—including a canopy bed. We also get a view into connecting rooms on both the right and the left. This is an interpretation of the project that takes us outdoors and imagines the space in an alley. The grid units double as paving stones. In this somewhat sci-fi example, we get the vanishing point pushed to the right. The floor plane's dramatically pulled back all the way to the vanishing point. And in this very playful response, ladders take us up and, down and in and out through space.

Even though we're into a new topic, perspective, we want to hold onto all the things we've already studied. You'll note that each of the drawings here has a specific format shape. None of the drawings are 18 × 24 inches, each is consciously composed. So you want to ask yourself where your drawing begins and ends. What kind of rectangle is it? How does it relate to your subject? Here, we get a peaceful and orderly bedroom. Bed's the focal point. Horizontal format expresses rest and stability. Good choice. Here, we get dynamic ladders popping in and out in space; the vertical format makes perfect sense.

And you want to remember to employ a compositional strategy. Give some thought to the large, flat shape divisions of the drawing and how they relate to the particular rectangle, and give consideration to the depth of the constructed space. Here, we have a relatively shallow space in the room; here, a very great depth indeed.

You'll also want to consider line weight. You'll have to make many construction lines, and you won't want them gumming up the works. And you'll also want to make sure to use line to reinforce the sense of spatial depth, and to create a hierarchy of focal points and focal areas. And just because we're using perspective; doesn't mean the lines should retain a ruled quality. Here, the cushion is drawn with a line quality that expresses the cushion's irregular form. No reason not to use different line attributes, they can be very expressive.

Remember, everything is made up of planes—windows, door handles, pictures on walls. There are lots of small planes, and they relate to the vanishing point just as the large planes do. Here, a window has multiple planes, all seen from below. All the boring things in our lives have planes. Here, wall molding seen from above, and door jambs, and bed and table legs have planes too.

So for you to get started, I want to show you how we can integrate quick gestural drawing with what we've learned about linear perspective. We want to be able to use gesture so we can move through different compositional ideas rapidly, just as we've done in prior drawings, like Rembrandt—no pressure there.

We'll imagine a room, but this method could equally be applied to a landscape, cityscape, or other spatial situation. First we want to imagine the major planes in the room—back wall, floor, ceiling, and two side walls. Then, imagine the rectangle they form—the format shape. For example, I could rough-in a fairly tall back wall. Then wide diagonals for the floor plane. These diagonals project to my vanishing point. The vanishing point reveals the top angles of both side walls. At this point, I could begin to approximate the shape of the drawing itself. You'll notice, I'm thinking perspectively, but I'm drawing gesturally.

Now, I might want to look at some variations—a wider back wall and a higher vanishing point, or the inverse, or I could equally try moving the vanishing point to the left or right. While I'm doing this, I'm thinking more about the specific room. I could add: a window or two; the horizon; some trees; a doorway; a carpet; a ceiling fixture; a lamp; a bookcase; a painting hung above the bookcase; molding on the walls; and maybe a desk in the middle of the room; and on the desk, a laptop; a trash can, and a stool by the desk.

And I'd begin to think about my grid unit. In the last drawing we moved from the ground line back into space, you could equally start at the back wall. Ask yourself how high the horizon is. Is it three feet? Six feet?—that's the viewer's eye level. Once you've made this determination, you divide the vertical distance between the horizon and the edge where the wall meets the floor into this number of units—that's your scale. Do this freehand gesturally; doesn't have to be perfect, you'll work out the specifics when you scale up. You can also divide the bottom edge of the back wall into these units, and project them forward to the ground line using the vanishing point.

That's about all we have time for; we're going to finish this discussion in the next lecture.

Additional Activities

Lectures 1–3

For those looking for a broad history of art as a companion to help situate what they're learning about drawing, *Janson's History of Art* is one the standards for the Western canon. Another is *The Story of Art* by E. H. Gombrich. For a more inclusive worldview, Stokstad and Cothren's *Art History*, weighing in at a hefty 1,240 pages, is highly regarded. It starts with prehistory and, in addition to the Western canon, covers Asia, Islam, Africa, and the Americas. Though out of print, Daniel Mendelowitz's 1966 book *Drawing* is a good introduction to the history of (mostly) Western drawing from prehistory to the early 20th century.

Quite a few books have good introductory sections on getting to know your materials. The chapter "Media and Materials" in Bernard Chaet's *The Art of Drawing* contains much useful information. Arthur Guptill's books *Rendering in Pencil* and *Rendering in Pen and Ink* have excellent sections, as well. In the first book see, chapter 2, "Equipment and Studio," and chapter 3, "Preliminary Exercises." In the book on pen and ink, see chapters 2 through 5.

Lectures 4–11

In the lectures, we covered only a fraction of the many artists who use line, shape, volume, and composition in compelling ways. Below are listed a few names, with search terms when applicable, that will bring up many more excellent examples.

Note: Specific sites are listed for some works. If a work is not easily found, its listing includes the name of a book from the bibliography for this course in which it appears.

Contour and Cross-Contour Line

Alexander Calder drawings
Juan Gris Line drawings
George Grosz drawings
Al Hirschfeld drawings

Jean-Auguste-Dominique Ingres line drawings
Gustav Klimt drawings
Gaston Lachaise drawings
Sol LeWitt drawings
Henri Matisse line drawings, including *Nude in the Studio* (pen and ink, 1935)
Pablo Picasso line drawings

Line and Volume

Luca Cambiaso, especially his preparatory drawings

Gestural Line

Honoré Daumier drawings
Willem de Kooning drawings
Frank Gehry drawings
Rembrandt van Rijn drawings

Shape

Arshile Gorky
Fernand Léger drawings
Henri Matisse cut-outs
Joan Miró drawings
Donald Sultan drawings

Positive and Negative Shape

Richard Diebenkorn drawings
M. C. Escher
Philip Pearlstein drawings
Fairfield Porter
Euan Uglow

Composition

Balthus (Balthazar Klossowski de Rola)

Max Beckman
Edgar Degas
Piero della Francesca
Lucian Freud
Edward Hopper
Rembrandt van Rijn drawings

Lectures 12–14

In his 2001 book *Secret Knowledge*, the artist David Hockney advanced the theory that the great changes evidenced in the Renaissance were traceable to the use of such optical devices as the *camera lucida* and *camera obscura* to project images onto a surface and trace them. As part of this project, he put together what he termed *The Great Wall* of art. It's a compilation of reproductions of art historical works arranged chronologically that shows a distinct change in the 15th century, when artists' ability to portray subjects naturalistically took off. A Google search will turn up a number of images of the wall, as well as articles about his project.

For those interested in the subject of mechanical devices used by Western artists, Martin Kemp's book *The Science of Art* has an excellent chapter on the subject.

Although the thought of drawing or painting a still life of books might not at first seem an exciting proposition, artists have done remarkable things with this idea. For example, the contemporary artist Vincent Desiderio painted a tour-de-force image titled *Cockaigne* that you can view at http://www.hirshhorn.si.edu/collection/vincent-desiderio-cockaigne/.

If you search the subject "still life of books," you'll find works by a number by 17th-century Dutch artists, including Jan Davidszoon de Heem. Many of the works you'll find fall within the larger category of *vanitas*. The idea expressed here is that knowledge is fleeting and, thus, a vain pursuit. Many of these images also contain skulls or snuffed-out candles to further illustrate the point.

Still life can be much more than just a bunch of random objects posed on a table. For additional inspiration, look for *Agnus Dei* by the 17th-century

Spanish artist Francisco de Zurbarán. Next, fast forward a couple hundred years to Frida Kahlo's still lifes of fruit. They're clearly set up and composed to bring out visual references to sexual organs and fertility. Finally, the contemporary artists Audrey Flack, Wayne Thiebaud, and Janet Fish each have a fresh take on the form.

Lectures 15–19
Perspective

Robert Bechtle drawings
Jacopo Bellini drawings
Leonardo da Vinci, *Study for the Adoration of the Magi* (c. 1481)
Rackstraw Downes drawings
Thomas Eakins, *Perspective Study for the Biglin Brothers Turning the Stake*, *The Pair Oared Shell*, *Perspective Study for Baseball Players Practicing*
M. C. Escher
Anselm Kiefer
Giovanni Battista Piranesi drawings

Three-Point Perspective

Charles Sheeler, *Delmonico Building* (lithograph, 1926, http://www.metmuseum.org/toah/works-of-art/68.728)

Lectures 20–30
As in the earlier section on formal language (Lectures 5–11), there are many excellent examples that could be added to what we looked at in this section of the course. Below are listed a few more individuals who are well worth looking up.

Value, General

Kent Bellows
Edgar Degas monotypes
Sidney Goodman
Francisco Goya drawings

Value, Compositional Use of Value

Akira Arita drawings
John Luke, *Self-Portrait* (pencil on paper, Mendelowitz, Faber, and Wakeman, *A Guide to Drawing*, p. 27)
John Singer Sargent, *Study of a Nude Man* (c. 1874–1880, Rockman, *Drawing Essentials*, p. 93)

Value, Chiaroscuro

Caravaggio
Alfred Leslie drawings
Georges Seurat drawings
Giovanni Battista Tiepolo drawings

Value, Black and White

Aubrey Beardsley drawings
Honoré Daumier, *Don Quixote and Sancho Panza* (c. 1850, http://www.metmuseum.org/collection/the-collection-online/search/333888)

Value, Positive and Negative Shape

Richard Diebenkorn drawings
Emil Nolde, *Harbor* (brush and ink, c. 1900, http://www.artic.edu/aic/collections/artwork/23101)
Notan
A. R. Penck drawings, black and white

Value, Gesture and Compositional Sketching

Edward Hopper, *Study for East Side Interior* (chalk and charcoal on paper, 9 x 11½ in., 1922, http://whitney.org/WatchAndListen/AudioGuides?play_id=845), *Study for Evening Wind* (1921, Mendelowitz, Faber, and Wakeman, *A Guide to Drawing*, p. 149) drawing for *Morning Sun* (1952, Brown and McLean, *Drawing from Life.* p. 29).

Planar Head

Planar heads are available from http://www.planesofthehead.com.

Texture and Mark

Texture and mark are used expressively in a range of drawing types. If you pull up the Charles Schulz characters Charlie Brown and Pigpen, you get a very clear illustration of how potently mark affects the character of the subject portrayed.

Texture and Mark, General

Pieter Bruegel, *The Beekeepers* (pen and brown ink, 1568)
Honoré Daumier drawings
Jean Dubuffet drawings
Alberto Giacometti drawings
Philip Guston drawings
William Kentridge drawings and animations
Roy Lichtenstein drawings
Henry Moore drawings
Saul Steinberg drawings

Texture and Mark, Cross-Hatching

Hiëronymus Bosch drawings
Pieter Breughel the Elder drawings
Paul Cadmus drawings
R. Crumb drawings
David Levine drawings
Raphael (Raffaello Sanzio) drawings
Peter Paul Rubens drawings

Texture and Mark, Simulated Textures

Kent Bellows
Vija Celmins

Audrey Flack
René Magritte, *The Thought Which Sees* (graphite, 1965, http://www.moma.org/collection/object.php?object_id=35714)
Catherine Murphy, *Paint Jacket Pockets* (pencil on paper, 2002, http://www.moma.org/collection/object.php?object_id=96790)
Sylvia Plimack Mangold drawings
Mark Tansey

Color

Pierre Bonnard
Yvonne Jacquette
Wayne Thiebaud
Édouard Vuillard

In addition, below are listed a number of color websites that may prove interesting:

- *ColorCube*, http://www.colorcube.com/illusions/illusion.htm. This site provides visual illustration of some optical effects.

- *Color Matters*, http://colormatters.com. This site focuses on color in relation to symbolism, marketing, and a number of other related subjects.

- *Color Palette Generator*, http://www.degraeve.com/color-palette/. This site allows you to upload an image and create a set of swatches related to the image.

- *A Breakdown of Color in Film Stills*, http://imgur.com/a/PyRly. Analyzes movie stills in terms of the color palettes used in the shots.

- *Movies in Color*, http://moviesincolor.com/. Like the preceding site, this one also analyzes movie stills in terms of the color palettes used in the shots.

The Figure, General

Jean-Auguste-Dominique Ingres drawings
Jacopo da Pontormo drawings
Raphael (Raffaello Sanzio) drawings

The Figure, Anatomy

Bernhard Siegfried Albinus
Andreas Vesalius

The Figure in Perspectival Space

Henri de Toulouse-Lautrec, *The Laundress* (1888, Mendelowitz, Faber, and Wakeman, *A Guide to Drawing*, p. 41)

The Figure, Foreshortened

Giovanni Paolo Lomazzo, *Foreshortened Nude Man* (Mendelowitz, Faber, and Wakeman, *A Guide to Drawing*, p. 43)
Andrea Mantegna, *Lamentation of Christ* (http://en.wikipedia.org/wiki/Lamentation_of_Christ_%28Mantegna%29)

Additionally, here is a list of some prominent artists who have done substantial work with the figure over the past 50 years. Their work represents a broad range of approaches.

Steven Assael
Paul Cadmus
George Condo
R. Crumb
John Currin
Richard Diebenkorn
Marlene Dumas
Eric Fischl
Lucian Freud

Additional Activities

Gregory Gillespie
David Hockney
John Koch
Alfred Leslie
Loretta Lux
Elizabeth Peyton
Alice Neel
Philip Pearlstein
Jenny Saville
Luc Tuymans
James Valerio

Lectures 35–36

To figure out where you want to go, it can be helpful to look at a wide array of work and see where you feel some kinship. The following three lists for further research include either contemporary artists who are currently active or artists who were active during the last 100 years. Most are artists who weren't mentioned in the lectures or in these accompanying notes. Needless to say, these lists are far from inclusive, and as you search each individual, you'll come up with 5 or 10 others artists who are or were in some way associated with your initial target.

The first list highlights abstraction because many people who otherwise have a real interest in art find abstraction challenging. However, some of what you've learned about drawing in this course should offer inroads to other work that might at first be difficult to appreciate. If you've kept abstraction at arm's length, here are some artists you might look up:

Willem de Kooning
Arthur Dove
Marsden Hartley
Howard Hodgkin
Franz Kline
Emma Kunz
Kazimir Malevich
Kurt Schwitters
Sean Scully

Terry Winters

Below are a few artists who straddle abstraction and figuration:

Louise Bourgeois
Cecily Brown
Richard Diebenkorn
Philip Guston
Philip Pearlstein
Gerhard Richter
Matthias Weischer

Finally, the following artists span some of the enormous range of figuration we've seen over recent decades:

Jean-Michel Basquiat
William Beckman
Paul Cadmus
James Castle
Vija Celmins
Sue Coe
John Currin
Tacita Dean
Jan De Vliegher
Rackstraw Downes
Marlene Dumas
Eric Fischl
Ann Gale
Gregory Gillespie
Ignacio Ituria
Yvonne Jacquette
William Kentridge
John Koch
Catherine Murphy
Alice Neel
David Park
Ed Paschke

Jenny Saville
James Valerio

A last note: Don't be afraid to change or try new things. Although some artists have been consistent over the decades of their lives, many others have embraced change. A look at the careers of such artists as Edvard Munch, Picasso, Matisse, Mondrian, or Philip Guston can be instructive in this regard.

Bibliography

Drawing: Contemporary Sources

Aristides, Juliette. *Classical Drawing Atelier.* Watson-Guptill, 2006. A solid and well-illustrated introduction to drawing based in post-Renaissance and pre-20th-century practices and techniques in the West.

———. *Classical Painting Atelier.* Watson-Guptill, 2008. A companion to Aristides's drawing book. For the purposes of this course, this volume has useful chapters on composition and value.

———. *Lessons in Classical Drawing.* Watson-Guptill, 2011. A third volume from Aristides that includes a DVD tutorial.

Bothwell, Dorr, and Marlys Mayfield. *Notan: The Dark-Light Principle of Design.* Dover, 1991. A good introduction to *notan*, discussed in Lecture 22.

Boyer, Sheri Lynn. http://www.artinstructionblog.com/drawing-lesson-a-theory-of-light-and-shade. Many of my students have found this site helpful. It provides an overview of value and light and shade.

Chaet, Bernard. *The Art of Drawing.* 3rd ed. Harcourt Brace Jovanovich, 1983. A good, straightforward text. Provides clear explanations and examples of line, value, texture, and figure-ground relationships. Also includes a good chapter on materials.

Character Design. http://pinterest.com/characterdesigh/. This site is popular among my students who have an interest in concept art, comics, manga, and video games.

Curtis, Brian. *Drawing from Observation.* McGraw-Hill, 2009. This source contains a great deal of good material, with a focus on observational drawing. The explanations are clear and in-depth. The many illustrations also help the reader understand the topics under discussion.

Eagle, Ellen. *Pastel Painting Atelier*. Watson-Guptill, 2013. Although a number of books in this bibliography have a section or chapter devoted to pastel, this book represents a comprehensive introduction to the subject with many fine illustrations by a range of artists.

Enstice, Wayne, and Melody Peters. *Drawing: Space, Form and Expression.* 2nd ed. Prentice Hall, 1995. This book contains all the materials commonly presented in a college-level drawing course. It's well-organized, with a wealth of reproductions of artists' works, including many contemporary examples.

Faber, David L., and Daniel M. Mendelowitz. *A Concise Guide to Drawing*, 8th ed. Cengage Learning, 2012. Another comprehensive college-level drawing book. Covers all the important formal elements with sections on still life, landscape, and the figure. Also contains many helpful visual examples, including contemporary ones.

Goldstein, Nathan. *The Art of Responsive Drawing*. 3rd ed. Prentice Hall, 1984. A thorough book with much useful information.

Guptill, Arthur L., and Susan E. Meyer, *Rendering in Pencil.* Watson-Guptill, 1977. This is one of my favorite books on drawing. It is thorough and provides clear explanations. Note: Arthur Guptill, Jack Hamm, and Andrew Loomis were all primarily illustrators and were first published in the early to mid-20th century. They each wrote multiple texts on drawing, many of which are listed in this bibliography. Their books are decidedly different in character from books published from the 1970s onward and geared to the college classroom (e.g., those by Enstice, Faber, Goldstein, Mendelowitz, Rockman, Sale, Smagula, and others.). Guptill, Hamm, and Loomis tend to be more prescriptive, with a greater reliance on recipes. Also, some of the drawing examples of female nudes veer toward the pin-up, and some drawings of different "ethnic types" would make most contemporary readers cringe. That said, these men were extremely knowledgeable and wrote in clear and concise terms. There is a wealth of good information in their respective volumes.

———. *Rendering in Pen and Ink.* Watson-Guptill, 1997. Like the book on pencil, an excellent work.

Hamm, Jack. *Drawing Scenery: Landscapes and Seascapes.* Perigee Trade, 1988. Hamm starts out with many basics about composition. He then goes on, in his encyclopedic way, to catalog 38 kinds of trees, many other kinds of rocks, and cloud types charted by altitude.

————. *First Lessons in Drawing and Painting.* Perigee Trade, 1988. Although this book is not comprehensive, it includes plenty of excellent information.

————. *How to Draw Animals.* Perigee Trade, 1983. If you want to draw animals, this is a good place to start. Hamm starts with some anatomical basics. Then, he runs through scores of different animals, pointing out differences among species. For example, he doesn't just give you one bear but contrasts the Kodiak with the polar, grizzly, black, Himalayan, sloth, and Malayan varieties.

The J. Paul Getty Museum. *Formal Analysis.* http://www.getty.edu/education/teachers/building_lessons/formal_analysis.html. This link provides an introduction to formal analysis.

The Kennedy Center. *Formal Visual Analysis.* https://artsedge.kennedy-center.org/educators/how-to/from-theory-to-practice/formal-visual-analysis. This site lists many formal language terms with concise definitions.

Loomis, Andrew. *Fun with a Pencil.* Titan Books, 2013. There's a fair degree of overlap in Loomis's books, but they all have excellent information, including this one. This volume concerns itself a bit more with cartooning than the others.

————. *Successful Drawing.* Titan Books, 2012. An excellent book with good sections on basic forms, form in light, linear perspective, and relating the figure to perspective.

Mendelowitz, Daniel M. *Drawing.* Holt, Rinehart and Winston, 1967. This is not a how-to book but, instead a good introduction to the history of (mostly) Western drawing from prehistory to the early 20th century.

Mendelowitz, Daniel, David L. Faber, and Duane Wakeman. *A Guide to Drawing.* 7th ed. Cengage Learning, 2006. From the same publisher and by some of the same authors as *A Concise Guide to Drawing*, above, this source has many of the same materials.

Pumphrey, Richard. *The Elements of Art.* Prentice Hall College Division, 1996. Though introduced as a book on design, not drawing, this volume provides an excellent introduction to formal language and many important aspects of two-dimensional art.

Rockman, Deborah. *Drawing Essentials.* Oxford University Press, 2009. A well-thought-out book with chapters on all the major topics generally covered in a college-level drawing course.

Sale, Teel, and Claudia Betti. *Drawing: A Contemporary Approach.* 5th ed. Thomson Wadsworth, 2004. A fairly comprehensive book, with many good explanations and illustrations.

Smagula, Howard J. *Creative Drawing.* 2nd ed. McGraw-Hill, 2002. Yet another thorough and well-illustrated book covering the major topics generally discussed in a university drawing course.

Stevens, Peter, S. *A Handbook of Regular Patterns.* MIT Press, 1981. An excellent and comprehensive book on pattern. The text is clear, analytical, and accompanied by a wealth of illustrations.

Drawing: Historical Sources

Ackerman, Gerald, and Graydon Parrish. *Charles Bargue and Jean-Leon Gérôme Drawing Course.* ACR, 2011. This is a reprinting of the 19th-century *Cours de Dessin* of Charles Bargue, a French lithogropher, and Jean-Léon Gérôme, the academician known for his orientalist paintings. The method involves copying drawings of plaster casts, starting with line to block out shape, then volume attached to planar structure. This is used as a guide to then apply value. The young Pablo Picasso made copies of a number of these drawings.

Alberti, Leon Battista, and Martin Kemp. *On Painting*. Penguin, 1991. A seminal 15th-century text on drawing and painting.

Cennini, Cennino d'Andrea. *The Craftsman's Handbook*. Dover, 1933. Among the first Western manuals on artistic materials and procedures. Written in 15th-century Italy, it describes many of the methods for making materials and their application.

da Vinci, Leonardo. *A Treatise on Painting*. Dover, 2005. http://www.treatiseonpainting.org. This is a translation of a text based, at least in part, on Leonardo's manuscripts. A number of versions were published in Europe during the 16th and 17th centuries. It is somewhat fragmented but interesting nonetheless. Multiple early editions can be viewed at the link listed above.

———. http://www.universalleonardo.org/. This site, curated by Martin Kemp, has an excellent selection of Leonardo's drawings and manuscript pages.

de Honnecourt, Villard. *The Sketchbook of Villard de Honnecourt*. Edited by Theodore Bowie. Indiana University Press, 1959. A 13th-century sketchbook of drawings with subjects spanning figures, animals, and architecture. This source is noteworthy for our course because it constitutes an early example of a draftsman using simple geometric shapes to draw more complex objects (plates 35 through 38). Plate 35 has the inscription "Here begins the method of representation."

Dürer, Albrecht. *Four Books on Human Proportions*. http://brbl-dl.library.yale.edu/vufind/Record/3783330. The entire 1528 volume containing Dürer's exploration of human proportions is available as a pdf at this site.

———. *Underweysung der Messung*. http://brbl-dl.library.yale.edu/vufind/Record/3529943. The original German text printed in 1525.

———. *Underweysung der Messung*. http://brbl-dl.library.yale.edu/vufind/Record/3529943. An additional eight pages published in 1538.

Dürer, Albrecht, and Walter Strauss. *The Human Figure by Albrecht Dürer: The Complete Dresden Sketchbooks*. Dover, 1972. https://archive.org/stream/

bub_gb_1vEEAAAAYAAJ#page/n51/mode/thumb. A collection of many of Dürer's annotated figure studies done in preparation for his 1528 publication *Four Books on Human Proportion*.

———. *The Painter's Manual.* Abaris Books, 1977. An English translation of Dürer's *Underweysung der Messung*.

Eakins, Thomas. *A Drawing Manual.* Philadelphia Museum of Art, 2005. This is an unfinished book written by Eakins based on his teaching at the Pennsylvania Academy of Fine Arts. Though fragmentary, it shows the kind of analytical and quantitative thinking that engaged him.

Koller, E. L. *Light, Shade, and Shadow.* Dover, 2008. This book was originally published in 1914. Though a slim volume, it covers the perspective of shadows in some detail.

Ruskin, John. *The Elements of Drawing.* Dover, 1971. Ruskin was better known as an art critic than an artist, but he was an accomplished draftsman nonetheless. His book, originally published in 1857, is heavier on text and has fewer illustrations than most contemporary books on drawing. That said, much of the information here is relevant.

Speed, Harold. *The Practice and Science of Drawing.* Dover, 1972. Originally published in 1917, this is a well-known text on drawing, much of it dealing with both line and mass.

Vasari, Giorgio. *Vasari on Technique.* Dover, 2011. This 1550 text on methods in architecture, sculpture, painting, and design was written by the well-known author of *Lives of the Artists*. It gives us a contemporary view of the materials, methods, and techniques used by Renaissance artists.

Linear Perspective

Auvil, Kenneth W. *Perspective Drawing.* 2nd ed. McGraw-Hill, 1996. A concise and thorough book with clear illustrations.

D'Amelio, Joseph. *Perspective Drawing Handbook*. Dover, 2004. This book was originally published in 1964. It is well-illustrated and covers many of the most important concepts related to one- and two-point perspective.

Montague, John. *Basic Perspective Drawing*. 6th ed. Wiley, 2013. Among the clearest and most thorough books on linear perspective. The newest edition includes a key code that gives you access to a website with instructional videos.

Norling, Ernest R. *Perspective Made Easy*. Dover Publications, 1999. This book was first published in 1939, and its illustrations may look somewhat dated. That said, the subject is well- presented. Both the text and illustrations communicate the essential points in a vivid way.

Robertson, Scott, and Thomas Berling. *How to Draw*. Design Studio Press, 2013. A good recent book on perspective. It covers all the basics and has detailed sections on drawing cars and planes.

Veltman, Kim H. *Linear Perspective and the Visual Dimensions of Science and Art*. Deutscher Kunstverlag, 1986. This is not a how-to book. Instead, it's a historical study of Leonardo's writings on, and use of, perspective and related subjects. Contains a great deal of fascinating material.

Figure Drawing and Anatomy

Bridgman, George B. *Bridgman's Complete Guide to Drawing from Life*. Sterling, 1952. Bridgman taught figure drawing and anatomy at The Art Students League in New York City for many years. This book includes his own drawings, accompanied by explanations of the major body parts. There is also a chapter on drapery.

Brown, Clint, and Cheryl McLean. *Drawing from Life*. 2nd ed. Harcourt Brace, 1997. A comprehensive guide to figure drawing. Many of the formal considerations are covered in the first section on fundamentals. This is followed by a section on anatomy and another on composition and expression.

Goldstein, Nathan. *Figure Drawing*. 4th ed. Prentice Hall, 1993. A good overview of figure drawing. Well-illustrated, with chapters on structural, anatomical, and expressive approaches

Hale, Robert Beverly. *Master Class in Figure Drawing*. Watson-Guptill, 1991. This text is distilled from Hale's anatomy classes at The Art Students League in New York. Hale moves through the major structures of muscle and bone in the human body, relating them to choices made in drawings by important artists from Leonardo to Rubens.

————. *Lectures on Artistic Anatomy and Figure Drawing*. http://www.jo-an.com/art_video.htm. These videos of Hale teaching at The Art Students League in New York provide excellent material. There are 10 talks in all, each covering a section of the body, as follows: Lecture 1, Rib Cage (78 minutes); Lecture 2, Pelvis (81 minutes); Lecture 3, Leg (74 minutes); Lecture 4, Foot (72 minutes); Lecture 5, Shoulder Girdle 1 (77 minutes); Lecture 6, Shoulder Girdle 2 (68 minutes); Lecture 7, Arm (76 minutes); Lecture 8, Hand (80 minutes); Lecture 9, Head and Skull (80 minutes); Lecture 10, Head and Features (97 minutes).

Hale, Robert Beverly, and Jacob Collins. *Drawing Lessons from the Great Masters*. Watson-Guptill, 1989. This book analyzes artists' drawings in relation to the use of line, light, plane, and anatomy.

Hamm, Jack. *Cartooning the Head and Figure*. Perigee Trade, 1986. As the title suggests, this book is all about cartooning. The examples are decidedly early to mid-20th century, but there's a great deal of excellent information here. Hamm had an encyclopedic personality. There are pages devoted to charting scores of cartoon noses, ears, and lips. A wonderful book to leaf through.

————. *Drawing the Head and Figure*. Perigee Trade, 1988. A great introduction to constructive figure drawing. In other words, the approach is not about observation but about using systems of measure and shape to draw figures from your imagination. Concerns itself a bit less with constructing three-dimensional form than either Loomis or Reed.

Loomis, Andrew. *Drawing the Head and Hands*. Titan Books, 2011. An excellent introduction to the subject.

————. *Figure Drawing for All It's Worth*. Titan Books, 2011. Contains a great deal of good information about measure, anatomy, constructing the figure from blocks, and drawing from observation.

Reed, Walt. *The Figure*. 30th ed. North Light Books, 1984. An excellent book with chapters on figure construction and anatomy.

Thomson, Arthur. *A Handbook of Anatomy for Art Students*. 5th ed. Dover, 2011. This book is primarily text with some illustrations. It contains thorough descriptions of the major anatomical structures of the body.

Vanderpoel, John H. *The Human Figure*. Dover, 1958. Considered one of the early-20th-century classics on the subject, this book was originally published in 1935. Like many books of the period, it has more text than illustration, and some contemporary readers find the prose difficult. That said, there is a wealth of good information to be found here.

Visiblebody.com. SkeletonPremium and MusclePremium. These apps let you move through all the important bones and muscles, which are rendered in three dimensions. You can rotate them and see them in motion, as well. This is one of the best ways to get a clear idea of how the various anatomical structures relate. The apps are compatible with many phones, tablets, and various operating systems.

Winslow, Valerie L. *Classic Human Anatomy*. Watson-Guptill, 2009. Among the most recent and comprehensive books on anatomy for the artist. It does a good job of outlining and illustrating the important bones and muscles.

Color

Albers, Josef. *Interaction of Color*. Yale University Press, 2006. Albers was a student, and later, a colleague, of Itten's (see below) at the Bauhaus. His book has become one of the standards used in art schools and universities in the United States. The strengths of his approach center on bringing out optical relationships, namely, how color is relative. A single color can be made to appear darker or lighter, warmer or cooler based on the surrounding colors—hence, the *Interaction* in the title.

A Breakdown of Color in Film Stills. http://imgur.com/a/PyRly. A good site that breaks down the color palettes in film stills into swatches.

Guptill, Arthur L. *Oil Painting Step-By-Step.* 9th ed. Watson-Guptill, 1978. Though primarily a book on oil painting, this source includes several useful chapters on color.

Guptill, Arthur L., and Susan E. Meyer, *Watercolor Painting Step-By-Step.* 2nd ed. Watson-Guptill, 1968. Similar to the oil painting guide above, this book has several excellent chapters on color.

Itten, Johannes, and Faber Birren. *The Elements of Color.* Van Nostrand Reinhold Company, 1970. Along with Albers's book, Itten's is one of those most used in U.S. academia today. The two approaches are similar.

Loomis, Andrew. *Creative Illustration.* Titan Books, 2012. As with all Loomis's books, there's excellent information here on many aspects of drawing, including line, tone, composition, and perspective. Also includes a useful chapter on color.

Robertson, Jean, and Craig McDaniel. *Painting as a Language.* Cengage Learning, 1999. Although primarily a book on painting, this source includes a good chapter on color, as well chapters on space, the picture plane, and abstraction.

Drawing and Painting Materials

Many of the contemporary drawing books listed above have excellent chapters on materials. In addition, several books that deal solely with this subject are listed below.

Chaet, Bernard. *An Artist's Notebook: Techniques and Materials*. Holt, Rinehart and Winston, 1979. This book has a lengthy chapter on drawing materials. Also includes a chapter on color.

Doerner, Max. *The Materials of the Artist*. Mariner Books, 1949. First published in 1921. Before Mayer published *The Artist's Handbook*, this source was among the most thorough and up-to-date texts on the subject. Like Mayer's work, it deals primarily with painting materials.

Eastlake, Sir Charles Lock. *Methods and Materials of Painting of the Great Schools and Masters*. Dover, 2001. This book, by a former president of the British Royal Academy, was originally published in 1847 as *Materials for a History of Oil Painting*. It is a lengthy volume—more than 1,000 pages—covering historical painting methods and techniques in the West.

Gettins, Rutherford J., and George L. Stout. *Painting Materials*. Dover Art Instruction, 2011. Originally published in 1942 and written by two specialists affiliated with the Department of Conservation at Harvard's Fogg Art Museum. This is a technical work with extensive information on pigments, mediums, and supports.

Gottsegen. Mark David. *The Painter's Handbook*. Watson-Guptill, 2006. Among the most recent, useful, and readable of the books listed here. The recipes are clear and concise. There is also a good introductory chapter on common drawing materials and papers.

Mayer, Ralph. *The Artist's Handbook*. 5th ed. Viking, 1991. First published in 1940, this book remains one of the standard references in the field. It is mostly concerned with painting materials but includes chapters on pastel and watercolor.

Speed, Harold. *Oil Painting Techniques and Materials*. Dover, 1987. First published in 1924, this book is regarded by many as a classic, covering traditional oil painting materials and techniques.

Turner, Jacques. *Brushes: A Handbook for Artists*. Design Press, 1992. A fairly comprehensive look at brushes used with a wide range of materials.

Bibliography

Van de Wettering, Ernst. *Rembrandt: The Painter at Work.* University of California Press, 2009. An interesting book that examines Rembrandt's materials and painting methods.

Health and Safety

McCann, Michael. *Artist Beware.* Lyons Press, 2005. This book has become a standard in the field.

Rossol, Monona. *The Artist's Complete Health and Safety Guide.* Allworth Press, 2001. Along with McCann's book, this is a well-reviewed and highly regarded text on the subject.

Artists' Writings, Interviews with Artists, and Artist Video Clips

Along with the more hands-on texts, it's useful to get a sense of what a range of artists actually think about. Below is a modest selection spanning artists' writings, interviews with artists, and clips of artists at work.

Ashton, Dore. *Picasso on Art*, De Capo Press, 1988.

Bacon, Francis. *Fragments of a Portrait*, https://www.youtube.com/watch?v=xoFMH_D6xLk. *Francis Bacon's Last Interview*, https://www.youtube.com/watch?v=p-d9TdRYUaQ. *Francis Bacon Rare Interview, 1971*, https://www.youtube.com/watch?v=aFDiemYxuvA.

Baselitz, Georg. *Georg Baselitz Talks about Farewell Bill*, https://www.youtube.com/watch?v=A6ipu0KzUds.

Cembalest, Robin. "How Edward Hopper Storyboarded *Nighthawks*." http://www.artnews.com/2013/07/25/how-edward-hopper-storyboarded-nighthawks/.

da Vinci, Leonardo. *The Notebooks of Leonardo da Vinci.* 2 vols. Edited by Jean Paul Richeter. Dover, 1970.

Desiderio, Vincent. *LCAD Vincent Desiderio Painting Demo*, https://www.youtube.com/watch?v=GxRN9tcN6pQ&list=PLnCjvdddc6_45 u4kYcwZJCbj_xmWcyfbr.

De Vliegher, Jan. http://www.youtube.com/watch?v=-T4ZW8NZOeA&feature=youtu.be.

Fischl, Eric. *Dive Deep: Eric Fischl and the Process of Painting.* https://www.youtube.com/watch?v=MWpYD4LWpVc.

Freud, Lucian. *An Exclusive Tour of Freud's Studio*, https://www.youtube.com/watch?v=4YMV4EyaPMM. *Lucian Freud's Rarest Interview*, https://www.youtube.com/watch?v=i5KcT4PBh2M.

Gaugain, Paul. *The Writings of a Savage.* Viking, 1978.

Henri, Robert. *The Art Spirit.* Basic Books, 2007.

Hockney, David. *David Hockney by David Hockney.* Abrams, 1977. *I Am a Space Freak*, http://channel.louisiana.dk/video/david-hockney-i-am-space-freak. *Photoshop Is Boring*, https://www.youtube.com/watch?v=oAx_aYGmpoM. *Who Gets to Call It Art*, https://www.youtube.com/watch?v=CjfIKymXMa4.

Kahlo, Frida, with an introduction by Carlos Fuentes. *Diary of Frida Kahlo.* Bloomsbury, 1995.

Katz, Alex. https://www.youtube.com/watch?v=p1bA6Sbk24Y.

Kiefer, Anselm. https://www.youtube.com/watch?v=qmn-w2J68pU.

Klee, Paul. *Diaries of Paul Klee.* University of California Press, 1968.

Kuspit, Donald. *Fischl: An Interview with Eric Fischl.* Vintage, 1987.

Lundin, Norman, and David Brody. *Norman Lundin: Selections from Three Decades of Drawing and Painting*. University of Washington Press, 2006.

Matisse, Henri. *Matisse on Art*. Phaidon, 1973.

Redon, Odilon. *To Myself: Notes on Life, Art, and Artists*. George Braziller, 1996.

Richter, Gerhard. *Gerhard Richter Painting*, http://www.youtube.com/watch?v=yF6EluMNR14. *Gerhard Richter in the Studio*, https://www.youtube.com/watch?v=ExfNJDh4K1g.

Richter, Gerhard, and Hans Ulbrich-Obrist. *The Daily Practice of Painting*. The MIT Press, 1995.

Shan, Ben. *The Shape of Content*. Harvard University Press, 1992. This volume contains six essays by Shahn delivered in 1956–1957 at Harvard University as part of The Charles Eliot Norton Lecture series. Shahn writes clearly and succinctly about art. Students of this course will find the final essay, "The Education of an Artist," of particular interest.

Sylvester, David. *The Brutality of Fact: Interviews with Francis Bacon*. Thames and Hudson, 1990.

Van Gogh, Vincent. *Letters of Vincent Van Gogh*. Penguin, 1998.

Wellington, Hubert. *The Journal of Eugene Delacroix*. Phaidon, 1995.

Compilations of Artists' Writings

Chipp, Herschel B. *Theories of Modern Art*. University of California Press, 1984. This volume includes writings by many 19th- and 20th-century artists, from Paul Cézanne to Henry Moore.

Goldwater, Robert, and Marco Treves. *Artists on Art*, Pantheon, 1974. This volume includes artists' writings from the 14th to the 20th centuries.

Harrison, Charles, and Paul Wood. *Art in Theory, 1900–1990.* Blackwell, 1995. As the title indicates, this book covers the period 1900–1990 with writings by many artists and writers, from Gaugain and Freud to Barbara Kruger and Richard Serra.

Art History and Criticism

This short list contains texts referenced in the course and a few others that are either comprehensive or will serve as introductions to aspects of art history or criticism.

Davies, Penelope. *Janson's History of Art.* 8th ed. Pearson, 2010. One of the standards used in university art history survey courses covering the Western canon at length.

Fineberg, Jonathan. *Art since 1940.* 3rd ed. Pearson, 2010. As the title indicates, this book covers art since 1940. Though not comprehensive, it's a readable overview that will give the reader a sense of the important individuals and ideas during this period.

Gombrich, Ernst. *The Story of Art.* 16th ed. Phaidon Press, 1995. One of the bestselling introductions to the history of (mostly) Western art. Well written and accessible.

Grove Dictionary of Art, Oxford University Press, 1996. This 34-volume work is as comprehensive as anything available. Not something you're likely to buy for your home library, but major libraries will have a copy. It's extremely useful for getting information and references for any topic you might become interested in.

Hickey, Dave. *Air Guitar: Essays on Art and Democracy.* Art Issues Press, 1997. A collection of essays by one of the more witty contemporary critics. It can serve as an introduction to some contemporary thought on art.

Hockney, David. *Secret Knowledge.* Studio, 2006. Artist David Hockney advances the theory that the great changes evidenced in the Renaissance were traceable to the use of such optical devices as the *camera lucida* and *camera obscura.* He argues that artists from Van Eyck to Caravaggio to Ingres used them to project images onto a surface and trace them. There is also a BBC documentary on the same subject that makes for interesting viewing (http://youtu.be/ynrnfBnhWSo).

Hughes, Robert. *Nothing If Not Critical.* Penguin Books, 1992. Hughes was the art critic for *TIME* magazine for many years and one of the most prominent art critics of the late 20th century. This is a collection of his essays on both historical and more contemporary artists. The prose is unusually lucid.

————. *The Shock of the New.* Knopf, 1991. An excellent introduction for anyone interested in beginning to understand what might be termed "modern art."

Kemp, Martin. *The Science of Art.* Yale University Press, 1992. This is a fascinating book for those interested in many of the more quantitative aspects of art. It covers the relationship of science to art in the West from the Renaissance through the 19th century. It includes an interesting chapter on mechanical devices used in drawing and painting. The appendix boasts one of the most lucid and concise descriptions of the principles underlying linear perspective.

Kleiner, Fred S. *Gardner's Art through the Ages: A Global History.* 2 vols. 14th ed. Wadsworth, 2012. Another standard comprehensive text used in university art history courses.

Sewell, Darrel, ed. *Thomas Eakins.* Philadelphia Museum of Art, 2001. Include several excellent articles on Eakins's working methods.

Stokstad, Marilyn, and Michael Cothren. *Art History.* 4th ed. Pearson, 2010. An inclusive world history of art. Starting with prehistory, it covers Asia, Islam, Africa, and the Americas, in addition to the Western canon.

Notes

Notes

Notes

Notes

Notes